Frommer's®

W9-AXL-955

Napa & Sonoma
day BY **day**
1st Edition

by Avital Binshtock

Wiley Publishing, Inc.

Contents

18 Favorite Moments   1

1 Strategies for Seeing Napa & Sonoma   5
Napa & Sonoma   6

2 The Best Full-Day Tours of Napa & Sonoma   9
The Best of Napa in One Day   10
The Best of Sonoma in One Day   14
The Best of Napa & Sonoma in Three Days—Day 3   18
The Best of Napa & Sonoma in Five Days—Days 4 & 5   22
The Best of Napa & Sonoma in One Week—Days 6 & 7   26

3 The Best Special-Interest Tours   31
Wine Country for Foodies   32
Wine Country with Kids   36
The Big Splurge, Napa Style   40
Wine Country for First-Timers   44
Wine Country for Nondrinkers   46
Wine Country for History Buffs   50
A Day for Arts Aficionados   56
Wine Country for Romance   60
Wine Country without a Car   64
Wine Country on a Budget   68

4 The Most Charming Towns   71
Napa   72
Where to Dine   76
Sonoma   78
Where to Dine   81
St. Helena   82
Where to Dine   84
Healdsburg   86
Where to Dine   89
Guerneville   92
Where to Dine   93

CALISTOGA

Yountville 94
Where to Dine 96
Glen Ellen 98
Where to Dine 100
Calistoga 102
Where to Dine 105

5 The Great Outdoors 107
The Wine Country by Bike 108
The Best Wine Country Hike 110
From the Russian River to the
  Pacific Coast 112

6 Napa & Sonoma Lodging 115
Where to Stay in Wine Country 116
Napa Lodging A to Z 118
Sonoma Lodging A to Z 124

7 The Best Wineries 129
Wineries A to Z 132

8 San Francisco 161
The Best of SF in One Day 162
The Best of SF in Two Days 166
The Best of SF in Three Days 170
Lodging A to Z 176
Dining A to Z 179
Shopping A to Z 186
Nightlife & Arts A to Z 189

The Savvy Traveler 193
Before You Go 194
Getting There 197
Getting Around 198
Fast Facts 200
Wine Country: A Brief History 205
A Quick Guide to Wine Varietals 207

Index 210

Exclusive Online Content
Tour of Santa Rosa
www.frommers.com/tours

Published by:

Wiley Publishing, Inc.

111 River St.
Hoboken, NJ 07030-5774

Copyright © 2007 Wiley Publishing, Inc., Hoboken, New Jersey. All rights reserved. No part of this publication may be reproduced, stored in a retrieval system or transmitted in any form or by any means, electronic, mechanical, photocopying, recording, scanning or otherwise, except as permitted under Sections 107 or 108 of the 1976 United States Copyright Act, without either the prior written permission of the Publisher, or authorization through payment of the appropriate per-copy fee to the Copyright Clearance Center, 222 Rosewood Drive, Danvers, MA 01923, 978/750-8400, fax 978/646-8600. Requests to the Publisher for permission should be addressed to the Legal Department, Wiley Publishing, Inc., 10475 Crosspoint Blvd., Indianapolis, IN 46256, 317/572-3447, fax 317/572-4355, or online at http://www.wiley.com/go/permissions.

Wiley and the Wiley Publishing logo are trademarks or registered trademarks of John Wiley & Sons, Inc. and/or its affiliates. Frommer's is a trademark or registered trademark of Arthur Frommer. Used under license. All other trademarks are the property of their respective owners. Wiley Publishing, Inc. is not associated with any product or vendor mentioned in this book.

ISBN-13: 978-0-470-05021-7
Editor: Caroline Sieg
Production Editor: Heather Wilcox
Photo Editor: Richard Fox
Cartographer: Andrew Murphy
Anniversary Logo Design: Richard Pacifico
Production by Wiley Indianapolis Composition Services
Chapter 8 illustration by Mary J. Gillot

For information on our other products and services or to obtain technical support, please contact our Customer Care Department within the U.S. at 800/762-2974, outside the U.S. at 317/572-3993 or fax 317/572-4002.

Wiley also publishes its books in a variety of electronic formats. Some content that appears in print may not be available in electronic formats.

Manufactured in China

5   4   3   2   1

A Note from the Publisher

Organizing your time. That's what this guide is all about.

Other guides give you long lists of things to see and do and then expect you to fit the pieces together. The Day by Day guides are different. These guides tell you the best of everything, and then they show you how to see it *in the smartest, most time-efficient way*. Our authors have designed detailed itineraries organized by time, neighborhood, or special interest. And each tour comes with a bulleted map that takes you from stop to stop.

Hoping to taste the latest Cabernet straight from the barrel at a family-owned boutique winery, learn about the winemaking process on a vineyard tour, or visit the *Peanuts* gang with your kids at the Charles Schultz Museum? Planning a walk through downtown Sonoma, or dinner and a bottle where you can rub shoulders with winemakers and other Napa and Sonoma locals? Whatever your interest or schedule, the Day by Days give you the smartest routes to follow. Not only do we take you to the top attractions, hotels, and restaurants, but we also help you access those special moments that locals get to experience— those "finds" that turn tourists into travelers.

The Day by Days are also your top choice if you're looking for one complete guide for all your travel needs. The best hotels and restaurants for every budget, the greatest shopping values, the wildest nightlife—it's all here.

Why should you trust our judgment? Because our authors personally visit each place they write about. They're an independent lot who say what they think and would never include places they wouldn't recommend to their best friends. They're also open to suggestions from readers. If you'd like to contact them, please send your comments my way at mspring@wiley.com, and I'll pass them on.

Enjoy your Day by Day guide—the most helpful travel companion you can buy. And have the trip of a lifetime.

Warm regards,

Michael Spring
Publisher
Frommer's Travel Guides

About the Author

Avital Binshtock is a writer and editor who regularly contributes to many media outlets including the *Los Angeles Times,* where she was an associate editor, and Potentia Media, for which she provides and edits startling-but-true content. She has also done work for National Geographic Television and *Elite Traveler,* among a number of others. She counts global travel and exploring different cultures almost foremost among her passions, just second to spending time with—and telling the stories of—the people she loves. A California native to the core, Avital was educated at UCLA and Stanford University.

Acknowledgments

Special thanks to my editor, Caroline Sieg, who was instrumental in shaping this book and adroitly steering me through writing it. Many thanks also to Jennifer Anmuth, without whom I would not have gotten this wonderful assignment, and to authors Erika Lenkert and Noelle Salmi, whose previous work for Frommer's was tremendously helpful. Appreciation, too, goes to Tracy Sway, whose good taste and San Francisco knowledge was critical in constructing Chapter 8, and to Amanda Jones for her patience as I plowed through this project. I am eternally thankful to my entire family, including my mother and father, Ruth and Arie, and my brothers, Eyal and Leor, for all of their unconditional love and support, and my grandmother, Sheindel, who consistently inspires my writing with the riveting stories she tells. This book is for Tim Andrews, whose geographic expertise lovingly and patiently guides me along not only the highways on the map, but also through those more intricate, trickier-to-navigate crossroads of life.

An Additional Note

Please be advised that travel information is subject to change at any time—and this is especially true of prices. We therefore suggest that you write or call ahead for confirmation when making your travel plans. The authors, editors, and publisher cannot be held responsible for the experiences of readers while traveling. Your safety is important to us, however, so we encourage you to stay alert and be aware of your surroundings.

Star Ratings, Icons & Abbreviations

Every hotel, restaurant, and attraction listing in this guide has been ranked for quality, value, service, amenities, and special features using a **star-rating system.** Hotels, restaurants, attractions, shopping, and nightlife are rated on a scale of zero stars (recommended) to three stars (exceptional). In addition to the star-rating system, we also use a **kids icon** to point out the best bets for families. Within each tour, we recommend cafes, bars, or restaurants where you can take a break. Each of these stops appears in a shaded box marked with a coffee-cup-shaped bullet ☕ .

The following **abbreviations** are used for credit cards:

AE	American Express	DISC	Discover	V	Visa
DC	Diners Club	MC	MasterCard		

Frommers.com

Now that you have this guidebook to help you plan a great trip, visit our website at **www.frommers.com** for additional travel information on more than 3,500 destinations. We update features regularly to give you instant access to the most current trip-planning information available. At Frommers. com, you'll find scoops on the best airfares, lodging rates, and car rental bargains. You can even book your travel online through our reliable travel booking partners.

A Note on Prices

In the "Take a Break" and "Best Bets" sections of this book, we have used a system of dollar signs to show a range of costs for 1 night in a hotel (the price of a double-occupancy room) or the cost of an entree at a restaurant. Use the following table to decipher the dollar signs:

Cost	Hotels	Restaurants
$	under $100	under $10
$$	$100–$200	$10–$20
$$$	$200–$300	$20–$30
$$$$	$300–$400	$30–$40
$$$$$	over $400	over $40

An Invitation to the Reader

In researching this book, we discovered many wonderful places—hotels, restaurants, shops, and more. We're sure you'll find others. Please tell us about them, so we can share the information with your fellow travelers in upcoming editions. If you were disappointed with a recommendation, we'd love to know that, too. Please write to:

Frommer's Napa & Sonoma Day by Day, 1st Edition
Wiley Publishing, Inc. • 111 River St. • Hoboken, NJ 07030-5774

18 Favorite
Moments

18 Favorite **Moments**

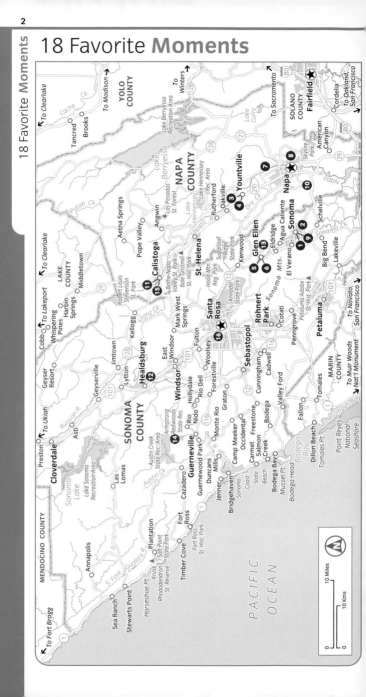

❶ **Reliving the Bear Flag Revolt and other significant parts of California history** while wandering Sonoma's historic town square. Seeing Mission San Francisco Solano, General Vallejo's home, and the Sonoma Barracks brings it all to life. *See p 17.*

❷ **Attempting a romantic tandem bike tour of Sonoma's charming wineries,** then enjoying an intimate lunch for two at Gundlach Bunschu's hillside picnic grounds. *See p 61.*

❸ **Savoring the perfectly crafted small dishes** off the tasting menu at one of Yountville's renowned restaurants, such as Thomas Keller's French Laundry (p 96), hailed by famously exacting celebrity chef Anthony Bourdain as the best restaurant in the U.S.

❹ **Trying to identify the 35 vintners** in the John Michael Keating painting on display at the Napa Valley Museum's permanent exhibit, *California Wine: The Science of an Art.* (Did you spot Robert Mondavi, Joseph Phelps, or Louis P. Martini?) *See p 53.*

❺ **Riding the tractor tram at Benziger Family Winery** through pastoral hills, learning about biodynamic wines and winemaking. Your tour ("the most comprehensive tour in the wine industry," according to *Wine Spectator*) winds through estate

Visiting a Farmer's Market is a fun way to embrace the local culture.

California has its own Old Faithful.

vineyards and into caves, and ends with a memorable tasting. *See p 135.*

❻ **Gasping at the beauty of spring wildflowers** bursting forth from Audubon Canyon Ranch's well-guarded Bouverie Preserve, in Glen Ellen—don't be surprised if you spot a wild egret or a bobcat. *See p 98.*

❼ **Enjoying a gourmet picnic** on the grounds of a winery on the Silverado Trail.

❽ **Losing yourself in a foodie reverie** at the Culinary Institute of America's expansive campus store, Spice Islands Marketplace. *See p 33.*

❾ **Embracing local culture, flavor, and music** at one of wine country's many farmers' markets. You can find one nearly every day of the week; the most popular is the Sonoma Plaza Friday Farmer's Market. *See p 21.*

❿ **Getting current on modern and regional art**—while enjoying a breath of fresh air—at Napa's 217-acre (87-hectare) di Rosa Preserve, where visitors enjoy local artists' works throughout fauna-rich meadows. *See p 57.*

⓫ **Jumping back in (anticipated) surprise at the eruption** of Calistoga's famous Old Faithful Geyser. Sure, it happens every half-hour, but when was the last time you've seen water this hot shoot 60 feet (18m) into the air? *See p 38.*

⑫ Kayaking down the Russian River on a lazy afternoon, looking for the perfect bank on which to savor your gourmet picnic and split of local sparkling wine. *See p 114.*

⑬ Feeling the exhilaration as you drive an open stretch of country highway like scenic Route 12, aka Valley of the Moon Highway; few windshield views surpass those that frame countless rows of grapevines fanning by.

⑭ Relishing a contemplative moment amidst the 1,000-year-old trees at the Armstrong Redwoods State Reserve. *See p 110.*

⑮ Immersing your body in min-eral hot springs or a soothing warm mud bath at one of Calistoga's thera-peutic spas. Dr. Wilkinson's Hot Springs Resort in Calistoga is one of the best. *See p 103.*

⑯ Chuckling at the antics of Lucy, Snoopy, and the rest of the *Peanuts* gang during a stroll through Santa Rosa's whimsical Charles M. Schulz Museum, which honors the cartoonist's prolific contribution to American culture. *See p 37.*

The best way to grasp the scope of Napa & Sonoma is to float above its vineyards in awe.

⑰ Floating aloft in a spectacularly colored hot-air balloon, serenely surveying miles of vineyards. The sensation is magical. *See p 64.*

⑱ Lingering over a bustling tast-ing room counter, quietly realizing you've just found the wine you'd like to use to toast your child's, or grandchild's, wedding. ●

The Peanuts *gang makes an appearance in Santa Rosa.*

Napa & Sonoma

Napa and **Sonoma** will bombard you with much to see and do, and not enough time to do it—it's easy to get overwhelmed by all there is to experience, and difficult to decide which of the region's 350-plus wineries seem most worthy and how best to experience it to the fullest. My best advice is to have an itinerary and a sense of what kind of vacation you want before you arrive. Use this book to chart your course and choose the special-interest tours that appeal to you.

Rule #1: Decide which county to focus on: Napa, Sonoma, or equal amounts of both.

Once you know that, determine which parts of each valley seem to beckon most (perusing this book's "Charming Towns" chapter, p 71, will help). Know that Napa Valley dwarfs Sonoma Valley in population, number of wineries, and sheer traffic. It's the more commercial region, boasting big names (Mondavi, Beringer,

Krug), more spas, and a generally superior selection of restaurants and hotels. Sonoma, however, is catching up quickly, although many people prefer its brand of under-doggedness. It's lower key, less snobby, and more backcountry—kind of like a Napa for insiders. Small, family-owned wineries are its mainstay; tastings are less expensive (sometimes free), and winemakers themselves are often in the tasting room pouring your flight. Choose Napa if you want an active touring schedule, and Sonoma for a restful, leisurely vacation.

Rule #2: Don't drink and drive—and don't speed, either.

Those tiny tastes add up. There are plenty of taxi and limo companies that will be more than happy to chauffeur you if you have too much to drink. Otherwise, designate a driver.

Rule #3: Visit wineries early in the day, if possible.

Most tasting rooms open around 10am and, even on the busiest weekends, remain empty in the morning, leaving staff free to discuss their product. If you come after noon, the tasting room may be packed (especially if it's high season), and many others will be waiting in line just to get a sample, much less the employees' prolonged attention.

Rule #4: To avoid the masses altogether, visit during off-season (Nov–May) or midweek.

The region's optimum time, "crush," the late-Aug–mid-Oct grape harvest, coincides with peak tourist season. If you can only get here on a high-season weekend, there are still ways to avoid the cattle drive: Opt for smaller, family-run wineries over the big boys. Even those along the Silverado Trail, which parallels Highway 29, receive significantly less traffic; locals use it as their main thoroughfare during high season. Another option is to stay in Sonoma. Though it, too, suffers from congestion, Sonoma gets less packed than Napa.

Note that most wineries are closed on major holidays, and many have restricted off-season hours, so call ahead if there's one you don't want to miss.

Rule #5: Be conscious of tasting fees.

Visitors didn't used to have to pay for sampling, but when Napa became a booming destination, wineries began collecting. To their credit, it wasn't so much to make a profit as to discourage visitors who, shall we say, preferred quantity over quality. Nowadays, the Napa norm is to charge about $2 to $8 per flight (though it's much higher at certain places), which is often refundable toward a purchase and sometimes includes a souvenir glass. Sonoma's wineries are less likely to charge for tasting.

Rule #6: Just because you're buying wine at the winery doesn't mean you're saving money.

In fact, you'll probably end up spending more at a winery than you would at stores that buy cases in bulk. Exceptions to this strategy are wineries that offer big discounts on cases and those that only sell their wines in the tasting room (that is, they have no distribution). **Note:** If you're able to ship your wine directly from the winery, you'll avoid having to pay sales tax.

Rule #7: Don't let your wine cook in the back of your car, or you'll be unpleasantly surprised at its new flavor.

Buy a cheap Styrofoam cooler and a couple of ice packs, place them in

A field of mustard seeds in Napa Valley.

Remember: A visit to wine country means you can (and should) drink champagne before noon. This is wine country—kick back and relax.

your car's trunk, and *Voilà!*—you own a portable wine cellar.

Wine shipping is an alternative to lugging around all that *vino* you bought, but it can be quite confusing, since it's limited by regulations that vary by state. Complicating the matter, shipping rules also differ from winery to winery. It's a good idea to check the current legal situation as it pertains to your home state before buying. Ask wineries and, if necessary, independent shipping companies about their wine-transporting policies.

Rule #8: Keep a light attitude.
If you don't yet know everything about wine and it seems that everyone around you does (to an

almost silly degree), don't fall prey to the sometimes-snobby attitude of those who deem themselves worthier than thou simply because they're better versed in what's essentially only a beverage. Wine country is about relaxing, having fun, learning, and taking in the spectacular scenery—not feeling intimidated. If you encounter a superior attitude pouring your taste, move on.

Rule #9: Make time to veer away from the wineries to explore the region's natural splendor.
You can hike through a redwood tree forest, kayak the Russian River, stroll along the rocky Pacific coastline in Bodega Bay, and more. See "18 Favorite Moments" (p 1) and chapter 5, "The Great Outdoors," for details.

Rule #10: Get to know the wine and the winery. Talk. Listen. Learn.
When at a winery, take the time to really get to know not only the wines but also the company's story: its history, its vineyards, and its colorful employees. Most staffers are quite willing to regale you with tales; if you want more, take a tour. You can drink California wine just about anywhere, but only by visiting a tasting room or touring a winery can you gain true appreciation for the painstaking and artistic processes that go into each bottle. ●

All roads lead to another fantastic winery.

The Best **Full-Day Tours of Napa & Sonoma**

The Best of Napa **in One Day**

To Robert Louis Stevenson Mem. St. Pk.

To Lake Berryessa

Pope Valley

Calistoga
To Petrified Forest

Lake County Hwy

Silverado Trail

Napa R.

Diamond Mountain Rd.

Bothe-Napa Valley State Park

Bale Gristmill St. Hist. Park

Spring Mountain Rd.

Bell Canyon Res.

Howell Mtn. Rd.

Angwin

Lake Posada State Forest

NAPA COUNTY

St. Helena

Hood Mountain Regional Park

Sulphur Springs

W. Zinfandel Ln.

Zinfandel Ln.

Conn Valley Rd.

Lake Hennessey Rec. Area

Lake Hennessey

Sage Canyon

Sugarloaf Ridge State Park

Rutherford ❼

Niebaum Ln.

❻

Rutherford Cross Rd.

Conn Creek Rd.

Oakville Cross Rd.

Conn Ck.

Rector Res.

SONOMA COUNTY

Sonoma Highway

Oakville Grade

Oakville

Dwyer Rd.

Glen Ellen

Jack London State Park

Mt. Veeder

Mt. Veeder Rd.

Dry Creek Rd.

Yountville Cross Rd.

Yountville ❽

❺ Washington St.

❾

Silverado Trail

Redwood Rd.

❹

Oak Knoll Ave.

❸

Trancas St.

SONOMA

SONOMA Map Area

NAPA

Carneros Ck.

Henry Rd.

Old Sonoma Rd.

NAPA

Napa Valley Wine Train ❶ ❷

Napa River

Cutting Wharf Rd.

To San Francisco

0 ____ 2 miles
0 ____ 2 kms

N

❶ Downtown Napa
❷ Napa General Store
❸ The Hess Collection
❹ Clos du Val
❺ Domaine Chandon
❻ Robert Mondavi Winery
❼ Rubicon Estate
❽ The French Laundry
❾ Bouchon

All you have is a day to make the most of Napa? It's a tall order because the valley is so rich with delightful towns, wineries, sights, and activities, but it can be done—and done well. This full-day itinerary, doable in a day by car, introduces you to the region's fundamental character. At the end of the day, rest assured that you've truly experienced the essence of Napa. But remember, drinking-and-driving rules still apply, so designate a driver, don't swallow the wine, or limit your intake and eat heartily. START: **1st & Main sts. Tour distance: About 36 miles (68km).**

❶ ★★ kids **Downtown Napa.** Not long ago, the actual town of Napa would never have been listed in a "best of Napa Valley" tour—but times have changed and the town's recent redevelopment merits it a spot right at the top. Hit select spots on the Napa walking tour (p 72): **Dwight Murray Plaza** for the clock tower and waterfront mural, **Napa Town Center** to get a feel for everyday life here, **Vintner's Collective** to kick off your wine-tasting day, and the striking Italianate-style **Opera House.** *Napa Valley Conference & Visitors Bureau, 1310 Napa Town Center, Napa.* ☎ *707/226-7459. www.napavalley.org. Mon–Sat 9am–5pm; Sun 11am–5pm.*

❷ ★ **Napa General Store.** End your downtown Napa visit at the Historic Napa Mill to pick up a box lunch ($15); choose from a variety of fresh sandwiches and salads that come with a house-baked cookie and utensils. **Note:** Box lunches must be ordered a day in advance. If you didn't pre-order, get something to go from the market's cafe (sandwiches, salads, pan-Asian specialties, and hand-tossed pizzas) or sit down and eat here—a cozy option if the weather's unsavory. *540 Main St., Napa.* ☎ *707/259-0762. $$.*

Take Hwy. 29 north and exit at Trancas St. Turn left on Redwood Rd., a 4-lane road that narrows into a 2-lane road. Turn left at the Hess Collection's sign.

❸ ★★★ **The Hess Collection.** The beautiful drive up provides a good example of the pristine scenery that characterizes much of northern California. The winery itself includes art galleries, a garden that fully blooms in summer, and a reflecting pond with water lilies. The

You are officially here!

WELCOME to this world famous wine growing region
NAPA VALLEY
...and the wine is bottled poetry...
OAKVILLE

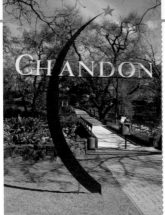

Stop off for a refreshing glass of sparkling wine at Domaine Chandon.

impressive stone-walled tasting room in the original 1903 winery features a maple bar, barrel-lined walls, and the true highlight: a full selection of Hess's current releases, including superb cabernet sauvignon and chardonnay. *4411 Redwood Rd., Napa.* ☎ *877/707-4377. See p 148.*

Wind back down Redwood Rd. and stay straight onto Trancas St., then turn left on Silverado Trail.

❹ ★ **Clos du Val.** You can't say you've done Napa's best without having seen at least one small, exclusive winery in the Stags Leap District along scenic Silverado Trail. Marked with both French and American flags to affirm that this estate is French-owned, Clos du Val's tasting room is behind ivy-covered walls. In it, try Ariadne, the winery's proprietary blend of sauvignon blanc and Sémillon. Ask tasting room staff for a tour of the demonstration vineyard, where you can learn about trellising techniques and how to identify different kinds of grapes. After trying the wines, settle into Clos du Val's beautiful olive grove and break out the food you bought earlier for a picnic lunch. *5330 Silverado Trail, Napa.* ☎ *707/259-2200. See p 141.*

Head southeast on Silverado Trail and turn right at Oak Knoll Ave., then left on Big Ranch Rd. Turn right to get back onto Oak Knoll Ave., and right again to get on Hwy. 29 N. Exit toward Yountville and turn left on California Dr. and head up the long, vineyard-flanked driveway.

❺ ★ **Domaine Chandon.** Cross a small footbridge over a life-filled pond (keep an eye out for egrets) and past some intricately placed sculptures (including a faux mushroom field) to enter the educational visitor center, complete with a 28-seat large-screen theater, a wall made entirely of bottles, and interactive exhibits. Domaine Chandon specializes in "sparkling wine"—technically, it can't be called champagne because it's not produced in that proprietary French province. But since this winery *is* owned by the venerable French company Moët et Chandon, what you get is pretty similar. The knowledgeable staff explains the nuances of effervescent wine. *1 California Dr. (at Hwy. 29), Yountville.* ☎ *707/ 944-2280. See p 143.*

Take California Dr. northeast to merge onto Hwy. 29.

❻ ★★ **Robert Mondavi Winery.** This mission-style winery gives the valley's most varied and comprehensive tours. Given today's time constraint, however, opt for the basic tour or simply visit the art gallery before or after tasting in the Appellation Room, an outdoor tasting area that's open in summer. If it's winter, taste in the upscale ToKalon Room. *7801 St. Helena Hwy. (Hwy. 29), Oakville.* ☎ *707/ 226-1395. See p 155.*

Keep following Hwy. 29 northwest.

❼ ★★★ **Rubicon Estate.** Still better known by its former name,

Niebaum-Coppola (and even to some, its historic name before that, Inglenook Vineyards), Rubicon is director Francis Ford Coppola's ivy-draped 1880s stone winery that exudes momentous grandeur. Inside, it's an impressive retail center promoting Coppola's products and, more subtly, his films. The Centennial Museum chronicles the wine-making estate's rich history, as well as Coppola's filmmaking—on display are Academy Awards and memorabilia from *The Godfather* and *Bram Stoker's Dracula*. Sample estate-grown blends, cabernet franc, and merlot—all made from organic grapes, but note the caveat: a $25 admission fee. For the price, you'll get a tour and a five-wine tasting flight. *1991 St. Helena Hwy., Rutherford.* ☎ *707/968-1100. See p 156.*

In 2006, Francis Ford Coppola changed the name of his winery from Niebaum-Coppola to Rubicon Estate.

⑧ ★★★ **The French Laundry.** If you want the *best* of Napa dining, there's only one place to go: a very, very famous little restaurant called The French Laundry. This is unlike any other dining experience you've ever had. Chef Thomas Keller's intricate preparations, often finished tableside, are presented with uncommon artistry. The prix-fixe dinners come in either five or nine utterly sublime courses, but when the check arrives, close your eyes as you slip your credit card into the folio and reassure yourself that this was a once-in-a-lifetime experience. **Reservations are required and should be made at least 2 months in advance.** *6640 Washington St., Yountville.* ☎ *707/944-2380. $$$$$. See p 96.* If you've still got next month's rent to pay, dine at humbler ⑨ ★★ **Bouchon.** You'll still be eating Keller's inspired creations, but in toned-down bistro environs that are far more friendly than froufrou. *6534 Washington St.* ☎ *707/944-8037. $$$. See p 96.*

Mr. Robert Mondavi in the barrel room.

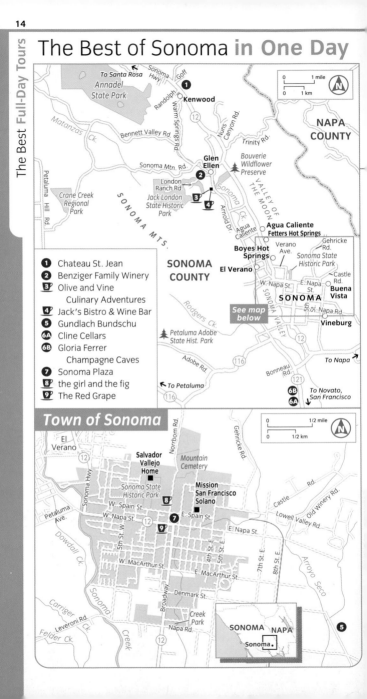

The Best of Sonoma **in One Day**

To Santa Rosa

Sonoma Hwy

Goff

Annadel
State Park

①

Randolph

Warm Springs Rd.

Kenwood

0   1 mile
0   1 km

**NAPA
COUNTY**

Matanzas   Ck.

Bennett Valley Rd.

Nuns Canyon Rd.

(12)

Trinity Rd.

Petaluma Hill Rd.

Crane Creek
Regional
Park

Sonoma Mtn. Rd.

**Glen
Ellen**

*Bouverie
Wildflower
Preserve*

②

VALLEY OF THE MOON

London
Ranch Rd.

*Jack London
State Historic
Park*

③

④

Sonoma Ck.

Arnold Dr.

Agua
Caliente

Agua Caliente
Fetters Hot Springs

Gehricke
Rd.

S O N O M A   M T S.

**Boyes Hot
Springs**

Verano
Ave.

*Sonoma State
Historic Park*

Castle
Rd.

**SONOMA
COUNTY**

El Verano

W. Napa St.

E. Napa
St.

SONOMA

**Buena
Vista**

① Chateau St. Jean
② Benziger Family Winery
③ Olive and Vine
　 Culinary Adventures
④ Jack's Bistro & Wine Bar
⑤ Gundlach Bundschu
⑥A Cline Cellars
⑥B Gloria Ferrer
　 Champagne Caves
⑦ Sonoma Plaza
⑧ the girl and the fig
⑨ The Red Grape

Rodgers Ck.

*Petaluma Adobe
State Hist. Park*

Adobe Rd.

(116)

**See map
below**

5th St.

Napa Rd.

Vineburg

(12)

Bonneau
Rd.

To Napa

←*To Petaluma*

(116)

(121)

⑥B
⑥A

*To Novato,
San Francisco*

Town of Sonoma

Northom Rd.

0   1/2 mile
0   1/2 km

El
Verano

(12)

*Mountain
Cemetery*

Gehricke Rd.

**Salvador
Vallejo
Home**

*Sonoma State
Historic Park*

**Mission
San Francisco
Solano**

Castle   Rd.

Old Winery Rd.

Sonoma Hwy

W. Spain St.

⑧

E. Spain St.

Lowell Valley Rd.

Petaluma
Ave.

W. Napa St.

(12)

⑦

E. Napa St.

Dowdall Ck.

5th St. W.

⑨

4th St. E.

5th St. E.

7th St. E.

8th St. E.

Arroyo Seco

W. MacArthur St.

E. MacArthur St.

Carriger

Sonoma

Leveroni Rd.

Broadway

Denmark St.

Felder Ck.

Creek
Park

Napa Rd.

(12)

Creek

SONOMA **NAPA**

Sonoma ■

⑤

Sonoma Valley is a bit like a younger sibling to Napa Valley; it's made up of the same kind of magic, but one gets the sense that it tries hard to live up to Napa's renown. The struggle to measure up has certainly paid off, to the degree that many visitors profess that Sonoma has actually surpassed Napa in charm—and wine. This one-day overview gives you a sense of the wineries, allows you to experience the small-town feel, and takes you along breathtakingly bucolic stretches of highway. START: **Chateau St. Jean, 8555 Sonoma Hwy. (Hwy. 12), Kenwood. Trip Length: 26 miles (42km).**

① ★★ Chateau St. Jean. Notable for its grand buildings and expansive grounds, Chateau St. Jean is, in California, a pioneer in vineyard designation—the procedure of making wine from, and naming it for, a single vineyard. A private drive takes you to a well-manicured picnic lawn overlooking meticulously maintained vineyards. In the large tasting room, where there are plenty of housewares for sale, sample Chateau St Jean's wide array of wines, including chardonnay, cabernet sauvignon, Johannesburg Riesling, and gewürztraminer. "Sideways" notwithstanding, merlot is the winery's bestseller. *8555 Sonoma Hwy. (Hwy. 12), Kenwood.* ☎ *707/833-4134.* *See p 139.*

Continue southeast on Hwy. 12, turn right onto Arnold Dr., then make a slight right onto London Ranch Rd.

② ★★ kids Benziger Family Winery. This is a true family winery. At any given time, two generations of Benzigers may be present, and they instantly make you feel like part of the clan. The pastoral property presents an exceptional 45-minute tractor-tram tour ($10), which winds through the estate vineyards while providing a thorough explanation of why it's a certified biodynamic winery. The tram stops often so that visitors can see exhibits and walk into aromatic aging caves; the tour ends with an informative tasting. **Tip:** Tram tickets—a hot item in the summer—are available on a first-come, first-served basis, so if the next tram ride is full, taste wines in the tasting room first and take the tour after. *1883 London Ranch Rd., Glen Ellen.* ☎ *888/490-2739.* *See p 135.*

Striking structures define Chateau St. Jean.

From Benziger, take London Ranch Rd. northeast (toward Chauvet Rd.), then turn right onto Arnold Dr., where you'll find the quaint Jack London Village complex, and in it:

3 ★ Olive and Vine Culinary Adventures. Grab a tasty box lunch at this Glen Ellen cafe/catering company whose food emphasizes fresh, local ingredients. Focaccia or ciabatta sandwiches come with salad, fruit, and a homemade cookie. Carry out your meal and save it for the outdoor picnic grounds at the next stop. ☎ 707/996-9150. $$. If the weather's inclement, the cafe has a few indoor tables. Alternatively, eat at **4 ★★ Jack's Bistro & Wine Bar**, a lovingly refurbished French-inspired bistro. ☎ 707/933-3043. $$. Both at 14301 Arnold Dr. See p 101.

From Jack London Village, take Arnold Dr. south (toward Holt), then turn left onto Leveroni Rd. Two miles (3.2km) after Leveroni becomes Napa Rd., make a left onto Denmark St. You'll almost immediately see:

5 ★★ Gundlach Bundschu. If it looks like the people working here are enjoying themselves, that's because they are. Gundlach Bundschu is the quintessential Sonoma winery—nonchalant in appearance but obsessed with wine. Members of this winemaking family are known for their mischievousness: They've pulled stunts like holding up Napa's Wine Train (p 67) on horseback and serving Sonoma wines to their "captives." The small, often crowded tasting room plays rock music as carefree—but attentive—staffers happily pour

chardonnay, pinot noir, merlot, cabernet, and others. Now in its sixth generation, this is California's oldest continually family-owned and -operated winery. Unfold your lunch feast here; GB's wonderful picnic area is perched on the side of a small hill, giving it a sensational view of the Sonoma countryside. Work up an appetite by taking a short hike to the top of the knoll. *2000 Denmark St., Sonoma.* ☎ *707/938-5277. See p 147.*

Choose between visiting Gloria Ferrer or Cline, which are almost adjacent. Travel less than 2 miles (3.2km) north on Hwy. 121 and pull into either:

6A ★ kids Cline Cellars. If you're more interested in California history and tasting an array of unique wines, opt for this family-owned winery with a small, friendly tasting room and a small museum showcasing dollhouse-sized dioramas of all 21 California missions. *24737 Carneros Hwy. (Calif. 121), Sonoma.* ☎ *707/940-4000. See p 140.*

OR:

6B Gloria Ferrer Champagne Caves. If you have had it up to here with chardonnays and pinots—or are simply a big fan of champagne—choose Gloria Ferrer, which specializes in sparkling wine. It's a bit overrated as a tourist attraction—to see the eponymous caves, you merely stand at a railing and flip on a light switch, then wonder to yourself, "That's *it*?" But the bubbly's good, so come expecting just that, and you won't be disappointed. Also note that the tasting room only offers wine by the glass (not flights), so it's not the best choice if you want to try a variety. *23555 Carneros Hwy. (Calif. 121), Sonoma.* ☎ *707/996-7256.*

A winemaker tops off barrels in Sonoma Valley.

www.gloriaferrer.com. Daily 10:30am–5:30pm. Guided underground cave tours (free) daily noon, 2 & 4pm. Tastings $2–$10. Map p 146.

Continue northwest on Hwy. 121/Carneros Hwy./Arnold Dr., then turn right onto W. Watmaugh Rd. After about a mile (1.6km), turn left onto Broadway and stay on it until it ends on Napa St. Turn left or right and look for parking:

7 ★★★ **kids** **Sonoma Plaza.** The 8-acre site of the 1846 Bear Flag Revolt is the pulse point of the entire county, and it hums with history and local culture. Despite the tense confrontation it commemorates, the plaza (California's oldest) couldn't be more relaxing; its park-like atmosphere promotes cheeriness, while well-preserved historic monuments—like the fascinating Mission San Francisco de Solano, City Hall, General Vallejo's home, and old army barracks—add wonder and mystique. You'll be hard-pressed not to leave the plaza lugging shopping bags, since the boutiques, bakeries, tasting rooms, and galleries are nearly irresistible. If your evening stroll is on a Tuesday in spring or summer, you'll catch the wonderful farmers' market and its

accompanying music shows. (For more on farmers' markets, see p 21.) *Sonoma Valley Visitors Bureau, 453 1st St. E.* ☎ *707/996-1090. www.sonomavalley.com. Daily 9am–6pm in winter; until 7pm in summer. For more on Sonoma, see p 78.*

8 ★★ **the girl and the fig.** For dinner, go with this local favorite right on the plaza. From its refusal to use uppercase letters to its insistence on using figs in many of its recipes, this warmly decorated eatery serving inventive nouveau French cuisine makes sure to defy convention, which works greatly to its benefit. Sit outside if the weather's pleasant, and save room for dessert. *110 W. Spain St. (in the Sonoma Hotel), Sonoma.* ☎ *707/938-3634. www.thegirland thefig.com. $$. See p 81.* If you're in the mood for great pizza, try **9** ★ **kids** **The Red Grape,** a casual, artsy space a half-block from the plaza. Its unconventional selection of crispy thin-crust pies made with fresh local ingredients in woodstone ovens gratifies even the snobbiest of pizza connoisseurs. *529 1st St. W., Sonoma.* ☎ *707/996-4103. www.theredgrape.com. $$.*

The Best of Napa & Sonoma in Three Days—Day 3

0 — 4 Miles
0 — 4 Kms

To Ukiah
Geyserville
To Napa, St. Helena
LAKE COUNTY
Robert Louis Stevenson St. Park
NAPA COUNTY
Jimtown
Lytton
Kellogg
Redwood Ck.
Old Faithful Geyser of California
Healdsburg
SONOMA COUNTY
Calistoga
Foothill Reg. Park
Safari West Wildlife Preserve
Bothe-Napa Valley St. Park
East Windsor
Petrified Forest
Bale Gristmill St. Hist. Park
Windsor
Mark West Springs
St. Helena Rd.
To Napa, St. Helena
Santa Rosa
To Sonoma
Annadel State Park
Map Area SONOMA NAPA

1. Bonaventura Balloon Co. *(see below)*
2. Old Faithful Geyser of CA
3. Schramsberg
4. Sterling Vineyards
5. Petrified Forest
6. Jordan Winery
7. Alexander Valley Grille
8. Quail Run Restaurant
9. River Rock Casino

Follow the previous two itineraries for your first couple of days. On the third day, this full-day up-valley Napa and Sonoma tour shows you the natural lay of the land from above (think balloons and aerial trams), below (from whence the geyser spews), and through. ***Tips:*** Plan ahead—advance reservations are required for ballooning and Jordan Winery. Ballooning requires rising around 5 or 6am. START: **Your hotel. Distance: 50 miles (81km; not including transport to, from, and during the hot-air balloon ride, or the drive from your hotel to Old Faithful).**

1 ★★★ ᴷᴵᴰˢ **Bonaventura Balloon Co.** If you've been in wine country this long, you've undoubtedly seen the colorful hot-air balloons floating above the vineyards. Sure, it means getting up at an ungodly hour—but once aloft, you'll know what true sanctity means.

Bonaventura's (the name means "good adventure") expert pilot maneuvers the balloon into the clouds, creating a sublime experience. A full champagne breakfast is served upon landing. **Reservations are required and should be made as far in advance as possible.**

The vineyards of Schramsberg are high up on the west side of Napa Valley.

📞 800/FLY-NAPA. www.bonaventura balloons.com. About $215 per person, including transportation. See p 65. Another good company providing rides is ★★★ kids **Adventures Aloft.** 📞 707/944-4408. www. nvaloft.com. $205 per person, including transportation to/from your hotel to the launch site. See p 64.

Ballooning Tip

When the valley's foggy, companies drive passengers outside the valley to launch. Though they cannot guarantee the flight path until hours before liftoff, they should refund your money if you decide not to partake.

Bonaventura will deliver you back to your hotel. From there, drive to

❷ ★ kids **Old Faithful Geyser of California.** At this natural wonder (it's one of only three "old faithful" geysers in the world) surrounded by pleasant kitsch, you can dependably see 60-foot-high (18m) eruptions every 40 minutes. If you want, buy treats at the snack bar to munch on between spews. Or linger at the gift shop, where you can watch a video all about California, get a penny stamped to remind you of

your visit, or buy California-themed mugs, key chains, and wine glasses. *1299 Tubbs Lane, Calistoga.* 📞 707/942-6463. See p 38.

Take Tubbs Lane southwest and turn left on Foothill Blvd /Hwy 128. Turn right on Peterson Dr., then right on Schramsberg Rd.

❸ ★★ **Schramsberg.** This 200-acre (80-hectare) estate has a wonderful old-world feel—in his heyday, Robert Louis Stevenson was a regular. Schramsberg is the label presidents serve when toasting dignitaries from around the globe, and there's plenty of historic memorabilia in the front room to prove it. But the real mystique begins when you enter the 2½-mile (4km) aging caves (reputedly the longest in North America), hand-carved by Chinese laborers in the 1800s. The comprehensive free tour ends in a charming tasting room, where you sit around a big table and sample varied selections of bubbly. *1400 Schramsberg Rd., Calistoga.* 📞 707/942-2414. See p 157.

Head northeast on Schramsberg Rd. to turn left on Peterson Dr. Turn left on Hwy. 29/128, then right on Dunaweal Lane.

❹ ★★ kids Sterling Vineyards.
An aerial tram brings you to this dazzlingly white Mediterranean-style winery, perched atop a 300-foot-high (90m) rocky knoll. On the way up, you'll marvel at breathtaking views spanning Napa Valley's vineyards. When you land, follow the multimedia self-guided tour (one of wine country's most thorough) detailing the winemaking process. This winery produces more than 500,000 cases per year (read: *huge* producer) and admission includes a sit-down wine tasting. *1111 Dunaweal Lane, Calistoga.* ☎ *707/942-3300. See p 158.*

Go south on Dunaweal Lane to turn right on Hwy. 29/128. Turn left on Petrified Forest Rd.

❺ ★★ kids Petrified Forest.
Volcanic ash blanketed this area after Mount St. Helena erupted more than 3 million years ago. As a result, the redwoods in this mile-long forest have turned to rock through the slow infiltration of silica and other minerals. If you look closely, you'll also see petrified seashells, clams, and other marine life, indicating that water covered this area before the redwood forest grew. Take the quarter-mile (.4km) walking trail to see a collection of petrified logs, the Pit Tree (a preserved pine in a 15-ft./4.5m-deep pit), a statue of Petrified Charlie (Charles Evans, this land's first

A vine grows on a wall at Jordan Winery.

owner), and other trees-turned-to-stone with names like The Giant (a redwood) and The Queen, which has an oak growing out of it. *4100 Petrified Forest Rd.* ☎ *707/942-6667. See p 37.*

Take Petrified Forest Rd. west and turn right on Porter Creek Rd./Mark West Springs Rd. Merge onto Hwy. 101 N, exit on Lytton Springs Rd. and turn right, then left on Lytton Station Rd., then left on Alexander Valley Rd.

❻ ★★ Jordan Winery. With ivy-covered buildings reminiscent of an18th-century French château and hilltop views of Alexander Valley, Geyser Peak, and Mount St. Helena, Jordan Winery is a must-see in the Healdsburg area. Formal French gardens and a variety of trees (picnic tables are set under a massive, stately oak) add to the experience. Tours of the winemaking facilities happen every day except Sunday and conclude with tastes of cab and chardonnay. **Reservations required.** *1474 Alexander Valley Rd., Healdsburg.* ☎ *707/431-5247. See p 149.*

❼ ★★ Alexander Valley Grille/Moving On Cafe. Have dinner at Francis Coppola's winery's restaurant, formerly Chateau Souverain's Alexander Valley Grille. The menu offers pizzas, salads, seasonal soups, small platters, and a gourmet buffet. *400 Souverain Rd., Geyserville.* ☎ *707/433-3141. $$.* For a more casual meal, dine at **❽ Quail Run Restaurant** at the River Rock Casino. It has a full 24-hour-a-day menu, plus a pretty typical casino buffet during more limited hours. *3250 Hwy. 128, Geyserville.* ☎ *707/857-2777. $$.*

Head east on Alexander Valley Rd. and turn left on Hwy. 128.

❾ ★ River Rock Casino. Open 24 hours a day, 365 days a year, this bungalow-style casino owned by the **Dry Creek Band of Pomo Indians** has more than 1,600 slot machines, a variety of card tables, and frequent live entertainment. Try your luck, but if it runs out, gain perspective on the outside deck overlooking the magnificent hills surrounding Alexander Valley. *3250 Hwy. 128, Geyserville.* ☎ *707/857-2777.*

Local Farmers' Markets

Wine country is alive and colorful with free farmers' markets from **Tuesday** through **Saturday.** Here's when to go where:

TUESDAY: The **Napa Downtown Farmers' Market** happens from 7:30am to noon in COPIA's south parking lot. In addition to fresh locally grown fruits and vegetables, baked goods, and coffee, there's live entertainment as well as a contingency representing nonprofit groups. *500 1st St.* ☎ *707/252-7142. May–Oct.* The **Sonoma Valley Farmers' Market** happens from 5:30pm to dusk; there's produce, food samples, flowers, crafts, nonprofit booths, and live music. *Sonoma Plaza.* ☎ *707/538-7023. Apr–Oct.*

WEDNESDAY: The energy-filled **Guerneville Farmers' Market** takes place on the town square from 4 to 7pm. ☎ *707/865-4171. May–Oct.* **Yountville's Farmers' Market** brings purveyors of organic produce, entertainment, wine tastings, and chef demonstrations from 4:30pm to dusk. *Vintage 1870 parking lot, Washington St.* ☎ *707/257-8481. June–Sept.* **Santa Rosa** holds two Wednesday farmers' markets: one operates year-round in the Veterans Building's east parking lot (at Maple St. and Hwy. 12) from 8:30am to noon (☎ 707/522-8629), and another downtown (May–Aug 5:30–8pm; 4th St. between B and D; ☎ 707/524-2123).

THURSDAY: **Santa Rosa's Downtown Market** happens again from 5 to 8:30pm. *May–Sept. See above for details.*

FRIDAY: **St. Helena's Farmers' Market** at Crane Park (on Crane St., off Hwy. 29) showcases fresh produce, flowers, baked goods, live entertainment, and arts and crafts from 7:30am to noon. ☎ *707/486-2662. May–Oct.* At **Sonoma Valley Friday Farmers' Market** you might see some of the valley's most prominent chefs eyeing the goods. It's open 9am to noon. *Depot Park (at 1st St. W.).* ☎ *707/538-7023.* At Napa's **Chef's Market,** farmers join musicians, artists, winemakers, brewers, and chefs to create a festive Friday-night event from 5 to 9pm. *1290 Napa Town Center (at 1st St.).* ☎ *707/257-0322. May–Aug.*

SATURDAY: **Calistoga Farmers' Market** happens at Old Gliderport from 8:30am to noon. *1546 Lincoln Ave.* ☎ *707/942-0808.* **Santa Rosa** holds another market in the Veterans Building's east parking lot. *See above for details.* In **Healdsburg** from 9am to noon, the town's excellent, sometimes crowded, farmers' market happens a block west of the Plaza (at North and Vine sts.). ☎ *707/431-1956. May–Nov.* The same **Napa Downtown Farmers' Market** also happens on Saturday from 8am to noon. *See above for details.*

The Best of Napa & Sonoma
in Five Days—Days 4 & 5

DAY 4
1. COPIA
2. American Market Café
3. Julia's Kitchen
4. Buena Vista Carneros
5. Sonoma Overlook Trail
6. Café La Haye
7. El Dorado Kitchen

DAY 5
8. Safari West Wildlife Preserve
9. Savannah Café
10. Delilah's
11. Mumm Napa
12. Paraduxx
13. Darioush
14. Redd
15. Pearl

After conducting your first 3 days as outlined on the preceding pages, Days 4 and 5 will serve to solidify your sense of the region, as well as expose you to both valleys' more distinctive attractions. For Day 4's gentle hike, bring drinking water and wear good walking shoes. It's helpful if you spend the night of Day 4 in Sonoma; consider even staying overnight at Safari West, the starting point of Day 5. (See p 124 for lodging details.) **DAY 4 START: COPIA, 500 1st St., Napa. Distance: About 50 miles (81km), including miles walked on the hike. DAY 5 START: Safari West Wildlife Preserve, 3115 Porter Creek Rd., Santa Rosa. Distance: About 32 miles (52km).**

DAY 4:

1 ★★★ COPIA: The American Center for Wine, Food & the Arts. Start your day at this downtown Napa attraction. It's preferable to get here in time for the half-hour orientation tour that begins at 10:15am in the atrium. After the tour, spend the next hour taking a self-guided walking tour through the well-labeled Edible Gardens or exploring the center's food-related artistic and educational exhibits. At 11:45, partake in the daily 25-minute wine program in the Staglin Family Vintage Room, which includes free tastings. (If you're horticulturally inclined and willing to cut short another of today's activities, there's also an hour-long garden tour at 12:15pm.) End your visit at the Cornucopia gift shop, where a classy array of food, wine, and gardenware lures even shopping-averse visitors. *Tip:* Check COPIA's website before visiting to find out about special events—lectures, concerts, and films are scheduled often. *500 1st St., Napa.* ☎ *707/259-1600 or 888/512 6742. www.copia.org. Daily 10am–5pm (closed Tues & holidays). Admission $5, $4 for students & seniors 62+, free for children 12 & under. See p 34.*

2 ★ **American Market Café.** You won't have to go far for lunch: COPIA has two excellent in-house dining options. This first one is casual; order a sandwich or salad at the counter, then picnic outside in abundant gardens. ☎ *707/265-5701. $.* Fancier **3** ★★ **Julia's Kitchen,** named for culinary legend Julia Child, is a sit-down venue where you can watch kitchen staff preparing your California-French food with bounty from COPIA's organic gardens. ☎ *707/265-5700. $$$. See p 77.*

Your scenic 25-minute drive from Napa Valley to Sonoma Valley starts westward on 1st St., then merges onto Hwy. 29 S. Turn right onto Hwy. 12/121, then make a slight right onto Napa Rd. Turn right on 8th St. E., then right again on E. Napa St., then make a quick left on Old Winery Rd.

4 ★★★ **Buena Vista Carneros.** America's oldest continuously operating winery was founded in 1857 and is worth a visit for its historical relevance. A restored stone press houses the tasting room; in it, try what the estate calls the "Carneros Quartet": its pinot noir, chardonnay, merlot, and cabernet sauvignon—all crafted by artisan methods. *18000 Old Winery Rd., Sonoma.* ☎ *800/926-1266. See p 137.*

Take Old Winery Rd. southwest, then turn right on E. Napa St. Turn right on 1st St. E. Just beyond the Veterans Memorial Building is a small lot adjacent to the Mountain Cemetery entrance. Park, then look for the trailhead sign.

5 ★ **Sonoma Overlook Trail.** Take in sweeping afternoon views from this well-maintained trail, an easy 2-mile-plus (3.2km) loop accented by interpretive signage,

COPIA is a food and wine cultural center founded by the Mondavi family.

Contemplate the black and white stripes of a zebra at Safari West Wildlife Preserve.

seasonal wildflowers, and manzanita trees. Not long ago, this hillside was doomed to be developed as a resort, but locals worked in conjunction with The Sonoma Ecology Center to preserve the scenic area. See if you can see San Pablo Bay and San Francisco's skyline; both should be visible on a clear day. Heartier tourists seeking a workout can experience this as a jog instead of a hike. If you're walking, though, allow about 2 hours. ☎ *707/996-0712. www.sonomaecologycenter.org.*

⑥ ★★ **Café La Haye.** You'll have worked up an appetite by now, so opt for dinner at this petite restaurant offering seasonal cuisine. *140 E. Napa St., Sonoma.* ☎ *707/935-5994. $$.*

Hit the patio at Mumm Napa.

⑦ ★★ **El Dorado Kitchen,** a Mediterranean-inspired bistro, is a bit more upscale and refined. *405 1st St. W., Sonoma.* ☎ *707/996-3030. $$$. See p 81.*

DAY 5:

⑧ ★★ **Safari West Wildlife Preserve.** Depending on season, tours at this 400-acre (160-hectare) home to more than 400 exotic animals—think zebras, giraffes, and gazelles—start at 9am or 10am. Though the organization's primary mission is wildlife preservation and breeding endangered species, it incorporates a strong belief that education and in-person contact with animals raises awareness about threatening issues that face them. During the preserve's daily Classic Safari Adventures, then, knowledgeable guides drive you around the surprisingly savannah-like environs in open-air vehicles from which you can see wildebeest, oryx, and ostrich, among many other species, freely roaming about. You'll want to take lots of pictures in the open-air aviary, and of all the lemurs and buffalo within view. If you or your travel companion is into zoology, you can pay extra ($200 for two people; $50 for each additional adult) for a behind-the-scenes tour and chat with the keepers. Advance reservations are essential for all tours,

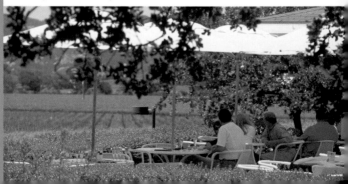

which are about 3 hours long. *3115 Porter Creek Rd., Santa Rosa.* ☎ *707/579-2551 or 800/616-2695. www.safariwest.com. Apr–Oct 28 tours daily at 9am, 1 & 4pm; Oct 29–Mar tours daily at 10am & 2pm. Safari Tours $68, children 3–12 $28.*

9 ★ **Savannah Café.** Power up before leaving Safari West at its on-site sit-down restaurant. ☎ *800/ 616-2695. $$$.* Reservations are required; if you haven't made them, and it's summer, grab a bite from **10** **Delilah's,** Safari West's deli, which offers sandwiches, salads, sides, and wines. ☎ *800/616-2695. $.*

Experience beautiful Silverado Trail. Drive about a half-hour to cross valleys again: Going east on Porter Creek, turn left on Petri fied Forest Rd., then right on Hwy. 28. Turn left on Deer Park Rd., then right on Silverado Trail. Once on the Silverado Trail, this portion of the tour can be done either by bicycle or by car.

11 ★★ **Mumm Napa.** This winery in a big redwood barn looks almost humble at first glance. Once through the door, however, you'll understand that Mumm means big business. Just beyond the extensive gift shop is the tasting room, where you can try sparkling wines. Appreciate vineyard and mountain views on the open patio, and don't miss the permanent Ansel Adams collection, a timeless staple amidst the winery's ever-changing photography exhibits. *8445 Silverado Trail, Rutherford.* ☎ *800/686-6272. See p 152.*

12 ★ **Paraduxx.** Rows of vineyards fan by as you travel farther south on Silverado Trail to reach this airy, chic tasting room. Try flavorful reds served in stemless crystal glasses alongside small plates of spiced almonds. *7257 Silverado*

Embrace California cuisine at Redd.

Trail, Yountville. ☎ *707-945-0890. See p 153.*

13 ★★ **Darioush.** Even farther south on Silverado Trail is this little-known winery that's sure to be huge in a few years. Its dazzling architecture is Persian-themed and wines worth trying include shiraz, merlot, cabernet sauvignon, viognier, and chardonnay, all served with Persian pistachios. Opt for the appointment-only private tasting with cheese pairing ($35), and you'll get tastes of local artisan cheeses with your wine, plus a tour of the stunning facilities. *4240 Silverado Trail, Napa.* ☎ *707-257-2345. See p 142.*

14 ★★ **Redd.** For an impeccable, dinner, go to Chef Richard Reddington's global-inspired Yountville restaurant. His seasonal California creations include signature dishes like butternut-squash ravioli with ragout. *6480 Washington St. Yountville.* ☎ *707-944-2222. $$$. See p 97.* A more casual option is Napa's **15** ★ **Pearl,** a treasure of a restaurant with big, creatively fashioned entrees. *1339 Pearl St., Napa.* ☎ *707-224-9161. $$. See p 77.*

The Best of Napa & Sonoma in One Week—Days 6 & 7

DAY 6
1. Healdsburg
2. Hop Kiln Winery
3. Korbel Champagne Cellars
4. Guerneville
5. Fort Ross State Historic Park
6. Hwy. 1
7. The Tides Wharf & Restaurant

DAY 7
8. Hoffman House Café
9. Locals
10. Russian River
11. Ferrari-Carano
12. Cyrus
13. Bear Republic Brewing Co.

If you've followed these daily tours until now, you've gotten a good sense for lower Sonoma. An extra 2 days gives you the luxury of being able to fully explore northeastern Sonoma, which you got a peek of at the end of Day 3. This itinerary expands on the 5-day tour to include posh Healdsburg, charming Guerneville, and the resplendent scenery that typifies much of California (frankly, it would be a crime to be this close to the Pacific and ignore the rocky coast edging the famed California Hwy. 1). You'll also gain more knowledge of state history at Fort Ross and taste wines from the Dry Creek and Russian River Valley appellations. **Tip:** If you're staying in wine country for a week or more, consider renting a vacation home instead of staying at a hotel. Consult chapter 6 for ideas, or check sites like www.beautiful-places.com and www.riverhomes.com. **DAY 6 START: Plaza St. & Healdsburg Ave., Healdsburg. Distance: About 62 miles (100km). DAY 7 START: Hoffman House Café, 21712 Geyserville Ave., Geyserville. Distance: About 21 miles (34km) not including river kayaking and shuttle.**

DAY 6:

❶ ★★★ Healdsburg. This up-and-coming town gets much of the credit for putting northern Sonoma on the tourist map. Until recently, it didn't even produce a blip on travelers' radar, but it's now a huge draw for those seeking true refinement in Sonoma. You'll find a plethora of tasting rooms (a few of the best are **La Crema, Chateau Felice, Cellar 360,** and **Gallo Family Vineyards**), excellent restaurants, fancy hotels, unique shops and galleries—and a modest small-town vibe. Everything surrounds **Plaza Park,** including chic markets like **Oakville Grocery** and **Plaza Farms.** You can even learn town history at the **Healdsburg Museum.** Before leaving, patronize **Powell's Sweet Shoppe** and **Flying Goat Coffee.** *See p 86 for a detailed walking tour.*

Head south on Healdsburg Ave. to turn right on Mill St. Stay straight to go onto Westside Rd.

❷ ★★ Hop Kiln Winery. Get your first taste of the Russian River Valley appellation at this California Historical Landmark. As its commemorative plaque says, this 1905 structure "represents the finest existing example of its type, consisting of three stone kilns for drying hops, a wooden cooler, and a two-story press for bailing hops for shipment." Indeed, this is a superb

You'll never forget the first time you stepped into a barrel room and inhaled.

example of a stone hop kiln. In the rustic tasting room, sample zinfandel, chardonnay, and the winery's gewürztraminer blend—for free. Also on site: a duck pond and the Old Fig Garden, both perfect for picnics. *6050 Westside Rd., Healdsburg.* ☎ *707/433-6491. See p 149.*

Head southwest on Westside Rd. When you get to River Rd., make a slight right.

❸ ★★ Korbel Champagne Cellars. Korbel, too, is within the Russian River Valley appellation, but it's been specializing in bubbly, produced by the *méthode champenoise,*

Hop Kiln Winery's distinct architecture and style is a must-see.

Korbel's is often flanked by colorful ivy.

since 1882. The winery's colorful rose garden and free tastings make for a delightful visit. If you're getting hungry for lunch, a tasty sandwich from the gourmet deli satisfies. *13250 River Rd., Guerneville.* ☎ *707/824-7000. See p 151.*

Take the beautiful short drive southwest on River Rd., which becomes Main St.

❹ ★★ **Guerneville.** This off-the-beaten-path village is perfect for a walking tour (p 92), and the town's predominantly gay and lesbian population is friendly, progressive, and proud.

Drive toward the ocean by heading southwest on Main St. (Hwy. 116) and making a slight right onto Hwy. 1.

❺ ★★ **kids Fort Ross State Historic Park.** What's now a historic park was the Russians' southernmost settlement in their attempt to colonize North America. See the Call Ranch House and its gardens, the Russian Cemetery, and Fort Ross's natural wonders. *19005 Hwy. 1, Jenner.* ☎ *707/847-3286. www. parks.ca.gov. Park grounds open daily a half-hour before sunrise & close a half-hour after sunset. Historical buildings, the visitor center & the bookstore open daily 10am–4:30pm. Parking $6. See p 114.*

> **Travel Tip: Fort Ross State Historic Park**
>
> Dress appropriately (in layers) for the ever-changing coastal weather, and wear shoes in which you'd be comfortable walking on wet ground.

❻ **Hwy. 1.** Yes, this 21-mile (34km) drive is spectacular enough to merit its own bullet point on this tour—especially during sunset. You'll pass Goat Rock Beach, the Russian River headwaters, the seaside towns of Jenner and Bridge Haven, and a natural cutout called Duncan Cove. End in the resort town of Bodega Bay for a dinner overlooking the water. (See p 113 in chapter 5 for a more detailed description of this drive.)

❼ ★ **kids The Tides Wharf & Restaurant.** All 150 seats at the Inn at the Tides's restaurant afford at least a decent view of the bay. Surroundings look familiar? You're perceptive: This dining room was the backdrop for scenes in one of Alfred Hitchcock's classic thrillers, *The Birds.* Menu options include seafood, pasta, and house-made desserts. *800 Hwy. 1, Bodega Bay. 707/875-3652. $$.*

DAY 7:

★★ **Hoffman House Café.** Buy a boxed lunch (about $10) from this family-owned restaurant specializing in California-style gourmet lunches and have a hot breakfast in this homey dining room, replete with a brick fireplace and stained-glass windows. *21712 Geyserville Ave. (at Geyserville Inn), Geyserville.* ☎ *707/857-3264. $$.*

Take Geyserville Ave. southeast.

❾ **Locals.** Taste Russian River–produced wines at this small, modern tasting room, which stocks more than 60 wines from about 10 tiny wineries. The educational—and free—tasting experience lines up varietal flights, which means you get to taste, say, five merlots or six sauvignon blancs (served in Riedel crystal), to determine how different producers interpret the same type of wine. Buy a bottle of your favorite to go with the lunch you bought at Hoffman House. *21023 Geyserville Ave., Geyserville.* ☎ *707/857-4900. www.tastelocalwines.com. Wed–Mon 11am–6pm (Tues by appointment).*

Follow Geyserville Ave. southeast and get on Hwy. 101 S. Exit on Westside Rd. and turn left on Westside Rd. Stay straight to go onto Mill St., then turn right on Healdsburg Ave. Across the street from the state beach entrance (before the bridge) is the

❿ ★★★ kids **Russian River.** Rent a canoe or kayak from a company called **River's Edge** (you can also buy box lunches directly from them if you didn't opt for the Hoffman House lunch, above) and float 15 miles (24km) from an Alexander Valley campground to River's Edge Beach in Healdsburg. Watch as the biome becomes wooded, and keep an eye out for swimming holes, vineyards, and a good riverbank on which to enjoy the food and wine you brought. The beach at Rio Lindo, 11 miles (18km) down, is a good option, but part of the fun is choosing a spot and making it your own. To leisurely experience the river, allow about 4 to 5 hours. Guided trips are available upon request. Reservations recommended. See chapter 5 (p 107) for more details. *13840 Healdsburg Ave. Healdsburg.* ☎ *800/345-0869. www. riversedgekayakandcanoe.com. Canoes & double kayaks $15 per hour; single kayaks $10 per hour. Rentals include paddles, life vests & shuttle rides.*

Head south on Healdsburg Ave. and get on Hwy. 101 N. Exit on Dry Creek Rd. and turn left on Dry Creek Rd. Turn left on Yoakim Bridge Rd. and right on Dry Creek Rd.

Goat Rock Beach is one of the Sonoma coast's spectacular beaches.

How to Wine-Taste Like a Pro

Stopping at tasting rooms to sample the goods, otherwise known as *wine tasting,* ranks as one of the top rituals in Wine Country touring. It provides pleasure and a chance to learn why the wines of Sonoma and Napa rank high among the wines of the world.

Precautionary notes would say "taste moderately," for there are literally 200 or so tasting rooms, and the virtues in wine take time to notice. Because we're all on a very pleasant learning curve, you can discover wine at many levels. If you should encounter a winery staffer with "attitude" (unfortunately, it happens), don't buy *any* of that wine and simply move on to the next stop.

The time-honored techniques for tasting wine involve three steps: a good look, a good smell, and a good sip of each wine. You'll learn about wine most quickly if you compare them, ideally side by side. Almost any comparison will reveal features of wines you might not see by tasting one wine at a time. You might think of it as the wines talking to one another ("I'm smoother than you are"; "I'm way more puckery than all of you"). By listening to these little conversations, you can discover just how smooth or how puckery you want your wines to be. Tasting rooms in Napa and Sonoma have their own regimens, usually offering a series of wines. When it seems appropriate, and when the tasting room is not too busy, ask your host if you can do some comparisons.

—John Thoreen

⓫ ★★ **Ferrari-Carano.** One of Sonoma's more beautiful wineries has an Italian château–style hospitality center. A highlight here, aside from tasting the chardonnay and other varietals, is walking through the wonderland of colorful flowers in the formal garden. Ponds, waterfalls, and walkways make your visit all the more magical. *8761 Dry Creek Rd., Healdsburg.* ☎ *800/831-0381. See p 144.*

⓬ ★★★ **Cyrus.** The most upscale restaurant in Healdsburg—and all of Sonoma, for that matter—is starting to be talked about as though it's this county's French Laundry. In the unreservedly classy Les Mars Hotel, dinners here are prix-fixe, but you can mix and match courses. Reservations recommended. *29 North St.* ☎ *707/433-3311. $$$$$.* A more laid-back Healdsburg option is

⓭ ★ **kids** **Bear Republic Brewing Co.** This high-energy American brewery with kitschy-but-fun decor is a great place for trying house-made beer and a greasy (in a good way) appetizer, burger, or pasta. *345 Healdsburg Ave.* ☎ *707/433-2337. $$.* ●

Ferrari-Carano is known for its pristine grounds and landscaping.

Wine Country **for Foodies**

1. Dutch Henry
2. CIA
3. Olivier
4. Woodhouse Chocolate
5. St. Helena Olive Oil Co.
6. Dean & Deluca
7. Long Meadow Ranch
8. Round Pond Estate
9. Oakville Grocery
10. The French Laundry
11. COPIA

I **f you're a foodie,** Napa's your ultimate vacation destination. Oodles of specialty food stores, farms, ranches, and culinary institutes will pique your interest. To whet your appetite further, there's a farmers' market virtually every day of the week (p 21). The endless food-and-wine pairings—mixed in with a smattering of some of the world's best restaurants and chefs—are the icing on the cake. **START: In Calistoga, at Dutch Henry. Distance: About 30 miles (48km), doable in a full day.**

1 ★ **Dutch Henry.** This small family-owned winery produces around 5,000 cases of wine annually and even fewer cases of its highly acclaimed olive oil, which is so distinctive that it has its own tasting notes. However, the expertly blended oil of Italian, Spanish, and Mexican olives, at $42 per bottle, isn't cheap, although you can taste it for free.

Reservations recommended. *4310 Silverado Trail, Calistoga.* ☎ *707/ 942-5771. www.dutchhenry.com. Wine tasting $5 for 5 wines, refundable with purchase. Olive oil tasting is free. Daily 10am–4:30pm.*

Head east on Silverado Trail. Turn right on Larkmead Lane. Turn left on Hwy. 29.

Chocoholics beware—Woodhouse will make you break out the emergency credit card.

palate, they're worth the price. Try the fan-shaped Thai ginger tidbit or the brown-butter *ganache* ($1.50 each). *1367 Main St.* ☎ *800/966-3468. www. woodhousechocolate.com. 10:30am– 5:30pm.*

⑤ ★★ St. Helena Olive Oil Co. True foodies will relish the many olive oils, vinegars, honeys, compotes, flavored salts, tapenades, syrups, and sauces available to try here. *1351 Main St.* ☎ *800/939-9880. www.sh oliveoil.com. Daily 10am–5pm.*

Head a bit farther south on Hwy. 29.

⑥ ★★ Dean & Deluca. California's only D&D outlet stocks fresh local produce, cheeses, and a fantastic array of international food products and gifts, not to mention 1,400 California wines. There's an espresso bar, too, if you need a pick-me-up after all of today's noshing. *607 St. Helena Hwy. (Hwy. 29), St. Helena.* ☎ *707/967-9980. www.deandeluca. com. Daily 7am–8pm.*

Keep heading south on Hwy. 29, then turn right on Whitehall Lane.

⑦ ★★ Long Meadow Ranch. This innovative organic farming operation is a winery known for its reds—but it's also an environmentally responsible ranch known for supplying the valley's best restaurants with

② ★★★ The Culinary Institute of America. America's heavyweight of food education. The West Coast arm of the New York institution (CIA, to insiders) is an imposing stone château to which wannabe executive chefs flock to sharpen their skills. Not an enrolled student? No worries: CIA has lots of attractions for day visitors, including chef cooking demos, historical displays of ancient food-producing tools, and an extensive marketplace with all kinds of specialty ingredients, cooking tools, unique utensils, and more cookbooks than you could get through in a long lifetime. *2555 Hwy. 29, St. Helena.* ☎ *707/967-2320. www.ciachef.org. Chef cooking demos $13; Greystone Restaurant entrees $18–$40. Daily 10am–6pm.*

Keep heading south on Hwy. 29. When it becomes St. Helena's Main St., park.

③ ★★★ Olivier. Sample, sample, sample at this French-inspired purveyor of epicurean delights. Big copper olive oil dispensers line the walls, so try mixing your own—or shop for beautiful kitchenware from Provence. *1375 Main St.* ☎ *707/967-8777. See p 83.*

④ ★★ Woodhouse Chocolate. The gourmet handmade confections here cost a pretty penny, but to a true

Buy yourself a new kitchen toy at CIA's California branch.

extra-virgin olive oil, eggs, and heirloom fruits and vegetables. Make a reservation (they're required) for the $35 wine and olive oil tour, which happens only on Saturdays and includes seeing the *frantoio* (olive mill), the valley's oldest olive orchards (planted in the 1870s), and gorgeous views. You'll taste current wine and olive oil releases, too. The $150 "Experience the Excellence" tour includes a hike and an estate-farmed picnic lunch. *1775 Whitehall Lane, St. Helena.* ☎ *707/963-4555. www.longmeadowranch.com. By appointment only.*

Head northeast on Whitehall Lane, then turn right onto Hwy. 29. Turn left on Rutherford Rd.

❽ ★★ Round Pond Estate. If it's not Saturday or you don't want to pay for Long Meadow's more expensive tour, make an appointment at Round Pond, which also makes artisan olive oil and premium red wine. During tours, guests see olive orchards and learn about harvesting techniques, growing olive trees, and oil-extraction processes. After, taste the Italian and Spanish olive oil varieties paired with estate-grown vegetables while an expert discusses the oils' many culinary uses. Reservations required. *886 Rutherford Rd., Rutherford.* ☎ *877/963-9364. www.roundpond.com. Tours ($20) by appointment only.*

❾ ★★ Oakville Grocery. If you didn't already picnic at Long Meadow, Napa's two true foodie options for lunch are on opposite ends of the fanciness scale. Oakville Grocery is a casual, crowded little store selling gourmet foodstuffs (much of it locally made and available for sampling) and sporting a nice wine selection in the back. Buy ready-made sandwiches and entrees, and at the espresso bar, coffee drinks to go. If you're lucky, you'll spot Martha Stewart, a regular here, shopping for flavored salts. *7856 St. Helena Hwy. (Hwy. 29), Oakville.* ☎ *707/944-8802. $.* The second option? You guessed it: **❿ ★★★ The French Laundry,** a culinary experience every gourmand should have, regardless of price or wait. **Reservations required.** Even if you can't get in, wander through Thomas Keller's herb garden across the street from the restaurant. *6640 Washington St.* ☎ *707/944-2380. $$$$$. See p 96.*

From Round Pond Estate, go north on Rutherford Rd./Hwy. 128, which becomes the Silverado Trail. Turn left on Trancas St., then right back onto the Silverado Trail. Turn right on 1st St.

⓫ ★★★ COPIA: The American Center for Wine, Food & the

Get a hands-on demonstration on the olive-oil-making process at Round Pond.

Arts. At today's last stop, experience a panoply of food programs, including tastings, demos, a rotating schedule of educational programs (such as "Chocolate as an Aphrodisiac" and "Catalan Cuisine"), lectures by famous guests, and daily food classes (with topics like "How to Tackle an Artichoke"). Its permanent interactive exhibition, **"Forks in the Road,"** looks at modern American culture within the context of food and drink. Temporary exhibits often explore food-related art and artifacts. *500 1st St., Napa.* ☎ *707/259-1600. www.copia.org.*

Is that a chardonnay- or cabernet-flavored bean? Anything is possible at the Jelly Belly store in Santa Rosa.

Admission $5, $4 students & seniors 62+, free for children 12 & under. Daily 10am–5pm (closed Tues & holidays).

A Foodie Tour of Sonoma

What with the newish "Sonoma Diet" trend plus the introduction of some new and spectacular Sonoma Valley food establishments, the food world is sitting up and taking note. If you're a foodie in Sonoma, here's your must-do list: Spend as much time as possible on **Sonoma County Farm Trails,** a network of local sustainable farms that encourages visitors to come and not only buy, but also have memorable experiences like picking berries, touring apiaries, taking hayrides, and petting farm animals. Visit the website to order a free map and guide. ☎ *707/571-8288 or 800/207-9464. www.farmtrails. org.* Try **El Dorado Kitchen**'s $30 three-course tasting menu, offered every Monday. Add $20 for your meal to be paired with featured wines. Thirty-two-year-old Chef Ryan Fancher was trained by Thomas Keller, who taught him to use French techniques while showcasing wine country's regional products. *405 1st St. W., Sonoma.* ☎ *707/ 996-3030 or 800/289-3030. See p 81.* If you're a fan of Italian, try **Della Santina's,** a family-owned trattoria just off Sonoma's town square. Its Northern Italian food has been a Sonoma staple for 16 years and is a local favorite. *133 E. Napa St., Sonoma.* ☎ *707/935-0576.* Visit **The Olive Press,** an exceptional Pieralisi olive-oil-pressing facility dedicated to making extra-virgin California oils, which are sold alongside culinary delights like tapenades, specialty crackers, and distinctive balsamic vinegars. *14301 Arnold Dr., Glen Ellen.* ☎ *800/965-4839. See p 100.* To satisfy a sweet tooth, visit Petaluma's **Jelly Belly store,** where you can concoct your favorite flavor blends at the sample bar, watch the entire candy-making process on a plasma TV, or simply stock up on all your favorite beans. (Buttered popcorn or cantaloupe, anyone?) *200 Petaluma Blvd., Petaluma.* ☎ *707/782-9700. www.jelly belly.com. Mon–Sat 10am–8pm; Sun 10am–6pm.*

Wine Country **with Kids**

DAY 1
1. Charles M. Schulz Museum
2. The Cantina
3. Fresh Choice
4. Petrified Forest
5. Old Faithful Geyser of California
6. Sterling Vineyards
7. Checkers
8. Pacifico

DAY 2
9. Train Town
10. Benziger Family Winery
11. St. Supéry Winery
12. Napa Firefighters Museum
13. Seguin Moreau Napa Cooperage
14. Downtown Joe's
15. Taqueria Rosita
16. Ben & Jerry's

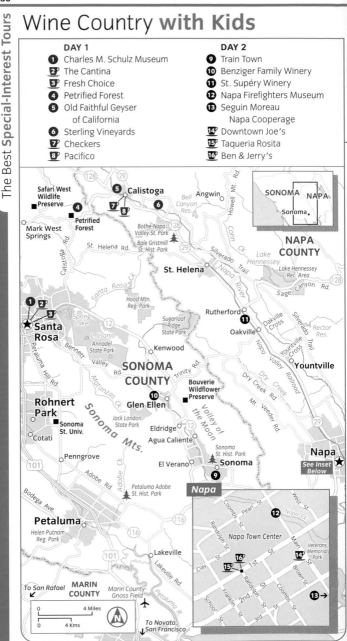

True, Napa and Sonoma are no Orlando or San Diego, but that doesn't mean there isn't lots to do for families wanting to spend quality time together. Some local attractions were in fact designed with kids in mind. Others, while not specifically aimed at entertaining children, can definitely accommodate kids while educating, even perhaps enthralling, them. **Tip:** Flip through this book for other attractions with the **kids** symbol. START: **Charles M. Schultz Museum. Time: 2 full days. Distance: About 20 miles (32km) on Day 1; 40 miles (64km) on Day 2.**

DAY 1

① ★★ Charles M. Schulz Museum. Charlie Brown is practically Santa Rosa's logo: Charles "Sparky" Schulz lived here most of his adult life. In his honor, town residents opened this museum in 2002, less than 2 years after he died. An introductory video, narrated by Schulz's wife, Jean, reveals the local rituals that were a part of the cartoonist's daily life, including his involvement with the **Redwood Empire Ice Arena** adjacent to the museum. Exhibits include a faithful re-creation of Schulz's studio (with his original drawing board, books, and photos); the "Morphing Snoopy Sculpture," an immense artwork portraying Snoopy's many personas; and a mural that, at first glance, looks like that ubiquitous image of Lucy holding the football for Charlie Brown. Look closer, however, and you'll see that the image is actually made of 3,588 comic images printed on small ceramic tiles. You can buy just about any "Peanuts"-themed product you can think up in the massive gift shop. Outside, a Snoopy-shaped contemplative labyrinth adds dimension. *2301 Hardies Lane.* ☎ *707/579-4452. www.schulzmuseum.org. Admission $8, $5 seniors & kids. Sept 25–May 28 Mon & Wed–Fri noon–5pm, Sat–Sun 10am–5pm; May 29–Sept 24 daily 11am–5pm (Sat–Sun opens at 10am).*

② The Cantina, a big, festive Mexican restaurant is particularly child-friendly. *500 4th St.* ☎ *707/523-3663.* Also worth a visit is **③ Fresh Choice,** a healthy buffet-style restaurant. *1018 Santa Rosa Plaza (at 4th St.).* ☎ *707/525-0912.*

From Hardies Lane, turn left on W. Steele Lane, left on Guerneville Rd., then left on Hwy. 101 N. Exit at River Rd. and turn right on Mark Springs Rd. (it turns to the right and becomes Porter Creek Rd.). Turn left at Petrified Forest Rd.

④ ★★ Petrified Forest. Kids can find interesting petrified specimens at this 3.4-million-year-old grove. Volcanic ash blanketed this area after the same eruptions that caused Mount St. Helena to burst forth. The giant redwoods here have since turned to stone through slow infiltration of silicates and other minerals. Take your kids on the quarter-mile

You're the greatest, Charlie Brown.

(.4km) walking trail and tell them to keep an eye out for the park's many marine fossils. There's also an interesting museum, as well as a discovery shop and picnic grounds. *4100 Petrified Forest Rd., Calistoga.* ☎ *707/942-6667. www.petrified forest.org. Adults $6, $5 seniors 60+, $5 kids 12–17, $3 kids 6–11, free for kids under 6. Daily 9am–7pm (5pm in winter).*

Head northeast on Petrified Forest Rd for nearly 4 miles, then turn left on Foothill Blvd./Hwy. 128. Turn right on Tubbs Lane.

❺ ★ **Old Faithful Geyser of California.** One of the world's three "old faithful" geysers is named for its dependable eruptions every 40 minutes, spewing 350°F (177°C) water as high as 60 feet (18m). Kids will be delighted during the 3-minute performance. While waiting, they can peruse educational exhibits about seismic activity and California history in the exhibit hall, which also houses a gift shop and snack bar. The site is also home to fainting goats, which look like regular goats until they're slightly startled; then they stiffen up and fall over. *1299 Tubbs Lane, Calistoga.* ☎ *707/942-6463. www.old faithfulgeyser.com. Admission $8, $7 seniors 60+, $3 kids 6–12, free for kids under 6. Daily 9am–6pm.*

Stone logs fascinate—and perplex—both children and adults.

From Tubbs Lane, turn right onto Hwy. 29, then left on Silverado Trail. Turn right on Dunaweal Lane.

❻ ★★ **Sterling Vineyards.** Now that your kids have developed a thorough affinity for the area, take them along for wine tasting. What's that? You can't do wineries with children? Think again. At Sterling, kids will love the aerial gondola that brings you to the winery. The $10 kids' admission fee includes a goodie bag (adults are $20, kids under 4 are free), and young ones might enjoy seeing the artifacts and videos along the multi-media self-guided tour. Parents will certainly enjoy tasting four wines in the panoramic tasting room. *1111 Dunaweal Lane, Calistoga.* ☎ *707/942-3300. See p 158.*

Go south on Dunaweal Lane to turn right on Hwy. 29/128. Turn left on Petrified Forest Rd.

❼ **Checkers.** Kids will love the pizza and calzones at this cheerful restaurant. *1414 Lincoln Ave.* ☎ *707/ 942-9300. $$. See p 105.* They'll also enjoy the Mexican fare at colorful ❽ ★ **Pacifico.** *1237 Lincoln Ave.* ☎ *707/942-4400. $$. See p 106.*

DAY 2

❾ ★ **Train Town.** It may not be all bells and whistles for adults, but that's exactly what Train Town is for tots. In this mini-amusement park, the theme is locomotion—as in train rides along a scale railroad around the wooded property, over bridges, and past doting parents. Other attractions include a petting zoo, a Ferris wheel, and a carousel. *20264 Broadway, Sonoma.* ☎ *707/938-3912. www.traintown. com. Tickets $3.75, other rides $1.75 per ticket (book of 8 tickets $10). Daily 10am–5pm.*

Take Broadway south to turn left on Leveroni Rd., then right on

A tram ride AND a wine tasting? Only at Benziger.

Arnold Dr. Turn left on London Ranch Rd.

⑩ ★★ Benziger Family Winery. At this family-owned winery, the 45-minute tractor-drawn tram tour will entertain kids and educate them about the agricultural processes that make wine. Tours are first-come, first-served, so if it's high season, come in the morning to buy tickets for later. *1883 London Ranch Rd., Glen Ellen.* ☎ *888/490-2739. See p 135.*

Go northeast on London Ranch Rd. and turn left on Arnold Dr. Turn left on Sonoma Hwy./Hwy. 12, then right on Trinity Rd., which becomes Dry Creek Rd. Stay straight onto Oakville Grade Rd., then turn left on Hwy. 29.

⑪ St. Supéry Winery. The emphasis here is on education. During the self-guided tour, kids wander through a demonstration vineyard and learn about growing techniques. Inside, they'll gravitate toward coloring books and SmellaVision, an interactive display that sprays out smells of different grape varieties to teach how to identify different wine ingredients. *8440 Hwy. 29, Rutherford.* ☎ *800/942-0809. See p 156.*

Take Hwy. 29 south and make a slight right on Solano Ave., then right onto W. Lincoln Ave. Turn right on Main St.

⑫ ★ Napa Firefighters Museum. Kids' never-failing fascination for all things fireman-related will be stoked at this small museum,

which exhibits antiquated as well as modern firefighting equipment, including a hand pumper from 1859, engines from the early 20th century, a 1904 horse-drawn steamer, plus uniforms and badges from all over the world. Little ones will particularly enjoy the collection of toy fire trucks and the two huge stuffed Dalmatian dogs. Older kids will take more pleasure in the model firehouse and the 1913 Model T Ford. *1201 Main St., Napa.* ☎ *707/259-0609. Free admission. Open Wed–Sun 11am–4pm. See p 74.*

⑬ ★ Seguin Moreau Napa Cooperage. If the Firefighters Museum is closed (Mon–Tues), take the kids to this facility, which offers a free tour that involves watching coopers make French-style wine-aging barrels using wood, fire, and water. *151 Camino Dorado, Napa.* ☎ *707/252-3408. www.seguinmoreaunapa.com. Tours Mon–Fri 9, 11:30am & 1pm.*

⑭ ★ Downtown Joe's. A short walk from the Firefighters Museum is this family-friendly (and pet-friendly) American grill and brewery. *902 Main St., Napa.* ☎ *707/258-2337. $$.* If the fam's in the mood for Mexican, popular **⑮ ★ Taqueria Rosita** is inexpensive, yet maintains a Napa feel. *1214 Main St., Napa.* ☎ *707/253-9208. $.* Afterward, stop at **⑯ Ben & Jerry's** for a big scoop of the Vermont-based company's latest flavor. *1299 Napa Town Center, Napa.* ☎ *707/253-0484. $.*

The Big Splurge, Napa Style

To Robert Louis Stevenson Mem. St. Pk.

↑ To Lake Berryessa

Pope Valley

Calistoga
← To Petrified Forest

Lake County Hwy.

Silverado Trail

Napa R.

Bell Canyon Res.

Angwin

Howell Mtn. Rd.

9A

Diamond Mountain Rd.

Bothe-Napa Valley State Park

Bale Gristmill St. Hist. Park

Spring Mountain Rd.

Lake Posada State Forest

NAPA COUNTY

Conn Valley Rd.

Lake Hennessey Rec. Area

Lake Hennessey

Hood Mountain Regional Park

Sonoma Hwy.

← To Santa Rosa

St. Helena

Sulphur Springs

W. Zinfandel Ln.

Zinfandel Ln.

Conn Creek Rd.

Sage Canyon

128

Rutherford

Niebaum Ln.

Rutherford Cross Rd.

Sugarloaf Ridge State Park

Oakville Grade

Oakville

Oakville Cross Rd.

Conn Ck.

Rector Res.

5

4

SONOMA COUNTY

12

Dwyer Rd.

6

Yountville Cross Rd.

Washington St.

10

7

Yountville

Glen Ellen

Mt. Veeder ▲

Mt. Veeder Rd.

Dry Creek Rd.

Silverado Trail

2

Oak Knoll Ave.

SONOMA Map Area NAPA

Redwood Rd.

Henry Rd.

3

Trancas St.

NAPA

Napa Valley Wine Train

SONOMA

Carneros Ck.

Old Sonoma Rd.

29

Cutting Wharf Rd.

12 121

Napa River

To San Francisco

0 — 2 miles
0 — 2 kms

N

1 Wine Country Helicopters
2 Darioush
3 Napa Valley Wine & Cigar
4 Shafer Vineyards
5 Paraduxx
6 Bistro Jeanty
7 Brix
8 St. Helena Wine Center
9A Viader Vineyards
9B Sterling
10 French Laundry

Napa can be the ultimate luxury vacation for those who have money and don't mind spending it. Because of its ever-present wine and food culture, as well as its physical beauty, this part of the world draws the world's most knowledgeable wine and food connoisseurs. This tour highlights just some of the exclusivity available in Napa. *Note:* This itinerary doesn't work on a whim, it requires **advance planning** to secure reservations, so read through to determine what needs to be done in advance. However, concierges at some of the area's luxury hotels would be happy to make the arrangements for you, provided you've already decided to stay in their hotel. START: **A helicopter. Distance: About 56 miles (90km), not including the helicopter ride. Doable in a full day.**

1 ★★★ **Wine Country Helicopters.** Start your day with an early-morning helicopter tour, one of the best ways to get an exclusive viewpoint of this stunning geographic area. WHC is a reputable company providing private, customized sightseeing flights that can include anything from **private reserve tastings at usually inaccessible wineries to breakfast on the Russian River to an aerial tour of San Francisco.** As the company's website puts it, "We are limited only by our collective imaginations and your credit card limit!" *2030 Airport Rd., Napa.* ☎ *707/226-8470. www.winecountry helicopters.com. Wine Tasting Tour $3,200; Russian River picnic $2,200; San Francisco tour $1,100. Tours accommodate 1–4 people. Arrange for the helicopter to pick you up near your lodging and drop you off at your next stop.*

2 ★★ **Darioush.** Arrange for the helicopter to leave you at this opulent Persian-inspired winery, which offers several signature ways to visit. The most comprehensive is called the **Private Tasting with Cheese Pairing Experience** ($35). In addition to a private tour of the visitor center and amphitheatre, a personal host leads you to the classy six-seat Barrel Chai (say "shay") Private Tasting Room, where Darioush's finest wines are

Get an aerial view of Napa & Sonoma on from a helicopter.

expertly paired with local cheeses. Appointments available 11am or 3pm Saturday through Thursday, or at 11am Friday. **Reservations required.** A luxurious purchase, at $408, would be a six-bottle hand-crafted pine case of the winery's 2002 Signature Napa Valley Cabernet Sauvignon. *4240 Silverado Trail, Napa.* ☎ *707/257-2345. See p 142.*

Pick up a fancy cigar to enjoy with your big wine splurge.

Limo Service

Arrange in advance for ★★ Antique Tours Limousine Service (☎ 707/226-9227; www.antiquetours.net), which operates an impeccable fleet of restored 1940s Packard convertibles and hard-top limousines ($105 per hour on weekdays and Sun, $120 per hour on Sat; 5-hr. minimum), to pick you up from Darioush.

❸ Napa Valley Wine & Cigar. Tell your driver to take you to this in-the-know shop, where you can pick out a full-flavored cigar to go with

The French Laundry is the ultimate place to splurge.

whichever luxury wine you choose. Options range from the $350 Two Worlds Napa Valley/Barossa Valley Red, which blends California and Australia grapes to very limited quantities of cult wines like the $725 Shafer 2001 Stags Leap District Hillside Select Cabernet Sauvignon. This is a great place to discover high-end, low-profile table wines, as well as vintage ports like a **1961 Warre's Colheita.** As for cigars, brands like **Montecristo** and **Arturo Fuente** are available. If you're buying many stogies, splurge on a beautiful humidor. *3780 Bel Aire Plaza, Napa.* ☎ *888/842-9463. www.napavalleywineandcigar.com. Sun–Fri 11am–6pm; Sat 11am–7pm.*

❹ ★ Shafer Vineyards. Next, have your driver take you to this upscale winery, where your visit ($25) includes a sit-down tasting of six wines, including the signature Hillside Select ($190 per bottle) and a short tour of the winery's cellar, barrel room, and cave. Reservations are required; you'd be well advised to set your appointment 4 to 6 weeks in advance, since Shafer hosts fewer than 20 guests per day. *6154 Silverado Trail, Napa.* ☎ *707/944-2877.* See p 157.

5 ★★ Paraduxx. Be one of the first to enjoy Duckhorn Wine Co.'s modern new sit-down tasting room, where vintages and limited-production wines are served in stemless Riedel crystal. Appointment required. *7257 Silverado Trail, Yountville.* ☎ *707/945-0890. See p 153.*

6 ★★ Bistro Jeanty. Order an array of exquisite French appetizers before savoring your main course from this proficient kitchen. *6510 Washington St.* ☎ *707/944-0103. $$$.* Or visit **7 ★★ Brix,** where food pairs well with wine in an elegant dining room. *7377 St. Helena Hwy.* ☎ *707/944-2547. $$$$. Also see p 96 for other Yountville dining options.*

8 St. Helena Wine Center. If your heart's set on taking home a bottle of elusive, expensive Screaming Eagle, you'll need to come to this well-stocked store, which also sells collectibles like the voluptuous $450 **2001 Bryant Family Cabernet Sauvignon.** *1321 Main St.* ☎ *707/963-1313. www.shwc.com. Daily 10am–6pm.*

9A ★★ Viader Vineyards. Make your next stop at this gorgeous estate, where you can try and buy an exclusive, difficult-to-find blend called "V" ($100 per bottle). Make reservations 3 to 4 weeks ahead. *1120 Deer Park Rd., St. Helena.* ☎ *707/963-3816. See p 160.*

9B ★★ Sterling Vineyards. If you didn't get a chance to make a reservation at Viader, head for Sterling. Aside from getting the valley's best sunset view from the aerial tram that takes you into the winery, you'll experience a multimedia self-guided tour that'll let you get to know the entire winemaking process at your own pace. *1111 Dunaweal Lane, Calistoga.* ☎ *707/942-3300. See p 158.*

10 ★★★ French Laundry. It's indisputable how to end your day: with dinner at what's often called the world's best restaurant. Make reservations as soon as you know you're coming to Napa; the waiting list is always months long—and be sure you're willing to pay for this truly one-of-a-kind dining experience: Dinner for two—without wine—costs an average $420. *6640 Washington St.* ☎ *707/944-2380. $$$$$. See p. 96.*

Driving along a scenic highway never gets dull.

Wine Country **for First-Timers**

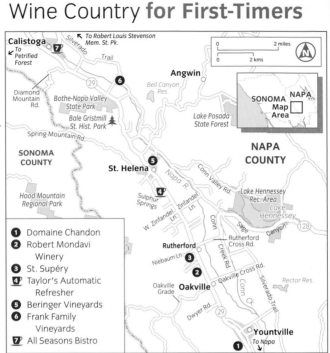

- **1** Domaine Chandon
- **2** Robert Mondavi Winery
- **3** St. Supéry
- **4** Taylor's Automatic Refresher
- **5** Beringer Vineyards
- **6** Frank Family Vineyards
- **7** All Seasons Bistro

A Napa novice? Not to worry: Highway 29 will show you the way. Following the path outlined below will up your wine-knowledge quotient and ensure that you leave wine country closer to "connoisseur" than ever before. Plus, you'll be able to go home assured that you've really gotten a sense for Napa Valley and its wineries. START: **Domaine Chandon, 1 California Dr. (at Hwy. 29), Yountville.** Distance: About 17 miles (27km), doable in a full day.

1 ★ **Domaine Chandon.** The comprehensive tour walks you through the entire bubbly-making process, from the cellars to the riddling room and bottling line. You'll also learn about the winery's history, including how the French champagne house Moët et Chandon founded it in 1973. *1 California Dr. (at Hwy. 29), Yountville.* 📞 *707/944-2280. See p 143.*

Drive northeast on California Dr., then merge onto Hwy. 29 N.

2 ★★ **Robert Mondavi Winery.** The basic 1-hour production tour thoroughly covers all aspects of the winemaking process and gives you a look at the destemmer-crusher, the tank room, the bottling room, and the vineyard. Top-notch guides consistently make sure you know what you're looking at. Make reservations in advance. *7801 St. Helena Hwy. (Hwy. 29), Oakville.* ☎ *707/226-1395. See p 155.*

Keep heading north on Hwy. 29.

③ ★ St. Supéry Winery. This straightforward winery is a great place for first-timers to learn more about oenology. Its emphasis is education, and while here, visitors can experience "SmellaVision," an interactive display that teaches how to identify various wine aromas and attributes; there's also a demonstration vineyard where visitors learn about growing techniques. *8440 St. Helena Hwy. (Hwy. 29), Rutherford.* ☎ *800/942-0809. See p 156.*

④ ★ Taylor's Automatic Refresher. For a quick bite, stop at this roadside burger shack with an impressive wine selection. *933 Main St.* ☎ *707/963-3486. $. See p 85.*

Keep heading north on Hwy. 29.

⑤ ★★ Beringer Vineyards. This winery pioneered the idea of public tours in 1934, and it's obvious that Beringer has since perfected that brainchild. Today, **Napa's oldest continually operating winery** offers four tour options ranging from a basic introduction to a thorough

Be sure to check out the stone mushrooms at Domaine Chandon.

exploration of Beringer's vintage legacy. *2000 Main St., St. Helena.* ☎ *707/963-4812. For details, See p 136.*

Keep heading north on Hwy. 29 for about 4 miles, then turn left on Larkmead Lane.

⑥ Frank Family Vineyards. Napa's least intimidating winery has exceptionally attentive staff members who take the time to explain anything you want to know about wine. *1091 Larkmead Lane, Calistoga.* ☎ *800/574-9463. See p 145.*

⑦ ★★ All Seasons Bistro. The bistro/CA cuisine menu (fresh, local ingredients) matches wines to dishes, so you'll know what's just right for the entree you choose. *1400 Lincoln Ave., Calistoga.* ☎ *707/942-9111. $$$. See p 105.*

Do oenophiles confuse you when they describe wine with words like grass or mineral? At Mondavi, you'll learn how to identify these aromas and flavors.

Wine Country **for Nondrinkers**

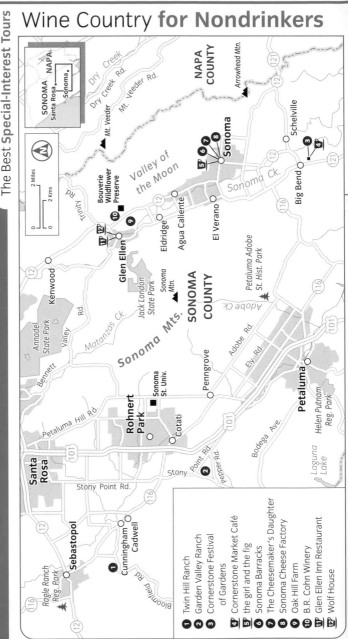

1 Twin Hill Ranch
2 Garden Valley Ranch
3 Cornerstone Festival of Gardens
4 Cornerstone Market Café
5 the girl and the fig
6 Sonoma Barracks
7 The Cheesemaker's Daughter
8 Sonoma Cheese Factory
9 Oak Hill Farm
10 B.R. Cohn Winery
11 Glen Ellen Inn Restaurant
12 Wolf House

Want to visit wine country but put off because you don't drink alcohol? Come anyway. Though wine initially put this region on the map, the tourism and agriculture industries have kept it there, ensuring that visitors are kept interested both before and after the tasting room. As a result, there's now a plethora of non-wine-related activities for those who just want to take a relaxing trip to the California countryside to do some nonalcoholic sampling and seeing. Here's how to get the wine country experience without the wine. **Note:** For nonalcoholic attractions in addition to these, also see the itineraries for foodies (p 32), history buffs (p 50), art aficionados (p 56), and outdoor enthusiasts (p 107). START: Twin Hill Ranch, 1689 Pleasant Hill Rd., Sebastopol. Distance: About 40 miles (64km), doable in a day.

1 ★ kids **Twin Hill Ranch.** Keep the doctor away with a visit to this Sebastopol operation that's been growing, packing, and shipping apples since 1942. In its country store (a perfect place to buy a gift for teacher), taste the ranch's signature apple bread, plus pies, cookies, juice, sauce, butter, and jelly, all made with the potassium-rich fruit grown on this ridiculously fertile land. Tours show you how the ranch produces and distributes 10 apple varieties, including Gravenstein, Gala, and Fuji. *1689 Pleasant Hill Rd., Sebastopol.* ☎ *707/823-2815. www.twinhillranch.com. Call ahead for tour appointments and pricing. Mon–Sat 8:30am–4:30pm (open Sun Thanksgiving to Christmas).*

Go west on Pleasant Hill Rd., which becomes Bloomfield Rd. Turn right on Lone Pine Rd., then right on Gravenstein Hwy./Hwy. 116. Turn right on Stony Point Rd., then right on Jewell Rd., then left on Pepper Rd.

2 ★★ **Garden Valley Ranch.** Did you know that apples are a member of the rose family? Continue the theme at this 9-acre (3.6-hectare) Victorian ranch, which has more than 8,000 rosebushes, a fragrance garden, and a test garden (where rosarians try to develop new species). On spring weekends, the ranch hosts "Tea in the Garden" ($25), during which a light meal is served alongside an assortment of

An apple a day...

teas in the fragrance garden, which overlooks thousands of roses. There's also a retail nursery where you can buy a variety of flowers, from antique, climbing, and miniature roses to floribundas, hybrid teas, and colorful annuals, as well as gardening supplies, seeds, and books. *498 Pepper Rd., Petaluma. ☎ 707/795-0919. www.gardenvalley.com. Self-guided tours ($5, including a descriptive booklet) Wed–Sun 10am–4pm; nursery open Wed–Sun 10am–5pm. Guided tours ($10, including a descriptive booklet) by appointment and require a minimum of 10 people.*

From Pepper Rd., get on Hwy. 101 S. Take Hwy. 116 E, then turn left on Frates Rd., which becomes Adobe Rd., which becomes Hwy. 116 again, then becomes Hwy. 121.

❸ ★★ Cornerstone Festival of Gardens. Nine acres (3.6 hectares) of 20 gardens were designed mostly by prominent landscape architects. These walk-through outdoor spaces are aimed at those interested in high-concept gardening—but they're enjoyable by all, as are the

Indulge in a cheese plate at the girl and the fig.

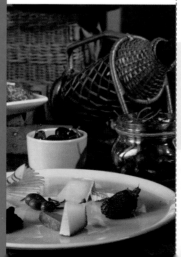

on-site shops and galleries. The **Barn Gallery** displays information about each installation and designer, while **A New Leaf Gallery** (☎ 707/933-1300) displays and sells beautiful indoor and outdoor modern sculptures by more than 50 artists. **Translations** (☎ 707/938-0888) sells outdoor furnishings and Asian-inspired landscape elements, and **Artefact Design & Salvage** (☎ 707/933-0660) offers antique garden pieces and found objects. *23570 Hwy. 121, Sonoma. ☎ 707/933-3010. www.cornerstone gardens.com. Admission $9 ($5 in winter), $7.50 seniors 65+ ($4 in winter), $6.50 college students ($4 in winter), $3 kids 4–17 ($2 in winter), free for kids under 4. Daily 10am–5pm (4pm in winter).*

❹ ★ Cornerstone Market Café. The seasonal lunch menu at this cute food shop lists panini sandwiches, soups, and salads; order from that or put together a meal from the artisan foods sold in the grocery section. *23584A Hwy. 121, Sonoma. ☎ 707/935-1681. $.*

Take Hwy. 121 northwest, then turn right on Watmaugh Rd. and left on Broadway. Turn right on E. Napa St.

For a more comprehensive sit-down meal, **❺ ★★ the girl and the fig,** just off Sonoma Plaza, is highly acclaimed. Cheese sampling at the restaurant's well-stocked *salon de fromage* is a great alternative to wine tasting. *110 W. Spain St. ☎ 707/938-3634. $$. See p 81.*

❻ ★★ kids Sonoma Barracks. Cross 1st Street again to get to this landmark, also part of Sonoma State Historic Park. Vallejo, whose assignment it was to secularize the mission, kept his Mexican troops here to guard against Native American tribes and rebuff possible threats (though none ever developed) from Russian settlers. During and after the revolt, these barracks were the Bear Flag Party's headquarters. When the U.S. took over, American soldiers moved in for a spell. Since then, it's been a winery, a law office, and a private residence, among other things. It became state property in 1958, and today there are two museum rooms and a theater in which you can catch the 22 minute video about General Vallejo. History buffs will appreciate the gift-shop merchandise. **Tip:** If possible, coincide your tour with the every-other-Saturday 2pm firing of the cannon. *E. Spain St. & 1st St. E. ☎ 707/939 9420. www.parks.ca. gov. Daily 10am–5pm. $2 admission for adults. Children under 17 free. Admission also includes Mission San Francisco Solano.*

❼ ★★ The Cheesemaker's Daughter. Try all kinds of nonwine wine country fare, from international artisanal cheeses to olive oils, vinegars, teas, coffees, cocoa, and honey. *127 E. Napa St., Sonoma. ☎ 707/996-4060. See p 79.*

❽ ★ Sonoma Cheese Factory. If you're not sick of sampling cheese yet (and, really, who could be?), walk across the plaza to this third-generation family enterprise, which was the first cheese producer west of the Mississippi to win a gold medal from the authoritative Wisconsin Cheese Makers Association. *2 E. Spain St., Sonoma. ☎ 800/ 535-2855. See p 80.*

From Spain St., turn left on 1st St., then right on Napa St. Make a slight right on Sonoma Hwy./ Hwy. 12.

❾ ★★ Oak Hill Farm. Head to this 45-acre (18-hectare) farm and its **Red Barn Store.** This business has existed since the 1950s and still grows its amazing heirloom vegetables entirely sustainably. The real highlight here is the century-old dairy barn housing the Red Barn Store. More than just an old-fashioned farm stand (though it's that, too), this is a unique place to buy organic produce, fresh flowers, beautiful wreaths, and handmade gifts amidst the farm's bountiful fields. *15101 Hwy. 12, Glen Ellen. ☎ 707/996-6643. www.oakhillfarm. net. Apr–Dec Wed–Sun 11am–6pm.*

❿ B.R. Cohn Winery. Yes, this *is* a winery, but the estate also specializes in gourmet (and pricey) olive oils and handcrafted vinegars. Taste them in the small tasting room, which is filled with framed platinum albums from vintner Bruce Cohn's *other* job as manager of the Doobie Brothers. His property is graced with groves of rare olive trees, terraced hills of plush lawn, and several picnic tables. Many musical events happen here; check the website. *15000 Hwy. 12, Glen Ellen. ☎ 800/330-4064. www.brcohn.com. See p 137.*

⓫ ★ Glen Ellen Inn Restaurant. This homey dining room serves seasonally changing cuisine. Reservations recommended. *13670 Arnold Dr., Glen Ellen. ☎ 707/996-6409. $$$. See p 100.* Another local option is **⓬ ★ Wolf House,** a classy-but-relaxed joint with local food and warm service. *13740 Arnold Dr., Glen Ellen. ☎ 707/996-4401. Reservations recommended. $$.*

Wine Country **for History Buffs**

DAY 1
1. Petaluma Adobe State Historic Park
2. Sonoma State Historic Park
3. Depot Park
4. Buena Vista Carneros
5. Sunflower
6. Depot Hotel-Cucina
7. Swiss Hotel
8. Jack London State Historic Park
9. Angèle

DAY 2
10. Napa Valley Museum
11. Veterans Home of CA
12. Beringer
13. Charles Krug
14. Bale Grist Mill State Historic Park
15. Schramsberg
16. The General's Daughter

To get to the real roots of the land, beyond tasting rooms and newfangled tourist attractions, and to see why so many from so far came here with dreams of paradise so many years ago, follow this northwest-bound county-crossing tour. It'll give you a sense of wine country's rich cultural, political, and agricultural history, and will help you get to know Sonoma and Napa's most colorful historical characters, including General Mariano G. Vallejo (California's last Mexican governor), the Bear Flag Party, Agoston Haraszthy, American veterans, and Jack London. START: Petaluma Adobe State Historic Park, 3325 Adobe Rd. Distance: About 40 miles (64km), doable in 2 days.

---

1 ★★ kids **Petaluma Adobe State Historic Park.** What's now a state-owned site was, in the mid-1800s, General Vallejo's working rancho, which he used for commercial ventures like growing crops, rearing cattle, raising sheep, and breeding horses. After Vallejo was taken captive during the 1846 Bear

Revolt, squatters took over. In 1857, after losing money while trying to regain control, Vallejo sold the rancho. Much later, after rejecting it as a site for a University of California campus in the early 1900s, the state acquired the land and made it a historic park, refurnishing many of the rooms in the adobe-and-redwood main building with authentic artifacts to bring history alive for visitors. Follow my tips to get a good sense of what rancho life was like:. Start at the **visitor center,** where exhibits portray some of the agricultural and domestic activities that took place here. Head into the **weaving room,** where ranch women spun wool into clothing, blankets, and rugs. The same room also functioned as a food pantry. Go out to the **courtyard,** where denizens cooked and made candles. Back inside, the **granary** is where corn, wheat, and barley were stored and ground; the workroom still contains its original gristmill. The adobe's first-floor north wing served as the **leather-working room;** here, cow tallow was made into belts and other accessories. Go upstairs to see the **married servants' quarters.** Living at the rancho was as communal as it gets, but workers of higher status got to sleep here, as opposed to the adjacent, darker **single servants' and artisans' quarters,** where lower-class laborers slept on straw mats. The **fandango area** was essentially the party room and was often made merry with music, dancing, and feasts. The **mayordomo's room** housed the *rancho*'s overseer, while the **dining room** is where

Old houses and wagons are just a few of the historical items you'll see at Petaluma Adobe State Historic Park.

Vallejo himself would entertain important guests. Finally, the **Vallejo family bedroom** is where the general's family slept all together. *3325 Adobe Rd. (off Hwy. 116), Petaluma.* ☎ *707/762-4871. www.parks.ca.gov. Admission $2 (also good at the mission, barracks, and Lachryma Montis).*

Take Hwy. 116 east and turn left onto Watmaugh Rd. Turn left onto Broadway/Hwy. 12 and continue 1 mile (1.6km) until you hit Sonoma. Park at the Plaza.

② ★★★ kids **Sonoma State Historic Park.** Less a park than it is a series of historic attractions throughout town, a thorough visit should include **Mission San Francisco Solano** (the 21st and last of the Franciscan *padres*' settlements, founded July 4, 1823, is a squat but impressive structure), the **Bear Flag Monument** (this imposing statue commemorates the 1846 hoisting of the rebel flag that swiftly ended Mexico's reign over California and made it an independent republic; not a month later, the American flag was raised in its stead), the **Sonoma Barracks** (p 48), the **Blue Wing Inn** (p 80), and if you're in town at the right time, a tour of **Toscano Hotel** (p 80). *Main office: 363 W. 3rd St. (at W. Spain St.).* ☎ *707/938-9560. www.parks.ca.gov. Admission $2 (includes all SHP sites), free for children under 17. Hours vary; call ahead.* Also part of the park is **Lachryma Montis,** where Vallejo lived with his wife after he was deposed by the Bear Flag Party in 1846. This comparatively modest house, whose name is Latin for "tears of the mountain," was what he could afford toward the end of his life. The frilly Gothic Victorian structure isn't exactly what one would imagine would house a former Mexican governor, but it was insulated with adobe and is still furnished with many of his personal possessions.

The Mission Solano is one of Sonoma's most famous landmarks.

In 1933, the state acquired the property and opened it to the public. Today, it (and an adjacent museum) continues to educate visitors. *W. Spain St., near E. 3rd St., Sonoma.* ☎ *707/938-9559. Admission $2 (includes all SHP sites). Occasional free docent-led weekend tours; call ahead for schedule. Daily 10am–5pm.*

3 Depot Park. Back on W. 1st St., a block north of the Plaza, is this little center, home to a historic railroad station and the Sonoma Valley History Museum. *270 1st St. W.* ☎ *707/939-1762. www.vom.com/depot. Free admission. Wed–Sun 1–4:30pm.*

The non-Swiss Swiss Hotel is a California historic landmark.

From 1st St., turn left on W. Spain St., then right on E. 2nd St. A left on E. Napa St. will bring you to Old Winery Rd. Turn left to get to

4 ★★★ Buena Vista Carneros. The nation's oldest continuously operating winery's historical significance extends to the fact that this is essentially the birthplace of California wine: In 1851, Hungarian colonel **Agoston Haraszthy** planted a few vines here. A decade later, he further bolstered the local winemaking culture by returning from a trip to Europe with thousands of cuttings of hundreds of varieties, many of which he planted at this winery that he founded in 1857. *18000 Old Winery Rd., Sonoma.* ☎ *800/926-1266. See p 137.*

5 Sunflower Caffe. Grab a sandwich or smoothie at this walk-up cafe located in Vallejo's historic adobe home. *421 W. 1st St.* ☎ *707/996-6645. $.* For a sit-down lunch, opt for the **6 ★★ Depot Hotel-Cucina Rustica's** Northern Italian cuisine. Its historic stone building 2 blocks from the plaza was once a destination for 19th-century train passengers. *241 W. 1st St.* ☎ *707/938-2980. $$.* If you feel like having a drink after lunch, head to **7 Swiss Hotel's** (p 80) old-fashioned watering hole, which is plastered with a photographic history of Sonoma. *18 W. Spain St.* ☎ *707/938-2884. $$.*

From Old Winery Rd., turn right on E. Napa St., then right onto Sonoma Hwy./Hwy. 12. Turn left onto W. Verano Ave., then right onto Arnold Dr., then left on London Ranch Rd.

⑧ ★★ kids Jack London State Historic Park. This is where the famous writer of *The Call of the Wild, White Fang,* and more than 50 other popular tales lived from 1905 until his 1916 death. In addition to 10 eucalyptus-laden miles (16km) of hiking trails, the park has a number of historic sites, including London's gravesite (a small copper urn), the remains of his burned-down dream house, the wood-framed cottage where London penned many of his later books while overseeing his estate's agricultural activities, and the stone House of Happy Walls, a museum dedicated to London's life (with a visitor center selling his books). Also at the park are sherry and stallion barns, a onetime piggery, early-20th-century silos, winery ruins, and an old distillery building. Even though much of what was here is now in various states of dilapidation, a visit still explains why London wrote, "I have everything to make me glad I am alive. I am filled with dreams and mysteries. I am all sun and air and sparkle. I am vitalized, organic." **Tip:** Pick up the $1 self-guided tour map on arrival to get acquainted with the grounds. Picnic tables are available. *2400 London Ranch Rd., Glen Ellen.* ☎ *707/938-5216. www.parks.ca.gov & www.jacklondonpark.com. Park admission $6 per car, $5 per car for seniors 62+. Park grounds daily 9:30am–7pm (during daylight saving), 10am–5pm (standard time). Museum daily 10am–5pm.*

⑨ ★★ Angéle. Finish the day at this rustic but upscale restaurant serving French country cuisine in the old boathouse of the Historic Napa Mill, built in 1884. Interior wood gives the restaurant a historic feel, as do beam ceilings and concrete flooring. *540 Main St., Napa.* ☎ *707/ 252-8115. $$$.*

DAY 2

⑩ ★ Napa Valley Museum. Though it's housed in a modern building, this museum gives a great overview of Napa history; its mission is to promote the valley's cultural and

At the House of Happy Walls in Jack London State Historic Park, you can take a peek into Mr. London's study.

Contemplate the dynamic winemaking process exhibit at the Napa Valley Museum.

environmental heritage. Upstairs, rotating exhibits have shown artists' interpretations of California's missions and sculptures of Mexican cowboys. You can also learn how Chinese, Jews, and other ethnic groups contributed to valley life. Downstairs is a permanent multimedia exhibit demonstrating the winemaking process. Before you leave, check out the painting by Michael Keating and see how many winemakers you can spot in it; among them are Robert Mondavi and Joe Heitz. *55 Presidents Circle, Yountville.* ☎ *707/944-0500. www.napavalleymuseum.org. Admission $4.50 adults, $3.50 students & seniors, $2.50 kids 7–17, free for kids under 7. Wed–Mon 10am–5pm.*

⑪ Veterans Home of California. Napa Valley Museum is actually on the grounds of one of Napa's best examples of living history: the home of some 1,100 ex-soldiers. Founded in 1884, this is America's largest veteran's home, with a years-long waiting list of people who fit the residency requirement: having served honorably and being 62 or older (younger if disabled). Also on-site is the excellent 1,200-seat **Lincoln Theater** (☎ 707/944-1300), a 9-hole golf course, a 35,000-volume library, a baseball stadium, bowling

lanes, and many other amenities. All the Spanish-style buildings are named after U.S. presidents. *100 California Dr., Yountville.* ☎ *707/944-4600. www.cdva.ca.gov.*

Continue north on Hwy. 29.

⑫ ★★★ Beringer. Founded in 1876, Beringer is the valley's oldest continually operating winery. *2000 Main St. (Hwy. 29), St. Helena.* ☎ *707/963-4812. See p 136.*

⑬ ★ Charles Krug. Walking distance from Beringer is Charles Krug, the valley's oldest working winery; it was founded in 1861 but ceased operation during Prohibition. *2800 Main St. (Hwy. 29), St. Helena.* ☎ *707/967-2229. See p 139.*

Continue north on Hwy. 29.

⑭ ★ kids Bale Grist Mill State Historic Park. This state park is worth a short stop for the sight of the massive wooden water-powered gristmill that was built in 1846 and was used until the early 1900s. Since Napa settlers gathered around the mill, it became the center of the valley's social activity and the site of Napa's first church. Dr. Edward Turner Bale owned the mill, having acquired it in a land grant from the Mexican government. He built a 36-foot (11m) waterwheel, operated on water diverted from nearby Mill Creek. On weekends, you can see the mill in action as a miller performs demonstrations, then buy the stone-ground flour you watched being made. *3369 Hwy. 29, St. Helena.* ☎ *707/942-4575. www.parks.ca. gov. Free admission to park; mill admission $2, free for kids under 17. Park daily 10am–5pm. Mill Sat–Sun 10am–5pm.* A 1-mile (1.6km) History Trail links this park to ★ **Bothe-Napa Valley State Park** (☎ 707/942-4575); if you're motivated and have time, take it to see ★★ **Pioneer Cemetery,** where many Napa settlers, including George C. Yount (p 94), are buried in a typical mid-1800s graveyard.

⓯ ★★ **Schramsberg.** If you have time and inclination for another historic winery, visit this sparkling-wine producer. It was founded in 1862 and frequented by the likes of Robert Louis Stevenson, who depicted the winery in his "Silverado Squatters." *1400 Schramsberg Rd., Calistoga.* ☎ *707/942-2414. See p 157.*

Schramsburg is a sprawling estate that produces sparkling wine.

⓰ ★★★ **The General's Daughter** is a beautiful dining room in Vallejo's daughter's early-1900s home. *400 W. Spain St.* ☎ *707/938-4004. $$$. See p 81 for detailed review.*

Have you ever seen such an enormous mill? Stop by Bale Grist Mill State Historic Park for a glimpse—and on weekends, a demonstration—of how the mill works.

A Day **for Arts Aficionados**

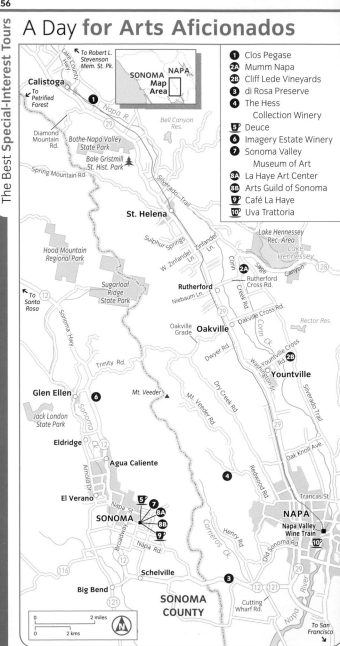

1 Clos Pegase
2A Mumm Napa
2B Cliff Lede Vineyards
3 di Rosa Preserve
4 The Hess Collection Winery
5 Deuce
6 Imagery Estate Winery
7 Sonoma Valley Museum of Art
8A La Haye Art Center
8B Arts Guild of Sonoma
9 Café La Haye
10 Uva Trattoria

To Robert L. Stevenson Mem. St. Pk.

SONOMA | NAPA
SONOMA Map Area

Calistoga
To Petrified Forest

Napa R.

Bell Canyon Res.

Diamond Mountain Rd.

Bothe-Napa Valley State Park

Bale Gristmill St. Hist. Park

Spring Mountain Rd.

St. Helena

Sulphur Springs

Silverado Trail

Hood Mountain Regional Park

W. Zinfandel Ln.

Zinfandel Ln.

Lake Hennessey Rec. Area
Lake Hennessey

Sugarloaf Ridge State Park

Conn

Sage

Canyon

Rutherford

Rutherford Cross Rd.

Conn Creek Rd.

Niebaum Ln.

Oakville Cross Rd.

Rector Res.

To Santa Rosa

Sonoma Hwy.

Oakville Grade

Oakville

Dwyer Rd.

Dry Creek Rd.

Washington St.

Yountville Cross Rd.

Yountville

Silverado Trail

Trinity Rd.

Glen Ellen

Mt. Veeder

Mt. Veeder Rd.

Jack London State Park

Eldridge

Arnold Dr.

Agua Caliente

Oak Knoll Ave.

Redwood Rd.

Trancas St.

El Verano

Napa St.

SONOMA

Broadway

Napa Rd.

NAPA
Napa Valley Wine Train

Carneros Ck.

Henry Rd.

Old Sonoma Rd.

Schellville

Big Bend

SONOMA COUNTY

Cutting Wharf Rd.

Napa River

To San Francisco

0 — 2 miles
0 — 2 kms

Robert Mondavi wrote, "Wine is art. It's culture. It's the essence of civilization and the art of living." The land of viticulture also abounds with so many art forms, from the visual to the audible to the experiential. Though there's no way to list every wine country art venue—that's a whole other book—this tour gives you a taste of the many creative talents that find inspiration here. As novelist Paul Richetr wrote, "Art is indeed not the bread, but the wine of life."

START: Clos Pegase, 1060 Dunaweal Lane, Calistoga. Distance: about 90 miles (145km), doable in a day.

1 ★★ Clos Pegase. Named for Pegasus, the mythological winged horse-god, this winery's winning design is a result of an architects' competition. Its stunning structures house a world-class fine-art collection, including a huge painting behind the tasting bar. There's also a remarkable sculpture garden. *1060 Dunaweal Lane, Calistoga.* ☎ 707/942-4981. See p 141.

Take Dunaweal Lane south to turn left on Hwy. 128/29. Turn left on Deer Park Rd., then right on Silverado Trail.

2A ★★ Mumm Napa. Explore Mumm's photography gallery, which displays original Ansel Adams works in long Spanish-style hallways, then enjoy sparkling wine in the glass-enclosed tasting room. *8445 Silverado Trail, Rutherford.* ☎ 800/686-6272. See p 152.

OR:

From Silverado Trail, turn right on Oak Knoll Ave., then left on Big

Ansel Adams paintings line the hallways at Mumm Napa.

Cliff Lede is known for the eclectic sculptures peppering its grounds.

Ranch Rd., then right back on Oak Knoll Ave. Turn left on Hwy. 29, then right on Hwy. 12/121 (Carneros Hwy.).

2B ★★ Cliff Lede Vineyards. This winery's gardens are graced with rosebushes and sculptures by artists like Keith Haring, Jim Dine, and Lynn Chadwick. A new wine-making facility opened in 2005, and the former one is now a modern art gallery displaying rotating 6-month shows of rising-star artists. *1473 Yountville Cross Rd., Yountville.* ☎ 800/428-2259. See p 140.

From Mumm, head south on the Silverado Trail, turn right onto Yountville Cross Rd., and follow directions from Cliff Lede. From Cliff Lede, take Yountville Cross Rd., then turn left on Yount St. and turn right on Madison St. Turn left onto Hwy. 29 S. At Carneros Hwy./ Hwy. 12/121, turn right.

3 ★★★ di Rosa Preserve. Yale-educated founder Rene di Rosa (he's now in his late 80s and lives on-site) opened his iconoclastic personal collection to the public in a confluence of art and bucolic nature. He started buying works by young up-and-comers in the 1960s so that now he has more than 2,300 extremely avant-garde pieces by upwards of 900 artists, spanning media from canvas to stained glass to porcelain—even to old cars. The art spreads from three galleries (one housing a photography hall) out into the 217-acre (87-hectare) preserve with sculpture-laden meadows set against vineyards and a palm-tree-lined lake. There are no identifying labels on or near the art, so, according to di Rosa's intention, visitors have to contextualize pieces without reference to who made what when—though a folder in each gallery makes it clear for those that absolutely need to know. Don't miss the former di Rosa residence, where art is so pervasive that paintings are even hung on the ceiling. *5200 Carneros Hwy (Hwy. 12/121/ Sonoma Hwy.), Napa.* ☎ *707/226-5991. www.dirosapreserve.org. Admission $3, free on Wed. Gatehouse Gallery Tues–Fri 9:30am–3pm; tours of galleries ($12, free on Wed; reservations recommended) Tues–Fri 10, 11am & 12:30pm; tours of galleries ($15, reservations required) Sat 10, 11am & noon; tours of sculpture meadows ($12, reservations recommended) Apr–Aug Tues & Thurs 10am.*

Head east on Sonoma Hwy. (12/ 121). Turn left onto Old Sonoma Rd., left onto Buhman Ave., left onto Browns Valley Rd., and again left onto Redwood Rd.

4 ★★★ The Hess Collection Winery. Architectural design here is contemporary to match Donald Hess's museum-quality art collection, acquired over more than 30 years, on the upper levels of the 1903 stone winery. Works on display include paintings and sculptures by contemporary American and European artists. *4411 Redwood Rd., Napa.* ☎ *877/707-4377. See p 148.*

Take Redwood Rd. southeast and turn right on Browns Valley Rd. Turn right on Buhman Ave., then right on Old Sonoma Rd. Turn right on Hwy. 12/121 and make a slight right on Napa Rd., then right again on Broadway/Hwy. 12.

5 Deuce. You'll be crossing county lines now, so if you're hungry, enjoy European-inspired cuisine at this intimate restaurant, where new works by local artists are shown on a 3-month rotating basis. *691 Broadway, Sonoma.* ☎ *707/933-3823. $$.*

A gallery and a winery? Yes, that's Hess.

Imagery's wine labels are works of art.

6 ★ Imagery Estate Winery.
Truly a winery for art lovers, each
Imagery bottle label is a tiny version
of an original painting commissioned specifically for the wine it
hugs. Each must somehow include a
replica of Benziger's Parthenon
(Imagery is Benziger's sister winery).
A curated collection of more than
175 artworks hangs in Imagery's
gallery. *14335 Hwy. 12, Glen Ellen.
☎ 707/935-4515. See p 149.*

Take Hwy. 12 southeast and turn
right on Broadway.

**7 ★★ Sonoma Valley
Museum of Art.** Walking distance from the plaza, this excellent
institution borrows local, international, and ethnic art of all media
from private collections, artists, and
other museums to create thematic
exhibits. In the past, showings have
ranged from the somewhat frivolous
("The Art of the Wine Label") to the
deeply emotional, like "Faces of the
Fallen," portraits of the thousands of
soldiers killed in Iraq. The museum
has also brought in works by Rodin
as well as exotic showings, like
cloths of Bali. However, SVMA
prides itself on bringing to light
lesser-known regional artists.
*551 Broadway, Sonoma. ☎ 707/
939-7862. www.svma.org. Admission*
*$5, free for kids under 18. Occa-
sional lectures, workshops, and
music performances; check website
for schedule. Wed–Sun 11am–5pm.*

8A ★ La Haye Art Center. Walking distance from the museum is this
nonprofit gallery cooperative that's
open only when artists are in residence, or by advance appointment.
148 E. Napa St. ☎ 707/996-4373.

OR:

8B Arts Guild of Sonoma is a
small, no-frills gallery featuring
mixed-media works by local artists.
*140 E. Napa St. ☎ 707/996-3115.
Sun–Mon & Wed–Thurs 11am–9pm;
Fri–Sat 11am–9pm.*

9 ★★ Café La Haye. This self-
appointed "place for food and art"
is a small but smartly designed
restaurant that enhances diners'
experiences with big, ever-changing
works of modern art. Reservations
recommended. *140 E. Napa St.,
Sonoma. ☎ 707/935-5994. $$. See
p 81.* If you're headed back to Napa
for your lodging, head to **10 ★ Uva
Trattoria** for after-dinner drinks
and live music (usually jazz). Perfor-
mances happen Wednesday to
Sunday nights. *1040 Clinton St.,
Napa. ☎ 707/255-6646. $$.*

Wine Country **for Romance**

Driving Tour

DRIVING TOUR
1. Sonoma Market
2. Enterprise Rent-A-Car
3. Schug Carneros
   Estate Winery
4. Arrowood
5. Chateau St. Jean
6. Ledson Winery
7. The General's Daughter

BIKE TOUR
1. Sonoma Market
2. Sonoma Valley Cyclery
3. Ravenswood
4. Sebastiani
5. Gundlach-Bundschu Winery
6. Della Santina's
7. Harmony
8. Bartholomew Park Winery
9. Buena Vista Carneros

Bike Tour

Whether you're trying to impress your new sweetie, seeking the perfect proposal moment, celebrating your honeymoon, or spending time with the longtime love of your life, wine country is the quintessential place for romance. This Sonoma-centric tour takes you to the wineries and restaurants most suitable for lovebirds. **Note:** Before you start this itinerary, the two of you need to decide whether you want to make this a biking or a driving tour. Then follow the appropriate travel plan below (the biking path is leisurely, mostly flat, and not too strenuous). START: Sonoma Market, 500 W. Napa St., Sonoma. Distance: Biking: 13 miles (21km), doable in a day. Driving: 26 miles (42km), doable in a day.

① ★★ **Sonoma Market.** Whether you're biking or driving, make a morning stop here to assemble lunch for later from the full deli and sandwich bar. If you order 24 hours in advance, the market can have a boxed picnic, including a deluxe sandwich, salad, and fruit ready and waiting ($16). The market itself is locally loved for its upscale selection of specialty foods, fresh breads, and reasonably priced wines. *500 W. Napa St., Sonoma.* ☎ *707/996-3411. Daily 6am–9pm.*

BIKE TOUR
From the market, take Napa St. east and turn right on Broadway.

② **Sonoma Valley Cyclery.** Sonoma's the perfect place to dually attempt a bicycle built for two—so rent a tandem bicycle. The experience is even more fun if you've never tried this kind of riding before; communication and listening are key to doing it successfully (just like in a relationship). *20093 Broadway, Sonoma.* ☎ *707/935-3377. www.sonomavalley cyclery.com. Tandem bikes $8 per hour, or $35 per day. Mon–Sat 10am–6pm; Sun 10am–4pm*

From the cyclery, pedal north on Broadway and turn right on E. Napa St., then left on E. 4th St. Turn right at Brazil St., then left on Gehricke Rd. (2½ miles/4km).

③ ★ **Ravenswood.** If strong wine makes for strong love, this is the place to bolster your affection. Take a tour together of the vineyards and cellar; barrel tasting is included. *18701 Gehricke Rd., Sonoma.* ☎ *707/933-2332. See p 155.*

Go ahead—give a tandem bike a try. You know you'll be laughing and smiling all day long.

The stone press house at Buena Vista is just one of the structures that makes this winery so romantic.

Head south on Gehricke Rd., turn right on Brazil St., then left on E. 4th St. (1⅓ miles/2.1km).

④ ★★ Sebastiani. The big tasting room might be crowded, but that'll just push the two of you closer together. Besides, after tasting the cabernet, merlot, and Barbera and strolling the historic grounds hand in hand, you both will forget all about it. If you plan in advance, though, you can arrange for customized private tastings (call for pricing). *389 E. 4th St., Sonoma.* ☎ *707/933-3230. See p 157.*

To get to Gundlach Bundschu, take 4th St. south and turn left on Patten St., then right on E. 5th St. Turn left on Napa Rd. and left on Denmark St. (3 miles/4.8km).

⑤ ★★ Gundlach Bundschu Winery. Unfold the picnic you bought from Sonoma Market at any of Gundlach-Bundschu's many picnic grounds. The remote hillside tables and the olive grove near a pond both overlook the valley. If it's spring or summer, you might be able to catch an after-lunch Shakespeare or Mozart performance in the outdoor amphitheater (check the website for schedules). *2000 Denmark St., Sonoma.* ☎ *707/938-5277. www. gunbun.com. See p 147.* If you prefer a restaurant lunch on the plaza, there's a romantic outdoor patio at **⑥ ★★ Della Santina's** *(133 E. Napa St., Sonoma;* ☎ *707/935-0576; $$)* and an elegant, love-inducing dining room at **⑦ ★★ Harmony** *(480 E. 1st St.;* ☎ *707/996-9779; $$$; p 81).*

From Gundlach Bundschu, take Denmark St. northwest and turn right on E. 7th St. Turn right on Castle Rd., which becomes Vineyard Lane (3 miles/4.8km).

⑧ Bartholomew Park Winery. Share tastes of limited-production wines, then explore the historical museum, memorial park, and hiking trails. Or simply sit and enjoy the views; on a clear day, you can see to San Francisco. *1000 Vineyard Lane, Sonoma.* ☎ *707/935-9511. See p 134.*

Take Vineyard Lane, which becomes Castle Rd., then turn left on Lovall Valley Rd. Turn left on Old Winery Rd. (2 miles/3.2km).

⑨ ★★★ Buena Vista Carneros. This estate inspires romance with its ivy-covered buildings, antique fountains, and restored 1862 press house, which houses the tasting room. *18000 Old Winery Rd., Sonoma.* ☎ *800/926-1266. See p 137.*

For recommendations for dinner venues, refer to the driving tour below.

DRIVING TOUR:
From the market, take W. Napa St. west and turn right on Sonoma Hwy./Hwy. 12.

② Enterprise Rent-A-Car. Evoke romance-movie scenes by

renting a convertible. Enterprise has a branch where you can rent open-top cars. They offer pickup service, too, so if you don't already have a car with you to get to the branch office, it won't be a problem. Additionally, all the gateway airports to wine country have many car-rental counters. *18981 Sonoma Hwy., Sonoma.* ☎ *707/938-0200.*

Take Sonoma Hwy. southeast to turn right on W. Verano Ave. Turn left on Arnold Dr., then right on Stage Gulch Rd. Turn left on Hwy. 116, then right on Bonneau Rd.

③ ★ **Schug Carneros Estate Winery.** In the cozy tasting room, share sips of European-style wines, then stroll hand in hand to see the herb garden, the duck pond, and the spectacular view. If it's clear out, see if your partner can spot Mt. Diablo in the distance. *602 Bonneau Rd., Sonoma.* ☎ *800/966-9365. See p 157.*

For where to have lunch, refer to the biking tour above.

Take Bonneau Rd. northeast and turn left on Hwy. 116/Arnold Dr. Turn right on Madrone Rd., then left on Sonoma Hwy./Hwy. 12.

④ ★ **Arrowood.** More than 20 years ago, a married couple founded this winery on a hillside overlooking Sonoma. Today, their love for each other and for wine evidences itself in the bright tasting room. After tasting, go out onto the veranda and gaze upon Sonoma Mountain, its valley—and each other. *14347 Sonoma Hwy. (Hwy. 12), Glen Ellen.* ☎ *800/938-5170. See p 133.*

Follow the highway northwest.

⑤ ★★ **Chateau St. Jean.** Romantic in the more academic sense of the word (it has a bit of a sentimental, nationalistic French feel about it,

though "Jean" is pronounced the American way), this château, which includes a fancy visitors' center, a small art gallery, and a formal garden with pond, provides a nice setting for you and your amour. *8555 Sonoma Hwy. (Hwy. 12), Kenwood.* ☎ *707/833-4134. See p 139.*

Keep following the highway northwest.

⑥ ★ **Ledson Winery.** Fairy-tale-like architecture, complete with a castle structure, regal gates, and a hyper-pruned fountain courtyard, is apt to evoke scenes of Prince Charming and his lovely maiden. If you're getting in the mood for an intimate dinner back at your hotel, pick up a to-go meal at this winery's gourmet market and picnic space—and don't forget a bottle of pinot noir or chardonnay. *7885 Sonoma Hwy. (Hwy. 12), Kenwood.* ☎ *707/537-3810. See p 151.*

⑦ ★★★ **The General's Daughter.** Sonoma's most romantic restaurant is in an early-1900s Victorian that used to be General Vallejo's daughter's house. The atmosphere is intimate and discreet—and the food is sublime. *400 W. Spain St.* ☎ *707/938-4004. $$$.* If you're headed back to Napa for your lodging, consider dining at 15-table ⑧ ★★ **La Toque,** which has an utterly romantic setting complementing chef Ken Frank's excellent French cuisine. *1140 Rutherford Rd., Rutherford.* ☎ *707/963-9770. $$$$$.*

Ledson is a castle AND a winery.

Wine Country **without a Car**

1. Adventures Aloft
   (Location varies. See bullet below.)
2. Artesa Vineyards & Winery
3. Domaine Carneros
4. Zuzu
5. High Tech Burrito
6. Far Niente Winery
7. Kuleto Estate Family Vineyards
8. Napa Valley Wine Train

Traffic is an increasing problem in Napa, and, hey, you didn't plan this getaway just to sit in more gridlock. Besides, if you're planning to try all the wine you'd like to, getting behind the wheel just doesn't factor in. So let others shuttle you around while you sip to your heart's content. Take this opportunity to see far-apart wineries that are off the main drag and experience some of Napa's best alternative ways to get around. **Note:** This itinerary requires **advance planning** to secure reservations. **Tip:** For other non-car transportation ideas (bikes, bus, and so on), refer to "Savvy Traveler" (p 193); for walking tours, see "Charming Towns" (p 71).

---

1. ★★★ kids **Adventures Aloft.** Wine country's ultimate mode of transportation is the hot-air balloon; in fact, Napa Valley is the busiest hot-air balloon flight corridor in the world. Northern California's temperate weather allows for ballooning year-round and on clear summer weekends in the valley, it's a rare day when you don't see at least one of the colorful airships floating above the vineyards. One of the best companies providing rides is Adventures Aloft. Though the company's headquartered in Yountville, its employees will pick you up from your hotel as long as it's in Napa Valley south of Calistoga

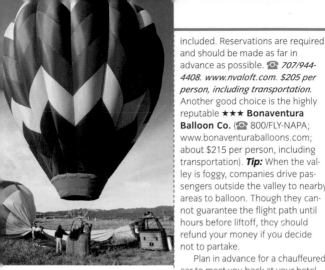

Up, up, and away!

(when you call to make your reservation, make sure to ask whether your lodging is within shuttling range). You'll have to get up before the sun, but it'll be worth it for the breathtaking serenity you'll experience as you float 3,500 feet (1,050m) above some of the world's most spectacular scenery. Skilled pilots double as informative tour guides, creating a highly personalized adventure. You'll get pastries and coffee before the flight and a full champagne breakfast after. Delivery back to your hotel is also

included. Reservations are required and should be made as far in advance as possible. ☎ 707/944-4408. www.nvaloft.com. *$205 per person, including transportation.* Another good choice is the highly reputable ★★★ **Bonaventura Balloon Co.** (☎ 800/FLY-NAPA; www.bonaventuraballoons.com; about $215 per person, including transportation). *Tip:* When the valley is foggy, companies drive passengers outside the valley to nearby areas to balloon. Though they cannot guarantee the flight path until hours before liftoff, they should refund your money if you decide not to partake.

Plan in advance for a chauffeured car to meet you back at your hotel after ballooning. **Beau Wine Tours and Limousine Service** (☎ 707/938-8001; www.beauwinetours. com) provides sedans, limos, vans, and SUVs; **California Wine Tours** (☎ 800/294-6386; www.california winetours.com) crafts personalized winery trips in town cars, SUVs, limos, and minibuses; **West Coach Limousine** specializes in luxury limos (☎ 707/548-2329; www.westcoach limo.net; around $75 per hour). *See p 203 for more options.*

❷ ★★ Artesa Vineyards & Winery. In a limo is a perfect way to visit the somewhat spread-out

The sculptures are funky and modern at Artesa.

Carneros appellation. **Artesa** is one of the few wineries directly east of Napa's downtown. A dramatically modern tasting room makes this Spanish-owned winery the "jewel of Carneros." Try the small-lot chardonnay and pinot noir, then explore the Carneros Center, which includes an exhibit on the region's history, a winemaking museum, and an art exhibit. *1345 Henry Rd., Napa.* ☎ *707/224-1668. See p 134.*

3 ★ **Domaine Carneros.** You can see this French-owned château beckoning you from the highway. Have your driver stop and ascend the grand staircase into the only tasting room to serve sparkling wines made exclusively with Carneros grapes. *1240 Duhig Rd., Napa.* ☎ *707/ 257-0101, ext.108. See p 143.*

4 ★★ **Zuzu.** For lunch, direct your chauffeur to this locals' favorite. Mini-Mediterranean plates meant for sharing are served in a comfortable, warm, and not remotely corporate atmosphere. Since you're not driving, indulge at the small but friendly wine and beer bar. *829 Main St., Napa.* ☎ *707/224-8555. $. See p 77.* For a quick to-go alternative, tell your driver to shift gears toward **5** ★ kids **High Tech Burrito,** an excellent fresh-Mex chain. If you like, take your healthy, creatively concocted wrap in the limo with you as you head north. *641 Trancas St., Napa.* ☎ *707/224-8882. $.*

6 ★ **Far Niente Winery.** Yes, this one's on the beaten path, but it has a faraway feel, created by its stone structure and Southern-style gardens with 8,000 azaleas and 100 ginkgo trees. And just because you're not behind the wheel today doesn't mean you can't ogle the amazing collection of classic automobiles in the **Carriage House.** After, taste Far Niente's current releases and late-harvest Dolce dessert wine. Appointment required. *1350 Acacia Dr., Oakville.* ☎ *707/944-2861.*

7 **Kuleto Estate Family Vineyards.** Bordering the far-flung (for Napa) Chiles Valley District appellation is this lovely spot for touring and tasting.

Vintage cars fill Far Niente's Carriage House.

Take a ride on the Napa Valley Wine Train.

Few wineries offer this great a view of Lake Hennessey, such mountainous scenery, or quite the possibility to glimpse wildlife. Appointment required. *2470 Sage Canyon Rd. (Hwy. 128), St. Helena.* ☎ *707/963-9750.*

Hit Napa's McKinstry Street Depot for ⑧ ★ kids **Napa Valley Wine Train's** 5:30pm check-in (boarding's at 6pm and the train departs for St. Helena at 6:30pm). Get to the station even earlier if you want to partake in the pre-boarding wine tasting. This rolling restaurant is one of the most leisurely ways to view Napa. The nonstop 3-hour journey through the vineyards of Napa, Yountville, Oakville, Rutherford, and St. Helena is a lazy 36-mile (58km) cruise on vintage-style cars finished with polished mahogany paneling and etched-glass partitions. The windows are slightly dirt-stained, but staffers are attentive, if not overly enthusiastic. Dinner's served with all the finery— linen, china, silver, and crystal—but the food itself is not quite memorable. The point here is the train ride, which means that this is a more interesting ride during daylight saving time. *Tip:* Sit on the west side for the best views. *1275 McKinstry St., Napa.* ☎ *800/427-4124. www. winetrain.com. Dinner packages*

$97–$140. Daytime rides, with or without meals, are available too; tickets range from $40–$125 ($25 for kids under 13). Boarding times Mon–Fri 11am & 6pm; Sat–Sun 9am, noon & 6pm. (The dinner schedule is abbreviated in Jan and Feb.) Check the website for special events.

Cabbing It

Napa Valley Cab (☎ 707/257-6444; www.napavalleycab.com).

A tractors makes its way through vineyards at Domane Carneros.

Wine Country **on a Budget**

SONOMA NAPA
Map
Area

Bale Gristmill
St. Hist. Park

Silverado

St. Helena

Lake
Hennessey

Lake Hennessey
Rec. Area

Napa R.

Sage Canyon Rd

Hood
Mtn.

Hood Mtn.
Reg. Park

Bald Mtn.

**Santa
Rosa**

Spring
Lake

Red Mtn.
Sugarloaf Ridge
State Park

Rutherford

**NAPA
COUNTY**

Oakville
Cross

Rector Res.

Llsanjo
Annadel
State Park
Bennett Mtn.

Kenwood

Oakville

Napa Valley Railroad

Yountville
Cross

Yountville

Bennett

Valley
Rd.

Sonoma
Cr.

Trinity Rd.

Dry
Creek
Rd.

Dry Creek

Mt.
Veeder

Silverado Trail

**Rohnert
Park**

Peluma Hill Rd

Bouverie
Wildflower
Preserve

Mt. Veeder Rd.

**Glen
Ellen**

Valley of the Moon

Eldridge

Agua Caliente

Sonoma
St. Hist. Park

El Verano

Sonoma

Napa

**SONOMA
COUNTY**

Schellville

Big Bend

Lakeville

Lave Veeder

❶ V. Sattui
❷ Sutter Home Winery
❸ The Silverado
   Museum
❹ COPIA
❺ Boon Fly Café
❻Ⓐ Cline Cellars
❻Ⓑ Navillus Birney
❼ Kenwood Vineyards
❽ Café Citti
❾ Fresh Choice

0   4 miles
0   4 kms

A **budget traveler** might not choose a region characterized
by splurging and expensive taste. While Napa and Sonoma
(especially Napa) are indeed those types of destinations, the budget-
conscious can still come here, indulge, and leave without breaking
the bank. Here's how. **START: V. Sattui, 1111 White Lane, St. Helena.
Distance: 53 miles (85km), doable in a full day.**

❶ ★★ **V. Sattui** offers free tastes
(eight wines!) and self-guided tours
all day. Explore the historic winery's
aging cellars, museum, and outdoor
spaces. At the deli and cheese shop,
there are free samples aplenty.
Tip: To fit everything in today, take
advantage of V. Sattui's 9am opening
time. *1111 White Lane, St. Helena.*
☎ *707/963-7774. See p 159.*

Take White Lane southwest and
turn right on St. Helena Hwy.
(easy walking distance).

❷ ★ **Sutter Home Winery.**
Tastings are free; enjoy them in the
original 1874 winery. Afterward,
take a self-guided garden tour (also
free) to see the estate's extensive
gardens, which were modeled after
Canada's **Butchart Gardens.**
The organic White Zinfandel
garden nurtures 125 rose species.
*277 St. Helena Hwy. (Hwy. 29), St.
Helena.* ☎ *707/963-3104, ext. 4208.
See p 159.*

Take St. Helena Hwy. northwest and turn right on Adams St. Turn left on Library Lane.

③ kids The Silverado Museum.
Dedicated to the life of Robert Louis Stevenson, this room-sized museum houses more than 8,000 writerly artifacts, including original manuscripts, photographs, and the author's copies of his own books. Free admission. *1490 Library Lane, St. Helena.* ☎ *707/963-3757.*

Go southeast on Library Lane to turn right on Adams St. Turn left on Hwy. 29 and take the ramp toward Lincoln Ave. Turn right on Solano Ave., then right onto Lincoln Ave. Turn right on Soscol Ave., then left on 1st St.

④ ★★★ COPIA.
Downtown Napa's main attraction is an exceptionally good deal. For a maximum of $5, you get to see downtown Napa's biggest attraction, a $55-million facility spearheaded by Robert Mondavi. Admission entitles you to the center's various exhibits, its vast Edible Gardens, its sensory stations offering "mini-tastings," and 30-minute introductory classes. **Tip:** Check out COPIA's website before visiting for the daily schedule. Also: Some culinary demonstrations, classes, and tastings cost extra; the website can tell you what's free and what's not. *500 1st St., Napa.* ☎ *707/259-1600. www.copia.org. Admission $5; $4 students of any age with valid ID & seniors 62+; free for children under 13; Wed half-price for Napa & Sonoma residents. Daily 10am–5pm (closed Tues & holidays).* See p 34.

To feel as though you've gone to an expensive restaurant, head to **⑤ ★★ Boon Fly Café,** which has upscale decor, white-linen tables, and classy California cuisine. *4048 Sonoma Hwy. (at Carneros Inn), Napa.* ☎ *707/299-4900. $$.*

From COPIA, go west on 1st St. onto Hwy. 29 S. Turn right on Carneros Hwy. (Hwy. 121/12), and turn left to stay on it.

⑥A ★ Cline Cellars.
Get here in time to take the 1 or 3pm free tour, or walk around yourself to see the quaint grounds, which include ponds, rosebushes, and the highlight: a small, woodsy museum (free admission) housing dioramas of all 21 California missions. Tastings are free, too, and they happen in a rustic 1850s farmhouse. *24737 Carneros Hwy. (Calif. 121), Sonoma.* ☎ *707/940-4000.* See p 140.

You'd never guess that V. Sattui's fancy grounds are home to free tastes!

Cline Cellars feels like more like a home than a tasting room.

OR:
From COPIA, go west on 1st St. onto Hwy. 29 S. Turn right on Carneros Hwy. (121) N; it becomes Arnold Dr.

6B Navillus Birney. Though this family-owned winery doesn't generally show guests its vineyards, its storefront tasting room in central Glen Ellen gives free tastings. Ask for sips of chardonnay and pinot noir, then examine the historic relics and photos documenting Glen Ellen's history—see if you can spot authors Jack London and M.F.K. Fisher in the mix. *13647 Arnold Dr., Glen Ellen.* ☎ *707/933-8514. See p 153.*

From Cline, head east on Hwy. 121 and turn left (north) on Hwy. 12. From Navillus, take Arnold Dr. northeast and turn left on Sonoma Hwy. (Hwy. 12).

7 ★ Kenwood Vineyards. The tasting room here is in a 1906 farmhouse, even though the winery's now a modern, high-production facility (most of it cleverly concealed in the original barnlike buildings). Though the winery looks modest, its output is staggering: nearly 500,000 yearly cases of wines well known throughout the U.S. Alas, tours aren't available, but free tastes include an array of varietals, including the popular

sauvignon blanc, a crisp, light wine with hints of melon. *9592 Sonoma Hwy. (Hwy. 12), Kenwood.* ☎ *707/ 833-5891. See p 150.*

8 ★ Café Citti. The high-quality Northern Italian cuisine at Citti (pronounced "Cheat-ee"), a roadside trattoria, is delightfully inexpensive. Order from the huge menu board above the open kitchen, then grab a table (the ones on the patio are best on warm evenings) and a server brings your hearty meal. Wine is available by the bottle, the espresso is plenty strong, and everything on the menu board is available to go. *9049 Sonoma Hwy., Kenwood.* ☎ *707/833-2690. $$.* It's a bit of a drive from central Napa and Sonoma, but another affordable option is **9 kids Fresh Choice,** where you won't pay more than $9 for a full dinner. What with the tremendous all-you-can-eat buffet, you'll definitely leave full; low prices ensure that your wallet does, too. There's a sliding price scale for kids, and since you serve yourself, you don't have to tip on the cost of your meal; just leave $1 to $2 for the busboy. *1018 Santa Rosa Plaza (at 4th St.).* ☎ *707/525-0912. $.* ●

TO
SAN FRANCISCO
71 7/10 M.

CALISTOGA

ELEVATION
365 FEET

Napa

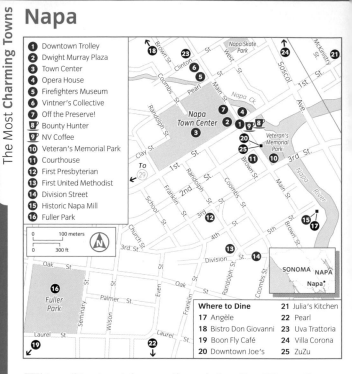

1 Downtown Trolley
2 Dwight Murray Plaza
3 Town Center
4 Opera House
5 Firefighters Museum
6 Vintner's Collective
7 Off the Preserve!
8 Bounty Hunter
9 NV Coffee
10 Veteran's Memorial Park
11 Courthouse
12 First Presbyterian
13 First United Methodist
14 Division Street
15 Historic Napa Mill
16 Fuller Park

Where to Dine		21 Julia's Kitchen
17 Angèle		22 Pearl
18 Bistro Don Giovanni		23 Uva Trattoria
19 Boon Fly Café		24 Villa Corona
20 Downtown Joe's		25 ZuZu

This walking tour takes you through the city of Napa—the town, not the region, the valley, or the county. The southern bookend to the ritzier towns above it, Napa is the more lived-in, real-life community that caters more to its ever-growing residential population than to its tourists. But that's exactly its charm: Visitors feel invited in rather than pandered to. Plant yourself here for a day, sip a glass of local cab, stroll among this riverside town's Victorian and Gothic landmarks, and mingle with Napans (or "Napkins," as locals call themselves). *For more information, contact the Napa Downtown Association. 1556 1st St. No. 102.* ☎ *707/257-0322. www.napa downtown.com or the Napa Valley Conference and Visitors Bureau (see* 3 *below).* 🕐 *6 to 7 hours.* **START: 1st & Main sts.**

1 ★ kids **Napa Downtown Trolley.** Start the day by getting a town overview on this vintage-style California streetcar—rides are free. If you board at the corner of 1st and Main (at Dwight Murray Plaza), you can stay on the trolley for about 45 minutes to see its full loop, which includes much of downtown, the Napa Town Center, COPIA, Napa Premium Outlets, the Wine Train station, Fuller Park, and the Historic

Napa's Main Street.

Napa Mill. The first pickup from the plaza is at 11am (11:15am Thurs–Sat) and about every 30 to 45 minutes thereafter. ☎ 707/255-7631. www. nctpa.net/trolley. Mon–Wed 11am–6pm, Thurs & Sun 11am–8pm, Fri–Sat 11am–11pm.

❷ **Dwight Murray Plaza.** Exit the trolley where you started and explore this community gathering spot, replete with a clock tower that chimes on the hour, various shops, a fountain, and picnic tables. Check out the waterfront mural depicting the Napa River waterfront in its early-1900s heyday.

❸ **kids Napa Town Center.** Head to this retail complex to grab a caramel apple at Rocky Mountain Chocolate Factory or gelato at Christopher's Fine Foods, and stroll past shops (don't miss the 50,000-sq.-ft./4,645-sq.-m McCaulou's Department Store, known for its selection of affordable clothes for the whole family). All the retailers are housed in historic buildings and connected by a pedestrian street. Look for the two huge oak trees that serve as town landmarks. Here you'll also find the overachieving **Napa Valley Conference and Visitors Bureau** (☎ 707/226-7459; www.napavalley.org; Mon–Sat 9am–5pm, Sun 11am–5pm). Stop in for a variety of local information,

money-saving coupons, and pamphlets outlining self-guided walking tours of the town's historic buildings. *1290 Napa Town Center* ☎ 707/255-9375. 1310 Napa Town Center.

❹ ★ **Napa Valley Opera House.** Cross the street to Main, and you'll see this Italianate-style building. Even if you don't see a show, this performance venue is worth a look for its historic value. Listed on the National Historic Register, it was originally built in 1879. Some nights, Jack London read aloud to rapt audiences; on others, traveling Vaudeville acts titillated delighted patrons. Due to poor attendance, however, it closed in 1914 and sat quiet and dilapidating until concerned local preservationists recently restored and reopened it—to the tune of $14 million. Today, operatic performances are still the minority at this 16-row venue, despite the establishment's name. Management prefers to bring in symphonies, musicals, and even country, rock, and R&B performers like Rosanne Cash, Los Lobos, and Boyz II Men. Occasionally, theatric and dance troupes come through as well. Check the website for show times and schedules. *1030 Main St.* ☎ 707/226-7372. www.napavalley operahouse.com. Box office open Mon–Fri 10am–5:30pm, Sat noon–4pm.

The Napa Valley Opera House is spectacular both night and day.

⑤ ★ kids Napa Firefighters Museum. Run by the Napa City Firefighters Association, this small museum is a loving tribute to the history of firefighting. Displays show antique and modern equipment used by lifesaving heroes. *1201 Main St., Napa.* ☎ *707/259-0609. Open Wed–Sat 11am–4pm. Free admission. Also see p 39.*

⑥ ★★ Vintner's Collective. Wine discoveries await at this 18-winery tasting room in the old Pfeiffer Building, which was built in 1875 and is Napa's first stone building (touch the native sandstone). After previous lives as a brewery, saloon, brothel, and Chinese-owned laundry, in 2002 it became an outlet for small, virtually unknown wineries like Judd's Hill, Melka, and Mi Sueno—in short, stuff you *won't* find at home. To boot, Keith Fergel (French Laundry's sommelier, aka the wine expert at the region's most famous restaurant) named this tasting room his favorite stop for finding new wines. *1245 Main St.* ☎ *707/255-7150. www.vintnerscollective.com. Wed–Mon 11am–6pm, Tues by appointment. Tastings $15–$25.*

⑦ Off the Preserve! Plucked from the modern art collection at the di Rosa Preserve (p 57), this gallery's contemporary exhibits are showcased in the circa-1886 Kyser-Williams building. *1142 Main St.* ☎ *707/253-8300. www.dirosa preserve.org. Wed–Sat 11am–6pm (9pm Fri–Sat). Free admission.*

⑧ ★★ Bounty Hunter Rare Wine & Provisions. A combination wine bar/eating joint/retail shop/tasting room, Bounty Hunter has bottles that even devoted collectors would be hard-pressed to find elsewhere. The thinking here is, "Find your own cult wine." Or just enjoy on-tap Guinness with a hearty sandwich. Before walking into this saloonlike space, admire its exterior: The brick Semorile Building, embellished with decorative cast-iron railing, was built in 1888 and is on the National Historic Register. *975 1st St.* ☎ *707/226-3976. www. bountyhunterwine.com. Daily Sun–Thurs 11am–10pm (1am Fri–Sat). Tastings $2.50–$19.*

⑨ Napa Valley Coffee Roasting Co. For a sweet fix after Bounty Hunter, or if you just need a caffeinated pick-me-up, this roastery in the adjacent **Winship Building** (also on the Historic Register) sells small-batch custom roasts and a selection of pastries. *948 Main St.* ☎ *707/224-2233. $.*

Get a java jolt at the Napa Valley Coffee Roasting Co.

The Napa Valley Mill is now home to a number of fun boutiques.

⑩ Veterans Memorial Park.
Savor your coffee on the river's
edge at this tranquil park. On holidays like Independence Day and
Labor Day, the site comes alive with
music and festivities. And when
Governor Arnold Schwarzenegger
comes to town, he holds press con-
ferences here. *Main & 3rd sts.*

⑪ ★ kids Courthouse. Napa's
Renaissance-style courthouse, built
in 1878, is still very much a working
court, complete with a law library,
hall of records, and mediation center. It's on the National Register of
Historic Places for its 19th-century
architecture and history—in 1897,
for example, this courthouse was
the site of California's last public
hanging. Explore the first-floor picto-
rial hall for a visual depiction of
Napa County history. On the east
lawn (2nd St.) look for the 1893 flag-
pole modeled after the Eiffel Tower,
as well as a Wappo Indian grinding
rock. *825 Brown St.*

**⑫ ★ First Presbyterian
Church.** Were it not for its protu-
berant steeple and ornamental
doorway, this pyramidal church,
built in 1874, would look like a big
rooftop sitting on the ground. It is
one of the county's best examples
of Victorian Gothic architecture—no
surprise, then, that this California
Registered Historical Landmark is

also in the National Register of
Historic Places. *1333 3rd St.* ☎ *707/
224-8693. www.fpcnapa.org.*

Heading from downtown into the
Napa Abajo District, you'll notice
larger city blocks and a high con-
centration of residential architec-
tural styles spanning the 1800s.
The entire district is on the
National Register of Historic
Places.

**⑬ First United Methodist
Church.** This mix of religious and
secular architecture done in late-
Gothic style is home to an elaborate
sanctuary and gorgeous stained-
glass windows. Be sure to try its
small labyrinth. *601 Randolph St.*
☎ *707/253-1411. www.napaumc.org.
Labyrinth hours 11am–2pm ($3 sug-
gested donation).*

Stroll riverward on **⑭ ★ Division
Street,** so named because it
divides Napa Abajo from downtown.
All the turn-of-the-20th-century
homes on this lane are historically
significant, from the **Hayman
House** (1227 Division St.) to the
Greek Revival–style **Lamdin Cottage** (1236 Division St).

⑮ ★★ Historic Napa Mill.
Abutting the Napa River are this
complex's Hatt buildings, also on
the National Register of Historic
Places (sensing a theme here?)—

they're good examples of the industrial false-front brick buildings that used to cluster the river's once-bustling wharves. The 1884 building used to house a grain mill (the old tin silos are still attached) and a roller-skating rink. These days, it's a smart commercial center including the "haunted" **Napa River Inn** (p 123) and a variety of shops: Stop at the upscale **Napa General Store,** the **Napa Valley Lavender Co.,** and the **Vintage Sweet Shoppe** for locally made non-wine souvenirs or gifts and ponder the exquisite mosaic fountain—its scenes portray Napa Valley's history. *500 Main St.* ☎ *707/251-8500. www.napariver inn.com/napamill.php*

⑯ kids **Fuller Park.** Take the trolley from COPIA to Napa's first park, which boasts more than 83 tree species, many marked with plaques commemorating important events. Named after Napa's 1905 mayor, John A. Fuller, the shaded park is a great spot to rest and unwind; kids will love its fountain and large playground. *Oak & Seminary sts.*

Where **to Dine**

★★ **Angèle** *FRENCH* This riverside spot has exciting food and surroundings to match; its combo of wood beams, concrete walls and floors, bright yellow barstools, and heated patio is great for intimate dining. The culinary ante is way up there: Think fabulous, crispy roast chicken with fresh corn and chanterelles or King salmon with arugula salad and heirloom tomatoes. If the chocolate soup's on the menu, it's a must-order for dessert. Reservations recommended. *540 Main St. (at Historic Napa Mill).* ☎ *707/252-8115. Entrees $10–$32. AE, MC, V. Daily 11:30am–10pm. Map p 72.*

★★★ **Bistro Don Giovanni** *ITALIAN* A bright, bustling restaurant highlighting quality ingredients and California flair. Entrees never disappoint, especially the thin-crust pizzas from the wood-burning oven and the house-made pastas. Begin with the salad of beets and *haricots verts.* If it's warm enough, dine alfresco in the vineyards. Reservations recommended. *4110 Howard Lane.* ☎ *707/224-3300. Entrees $12–$28. AE, DC, DISC, MC, V.* *Sun–Thurs 11:30am–10pm; Fri–Sat 11:30am–11pm. Map p 72.*

★ **Boon Fly Café** *AMERICAN* Along the rural Carneros Highway is a great bargain dining option: the gourmet roadhouse in front of the Carneros Inn. The slick and inviting interior is modern barn style, complete with a corrugated metal watershed-like pizza oven and light, airy surroundings accented with dark wood. The food similarly balances rustic and chic with fancy renditions of comfort classics like killer beer-battered onion rings and flatbread pizzas. Breakfast options include satisfying omelets and pancakes. If you're passing by and in a hurry, there are tasty to-go items like donut holes and breakfast sandwiches. *4048 Sonoma Hwy.* ☎ *707/299-4900. Entrees $8–$27. AE, DC, DISC, MC, V. Daily 7am–10pm. Map p 72.*

kids **Downtown Joe's** *AMERICAN* Foodies will want to steer clear, but those looking for a good heavy breakfast, a down-home atmosphere, and live entertainment during the evenings (Thurs–Sun) will appreciate this well-priced restaurant. Beers, such as the tart Golden Ribbon American, are made in-house, as are the breads and desserts. If the sun's out, request a table on the outside patio. Weekday happy hours feature specials such as $2 pints and half-price appetizers. *902 Main St.* ☎ *707/258-2337. Entrees $8–$19. AE, DC, DISC, MC, V. Mon–Fri 10:30am–11pm, Sat–Sun 8:30am–midnight. Map p 72.*

★★ **Julia's Kitchen** CALIFORNIA-FRENCH   This restaurant (part of Copia; p 34) is for serious foodies. Peer into the open kitchen and watch as an army of chefs, headed by young Victor Scargle (formerly of SF's acclaimed **Aqua** and **Jardiniere**), bustle to prepare your amazing meal. It's much more relaxing than it sounds; sit back and await the colorful parade of dishes headed your way, especially if you've ordered the $60 six-course tasting menu. *500 1st St.* ☎ *707/265-5700. Entrees $16–$30. AE, MC, V. Wed–Mon 11:30am–3pm, Thurs–Sun 5:30–9:30pm. Map p 72.*

★ **Pearl** CALIFORNIA ECLECTIC   If you prefer to skip the destination restaurants and head for a casual but quality meal among locals, head to Pearl, which has a warm, friendly dining room and a lovely enclosed patio. The seasonally influenced menu includes a selection of salads, sandwiches, and main courses; an excellent choice is the soft polenta with sautéed vegetables. Reservations recommended. *1339 Pearl St.,*

The entrance to Julia's Kitchen.

no. 104. ☎ *707/224-9161. Entrees $12–$27. MC, V. Tues–Thurs 11:30am–2pm, 5:30–9pm; Fri–Sat 11:30am–2pm, 5:30–9:30pm. Map p 72.*

★ **Uva Trattoria** ITALIAN   At this lively restaurant with a hopping music scene, jazz musicians perform almost every evening, making diners' reasonably priced meals a special occasion. To start, order *arancini* (breaded, fried basil-risotto balls filled with Teleme cheese); follow that with a gourmet pizza or house-made pasta. *1040 Clinton St.* ☎ *707/255-6646. Entrees $11–$21. AE, MC, V. Tues–Thurs 11:30am–10pm, Fri 11:30am–midnight, Sat 5pm–midnight, Sun 4–9pm. Map p 72.*

★ **Villa Corona** MEXICAN   A funky, colorful local favorite hidden in the southwest corner of a strip mall. Order at the counter, then wait for the huge burritos, enchiladas, and chimichangas to arrive at your table. *3614 Bel Aire Plaza (on Trancas St.).* ☎ *707/257-8685. Entrees $6–$11. MC, V. Tues–Sat 8am–9pm, Mon–Sun 8am–8pm. Map p 72.*

★★ **ZuZu** TAPAS   If you've had it with French and Italian fare and wine-country-themed dining rooms, this neighborhood haunt will refresh and restore you. Enjoy shockingly affordable Mediterranean-inspired small plates, like tangy paella, paired with intriguing by-the-glass wines and a friendly attitude. Desserts aren't as interesting, but with a bottle of wine and more delicious plates than you could possibly devour, who cares? Reservations not accepted. *829 Main St., Napa.* ☎ *707/ 224-8555. Tapas $3–$13. MC, V. Mon–Thurs 11:30am–10:30pm, Fri 11:30am–midnight, Sat 4pm–midnight, Sun 4–10:30pm. Map p 72.*

Sonoma

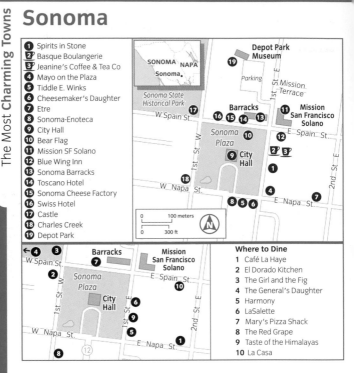

1. Spirits in Stone
2. Basque Boulangerie
3. Jeanine's Coffee & Tea Co
4. Mayo on the Plaza
5. Tiddle E. Winks
6. Cheesemaker's Daughter
7. Etre
8. Sonoma-Enoteca
9. City Hall
10. Bear Flag
11. Mission SF Solano
12. Blue Wing Inn
13. Sonoma Barracks
14. Toscano Hotel
15. Sonoma Cheese Factory
16. Swiss Hotel
17. Castle
18. Charles Creek
19. Depot Park

Where to Dine
1. Café La Haye
2. El Dorado Kitchen
3. The Girl and the Fig
4. The General's Daughter
5. Harmony
6. LaSalette
7. Mary's Pizza Shack
8. The Red Grape
9. Taste of the Himalayas
10. La Casa

At the northern boundary of the Carneros District, along Highway 12, is the centerpiece of Sonoma Valley: the midsized town of Sonoma, which owes much of its appeal to Mexican general Mariano Guadalupe Vallejo. Vallejo fashioned this pleasant, slow-paced community after a typical Mexican village—right down to its central plaza, which still serves as Sonoma's geographical and commercial center. The plaza sits at the top of a "T" formed by Broadway (Hwy. 12) and Napa Street. Most of the surrounding streets form a grid pattern around this axis, making Sonoma easy to navigate. The plaza's Bear Flag Monument marks the spot where the crude Bear Flag was raised in 1846, signaling the end of Mexican rule; the symbol was later adopted by the state of California and placed on its flag. The 8-acre (3.2-hectare) park at the center of the plaza, complete with two ponds that are populated with ducks and geese, might make you want to take an afternoon siesta—but don't. There's too much to see here. Depending on your pace, allow a half- to a full day. START: **Sonoma Valley Visitors Bureau, 453 1st St. E. Distance: Less than a half-mile (.8km) of walking.**

1 ★ Spirits in Stone. Cross the street to get to this gallery selling African sculptures, paintings, baskets, and ethnic jewelry. It'll make you want to go to Kenya. *452 1st St. E. ☎ 707/938-2200. www.spiritsin stone.com. Daily 10am–6pm (open until 8pm Fri–Sat).*

2 Basque Boulangerie. Grab lunch at this crowded little bakery with fresh sandwiches and good coffee. *460 1st St. E. ☎ 707/935-7687. Daily 7am–6pm. $.* Also offering exceptional coffee is tucked-away **3 Jeanine's Coffee & Tea Co.,** which roasts its own beans and shares a quirky storefront with a tobacconist. *464 1st St. E. ☎ 707/996-7573. $.*

4 ★★ Mayo on the Plaza. At Mayo Family Winery's friendly, fragrant tasting room, $5 gets you six tastes; it's free to peruse the nice gift selection, so pick out a book, table linen, or candle to take home. *498 1st St. E. ☎ 707/996-9911. www.mayofamilywinery.com. Daily 10am–6pm.*

5 ★★★ kids Tiddle E. Winks Vintage 5 & Dime. A treasure trove of nostalgic paraphernalia. Marvel at the meticulously kept tchotchkes, including authentic college pennants (some date back to the 1940s), decades-old board games, and old-fashioned candies and sodas. This place is like a hands-on museum; kids love it as much as adults do. *115 E. Napa St. ☎ 707/939-6933. www.tiddlewinks. com. Mon–Sat 11am–6pm, Sun 11am–6pm.*

6 ★★ The Cheesemaker's Daughter. This small country-style store has artisanal cheeses from around the world. Proprietress Ditty Vella knows her stuff; she was born into Sonoma's Vella Cheese Co. family.

Also try the shop's oils, teas, cocoas, honeys, and pastas. *127 E. Napa St. ☎ 707/996-4060. www.cheese makersdaughter.com. Tues–Sat 10am–6pm, Sun 11am–5pm.*

7 ★★ Etre. Some store-design expert must've planned this delight-filled boutique; it's in a restored 1880s bungalow with a singular selection of hard-to-find home wares, books, cosmetics, fragrances, and other excellent ware. *156 E. Napa St. ☎ 707/939-2700. www.etresonoma. com. Wed–Mon 11am–6pm.*

8 ★ Sonoma-Enoteca. Back on the plaza, a staffer behind this wine bar hands you a sheet listing the 20 wine selections of the day, all from small-lot wineries; your task is to select 6 to try. Also taste a variety of olive oils and browse the home decor selection. *35 E. Napa St. ☎ 707/935 1200. www.sonoma-enoteca.com. Wed–Mon 11am–6pm (last tasting at 5:30pm). $5 for 6 tastes, $10 with a cheese plate.*

Walk past **9 City Hall,** which looks like something out of "Back to the Future," and through a children's park, after which you'll see the **10 ★★ Bear Flag Monument,** representing the end of Mexico's rule.

Will it be cheddar or stilton? Sample both at The Cheesemaker's Daughter.

⑪ ★★★ kids Mission San Francisco Solano. The plaza's crowning jewel, and its reason for being, is this must-see landmark, known also as **Sonoma Mission.** *363 3rd St. W.* ☎ *707/938-1519. www.parks.ca.gov. Daily 10am–5pm. $2 admission for adults. Children under 17 free. Admission also includes the Sonoma Barracks. For details, see p 51.*

⑫ ★ Blue Wing Inn. Across the street from the mission is this pleasantly dilapidated building, commissioned by Vallejo around 1840 to accommodate "emigrants and other travelers," as its inscription states. Notable guests included John C. Frémont (an explorer, general, senator, and presidential candidate) and Western legend Kit Carson, as well as members of the Bear Flag Party—not to mention outlaws and bandits. Admire it from the outside. *133 E. Spain St.*

⑬ ★★ kids Sonoma Barracks. This Sonoma landmark is a must-see during your stroll through this historic town. *See p 48 for details.*

⑭ Toscano Hotel. Built in 1851 as a general store and library, this became a hotel in 1886. In 1972, the

The Sonoma Mission and it's trademark bell.

Sonoma Plaza marks the center of town.

Sonoma League for Historic Preservation faithfully refurbished the building and opened it for public tours. *20 E. Spain St.* ☎ *707/938-9560 (Sonoma State Historic Park). www.parks.ca.gov. Tours Sat & Sun 1–4pm, Mon 11am–1pm. Free.*

⑮ ★ Sonoma Cheese Factory. This huge marketplace, a 75-year-old institution, has more cheese varieties than conceivably imaginable. Many are available for sampling, alongside snacks and wine. There's also a small coffee and gelato bar. *2 E. Spain St.* ☎ *800/535-2855. www.sonomajack.com. Daily 8:30am–5:30pm.*

⑯ Swiss Hotel. Built in 1840, the Swiss Hotel was home to Vallejo's brother and vintner. Though it has nothing to do with Switzerland (the name was adopted from another local hotel that burned down), it's been a hotel and restaurant since 1909. Step into the bar to see a bevy of historic Sonoma photos. *18 W. Spain St.* ☎ *707/938-2884. www.swisshotelsonoma.com. See below for restaurant hours.*

⑰ Castle Vineyards & Winery Tasting Room. Tastings of European-style current releases are $5, but if you buy a bottle, the fee is waived. *122 W. Spain St.* ☎ *707/996-1582. www.castle vineyards.com. Daily 10am–5pm.*

⑱ Charles Creek Vineyard Tasting Room & Gallery. Even if you're done tasting for the day, step in to see the cow made of corks. If you *are* tasting, it's $5 for about six samples—but that fee's refundable upon purchase.

483 1st St. W. ☎ *707/935-3848. www.charlescreek.com. Daily 11am–6pm.*

Where **to Dine**

★★ **Café La Haye** *CALIFORNIA/ MEDITERRANEAN* Despite its limited hours and somewhat high prices, this tiny, artsy dining room is worth a visit for its top-notch food and wine. The baked almond-crusted goat cheese with roasted beets is a menu highlight. *140 E. Napa St.* ☎ *707/ 935-5994. Entrees $16–$19. AE, MC, V. Tues–Sat 5:30–9pm. Map p 78.*

★★★ **The General's Daughter** *NEW AMERICAN* This turn-of-the-20th-century Victorian home was once the home of General Vallejo's daughter (hence the name)—but there's nothing passé about the all-organic menu and refined decor. An utterly romantic dining experience. *400 W. Spain St.* ☎ *707/938-4004. Entrees $15–$30; tasting menu $45–$65. MC, V. Tues–Sun 5:30–10pm. Map p 78.*

★★★ **El Dorado Kitchen** *CALIFORNIA* El Dorado Hotel's in-house establishment presents exquisite plates in a thoroughly comfortable space. The personalized six-course tasting menu is highly recommended. *405 1st St. W., Sonoma.* ☎ *707/996-3030 or 800/289-3030. Entrees $12–$26; tasting menu $60. AE, MC, V. Daily 11:30am–2:30pm, 5:30–10pm (bar open later). Map p 78.*

★★ **the girl and the fig** *FRENCH* This cozy restaurant's gotten a lot of attention, and for good reason: The food's fantastic and imaginative. After dining, sample cheeses at the *salon de fromage. 110 W. Spain St.* ☎ *707/938-3634. Entrees $10–$22. AE, DISC, MC, V. Daily 11:30am–*

10pm (11pm Fri–Sat). Brunch Sun 10am–3pm. Map p 78.

★★ **Harmony** *CALIFORNIA* Ledson Hotel's sophisticated restaurant has marble decor and a seasonally changing menu. If it's available, try the ricotta-mint ravioli as an appetizer. *480 E. 1st St.* ☎ *707/996-9779. Entrees $23–$33. AE, DISC, MC, V. Wed–Mon 11:30am–9pm (10pm Fri–Sat). Map p 78.*

★ **LaSalette** *PORTUGESE* One of wine country's only Portuguese restaurants has a pleasant dining room decorated with hand-painted tiles. Choose from a large selection of cheeses and ports for a perfect ending to the inspired dishes. *452 E. 1st St.* ☎ *707/938-1927. Entrees $11–$25. AE, MC, V. Tues–Sun 11:30am–9pm. Map p 78.*

kids Mary's Pizza Shack *ITALIAN* Belying its name, this place has more pasta and sandwich choices than it does pizza options. Neither is it a shack; its bright and inviting interior is quite comfortable. *8 W. Spain St.* ☎ *707/938-8300. Entrees $6–$15.25. Pizzas $6–$24. AE, DISC, MC, V. Daily 11am–10pm (11pm Fri–Sat). Map p 78.*

Taste of the Himalayas *INDIAN/ NEPALI/TIBETAN* This friendly restaurant, whose founders are descendents of Nepali Sherpas, is a good place to try momos, curry, or tandoori. *464 E. 1st St.* ☎ *707/996-1161. Entrees $9.50–$18. AE, MC, V. Daily 11am–2:30pm, 5–10pm. Map p 78.*

St. Helena

1 NV Coffee
2 River House
3 Murray n' Gibbs
4 Olivier
5 Woodhouse Chocolate
6 Art on Main
7 St. Helena Olive Oil Co.
8 Market
9 St. Helena Wine Center
10 Hotel St. Helena
11 Findings
12 Jan de Luz
13 Vintage Home
14 Tasting on Main
15 Martin
16 I. wolk Gallery

Where to Dine
1 Ana's Cantina
2 Cindy's Backstreet Kitchen
3 Wine Spectator
   Greystone Restaurant
4 Giugni's
5 Martini House
6 Taylor's Automatic Refresher
7 Terra
8 Tra Vigne

A first glance of St. Helena (say "Saint Hel-*een*-uh") gives the impression that this could be a pleasant Anytown, USA. But a step into any of its myriad boutiques, galleries, and showrooms reveals otherwise; their brand of ritziness couldn't be afforded many other places. This walking tour starts just off Main Street, then takes you through a foodie's delight. Crossing the street allows you to take in wine country's artsy side. Allow a half-day. **START: Napa Valley Coffee Roasting Co., 1400 Oak Ave. St. Distance: Less than a half-mile (.8km) walk.**

1 ★ Napa Valley Coffee Roasting Co. Coffee and pastries fuel you in this relaxing and sunny ambience, bettered by an antique coffee press on display in the back and a communal book swap in the front. *1400 Oak Ave. St. ☎ 707/963-4491. $.*

2 ★ River House Books. Peruse the well-rounded travel and architecture sections at this inviting bookstore. *1234 Adams St. ☎ 707/963-1163. www.riverhousebooks napavalley.com. Mon–Sat 10am–5:30pm, Sun 11am–5pm.*

3 ★ Murray n' Gibbs. A unique and global selection of gifts, bedding, and kid stuff. *1220 Adams St. ☎ 707/963-3115. Mon–Sat 10am–5:30pm, Sun 11am–5pm.*

④ ★★★ Olivier. This beautiful French-style store is where to sample a wide array of epicurean savories. The big copper vats lining the walls are actually olive oil dispensers; feel free to mix your own. Olivier also offers bath goods, as well as upscale dishware imported from Provence. *1375 Main St. ☎ 707/967-8777. www.oliviernapa valley.com. Mon–Sat 10am–6pm (5pm on Sun).*

⑤ ★★ Woodhouse Chocolate. This salon showcases gorgeous handmade chocolates: Try the fan-shaped Thai ginger confection or the brown-butter *ganache* ($1.50 each). These decadent treats in delicate boxes can be shipped anywhere in America. *1367 Main St. ☎ 800/966-3468. www.woodhousechocolate. com. Daily 10:30am–5.30pm.*

⑥ Art on Main. A small gallery with striking art is a draw for fans of modern or wine-related works. *1359 Main St. ☎ 707/963-3350. www.imagesnapavalley.com. Daily 10am–5pm.*

⑦ ★★ St. Helena Olive Oil Co. Between stone walls, helpful staffers guide you through tastings of vinegars, honeys, fruit relishes, compotes, flavored salts, tapenades,

Sample olive oil at St. Helena Olive Oil Co.

The road to St. Helena is picturesque.

syrups, sauces—oh, and olive oils. *1351 Main St. ☎ 707/968-9260. Mon–Fri 10:30am–5pm, Sat–Sun 10:30am–6:30pm.*

⑧ ★ Market. This long restaurant with a wooden bar and stone walls has helpful waitstaff and playful American cuisine. Try the "Very Adult Macaroni and Cheese," and save room for desserts that'll take you back to childhood: homespun cotton candy (made at your table), s'mores, or butterscotch pudding. *1347 Main St. ☎ 707/963-3799. Entrees $9.50–$20. AE, MC, V. Daily 11:30am–10pm. Map p 82.*

⑨ St. Helena Wine Center. More than your typical wine shop, this one has rare and high-end wines in the back (think Screaming Eagle), unique vodkas (like Charbay's green tea flavor), and yummy liqueurs. *1321 Main St. ☎ 707/963-1313. www.shwc.com. Daily 10am–6pm.*

⑩ Hotel St. Helena. Step into this dark B&B to see the eccentric, almost creepy, decor (old dolls and mounted animal heads abound) and maybe to sip coffee at the small wine bar. *1309 Main St. ☎ 707/963-4388. www.hotelsthelena.com. Wine bar daily 3–8pm.*

11 Findings. Eclectic offerings combine the antique and the new; check out the jewelry, frames, and furniture. *1269 Main St. ☎ 707/963-6000. Daily 10am–6pm (until 7pm Fri–Sat).*

12 ★ Jan de Luz. This impressive home-decor store features custom-embroidered table linens, upscale furnishings, even fountains and fireplaces. *1219 Main St. ☎ 707/963-1550. www.jandeluz.com. Daily 9:30am–5:30pm.*

13 ★ Vintage Home. An inspiring store with distinctive home goods, like pillows, linens, candles, and books. *1201 Main St. ☎ 707/963-7423. Daily 10am–5:30pm (Sun until 4pm).*

Now that you've walked the most interesting part of Main Street's south side, cross the street and slip into **14 ★ Tasting on Main,** where, for $10, you can taste somewhat obscure wines selected by this tasting room's manager. Wine-tasting classes are offered too: They're $15 and include a flight of four wines (call for reservations). This is a great way to discover the products of closed-to-the-public wineries. *1142 Main St. ☎ 707/967-1042. www.tastingonmain.com. Fri–Sat 10:30am–8pm; Sun–Thurs 10:30am–6pm.*

15 ★★ Martin. A true showroom, this lavish store displays everything from art books to large furnishings. *1350 Main St. ☎ 707/967-8787. Wed–Mon 10am–6pm (Sun until 4pm).*

16 ★ i. wolk gallery. A sparse space with lighthearted art. *1354 Main St. ☎ 707/963-8801. www.iwolkgallery.com. Daily 10am–5:30pm.*

Where to Dine

Ana's Cantina *MEXICAN* A friendly joint with great Mexican food, billiards, darts, beer, and a fun crowd. Live entertainment Wednesday through Saturday. *1205 Main St. ☎ 707/963-4921. Entrees $2–$7. MC, V. Food served Thurs–Mon 11am–2pm; bar open daily 10am–2am (winter hours may vary). Map p 82.*

★★ Cindy's Backstreet Kitchen *CALIFORNIA/AMERICAN* An upscale down-home type of place, this restaurant with a darling dining room presents unfussy yet creative dishes made with local ingredients. *1327 Railroad Ave. ☎ 707/963-1200. Entrees $11–$25. DC, DISC, MC, V. Daily 11:30am–10pm (9pm Sun–Thurs in winter). Map p 82.*

★★ Wine Spectator Greystone Restaurant *CALIFORNIA* You know a restaurant at the Culinary Institute of America (where culinary pros go to become executive chefs) has got to be good—and oh, is it ever. Watch as chefs prepare small plates, then try them with a new-to-you wine. *1304 Main St. ☎ 707/967-1010. Entrees $18–$40. AE, DC, DISC, MC, V. Daily 11:30am–9pm (10pm Fri–Sat). Map p 82.*

Giugni's *SANDWICHES* Locals come here for a satisfying bite and an escape from pretense; there's always a long line at the counter. Don't be surprised if you get hit by a touch of nostalgia here: Historical political posters clutter the walls, and among the grocery items for sale are Cokes in glass bottles and old-time jawbreakers. *1227 Main St. ☎ 707/963-3421. Sandwiches $5.45–$6.45. No credit cards. Daily 9am–5pm. Map p 82.*

Tra Vigne is a local favorite.

★★ Martini House NEW AMERICAN

One of the area's more renowned restaurants, Martini House is well designed both in terms of decor and cuisine. Chef/owner Todd Humphries's comprehensive seasonal tasting menus ($45–$65) can be ordered with a sommelier wine pairing, which can bump the per-person price up to $100. There's also an excellent prix-fixe dinner ($45), or just order an a la carte entree with one of the divine soups or salads. *1245 Spring St.* ☎ *707/963-2233. Entrees $25–$34. AE, DC, DISC, MC, V. Daily 11am–10pm. Map p 82.*

★ Taylor's Automatic Refresher

DINER It isn't every day that a roadside burger shack gets a spread in *Food & Wine* magazine, but then, this outdoor diner built in 1949 isn't your average fast-food stop. Its excellent hamburgers on soft but sturdy buns are known the valley over. Vegetarians need not sigh when their dining companions opt for Taylor's: There are at least five veggie options, including a burger and a taco. *933 Main St.* ☎ *707/963-3486. Entrees $3.25–$14. AE, MC, V. Daily 10:30am–9pm. Map p 82.*

★★ Terra NEW AMERICAN

Terra manages to be humble even though it serves some of northern California's most extraordinary food. The dining room is rustic-romantic with stone walls. The menu, by James Beard Award–winning chef Hiro Sone, reflects the region's bounty as well as European and Japanese influences. Desserts are sublime, especially orange risotto in brandy snap with passion-fruit sauce. Reservations recommended. *1345 Railroad Ave.* ☎ *707/963-8931. Main courses $19–$29.50. AE, DC, MC, V. Wed–Mon 6pm–close. Map p 82.*

★★ Tra Vigne ITALIAN

Its combination of good food and high energy makes Tra Vigne a long-standing favorite among visitors and locals. Whether guests dine in the Tuscan courtyard or in the enormous dining room, they're treated to wonderful bread with house-made olive oils and robust California dishes cooked Italian-style. Try the heirloom tomato salad, the daily oven-roasted pizza special, or fresh pasta. Reservations recommended. Adjoining **Cantinetta** offers sandwiches and lighter meals. *1050 Charter Oak Ave.* ☎ *707/963-4444. Main courses $15.95–$26.50. DC, DISC, MC, V. Daily 11:30am–9pm (until 10pm Fri–Sat).*

The heirloom tomato & mushroom salad at Martini House.

Healdsburg

1. Kendall-Jackson
2. La Crema
3. Plaza Farms
4. Plaza Park
5. Hand Fan Museum
6A. Thumbprint
6B. Toad Hollow
7. Costeaux
8. Flying Goat
9. Downtown Bakery & Creamery
10. Healdsburg Museum
11. Cellar 360
12. Gallo
13. Powell's
14. Chateau Felice

Where to Dine
1. Barndiva
2. Bear Republic
3. Bistro Ralph
4. Bovolo
5. Cena Luna
6. Ctr. St. Café & Deli
7. Cyrus
8. Dry Creek Kitchen
9. Healdsburg Bar & Grill
10. Manzanita
11. Oakville Grocery
12. Restaurant Charcuterie
13. Taqueria El Sombrero
14. Willi's Seafood & Raw Bar
15. Zin

Healdsburg is a town on the rise. Not long ago, it was just another agricultural Sonoma borough, content to quietly produce some of the world's best food and wine. But word got out about where all that refined alimentation was coming from, and local tourism-minded entrepreneurs picked up on the excitement. Hence, recent arrivals of fancy hotels (especially Les Mars and Hotel Healdsburg) and their respective restaurants (Cyrus and Dry Creek Kitchen) drew big names like Martha Stewart and Bob Dylan, definitively stamping the town onto the jet-setter map. And Healdsburg's status just keeps rising, thanks to all the famous wineries that keep opening tasting rooms downtown, new shops targeting well-heeled patrons, and perennial attractions like the jazz festival each June and the twice-weekly organic farmers' market (p 21). Still, Healdsburg gracefully maintains a friendly small-town personality that also has reverence for the area's rich history—and just a touch of quirkiness. This full-day walking tour highlights the town's best tasting rooms and historical spots. START: **Toad Hollow Vineyards's tasting room, 409A Healdsburg Ave. Distance: Less than a half-mile (.8km).**

❶ ★ **Kendall-Jackson.** Try one of America's most recognizable wine brands (p 150) in this tasting room. Your eyes will be drawn to the particleboard floor and the agreeable selection of wine-related merchandise, but once your nose whiffs the wines, your body and soul will be stationed at the expertly staffed bar. Print free tasting coupons from the website. *337 Healdsburg Ave.* ☎ *707/433-7102. www.kj.com. Daily 10am–5pm. $2 for 4 tastes ($10 for reserves).*

❷ ★★ **La Crema.** Modern design sets this tasting room apart, as do coastal artisan wines. The winery specializes in Burgundian varietals, so try chardonnay and pinot noir. *235 Healdsburg Ave.* ☎ *707/ 431-9400. www.lacrema.com. Daily 10:30am–5:30pm. Free tastings.*

❸ ★★ **Plaza Farms.** An intimate marketplace where small producers of artisan foods and beverages showcase their goods. Occupying the stalls: a gourmet mushroom purveyor, an olive oil producer, a creamery, three wineries, a chocolatier, and a maker of specialty teas. The best part? Lots of free samples, and staffers explaining everything you try. In the back is Bovolo (p 90). *106 Matheson St.*

☎ *707/433-2345. www.plazafarms. com. Daily 10am–8pm (6pm in winter). Free tastings.*

❹ ★ **Plaza Park.** There are plenty of picnic benches in Healdsburg's acre-wide focal point. At this site of Healdsburg's fairs, festivals, and concerts, find the Olympic flame statue honoring local athletes. On the other end of the park is the 1847 millstone from Cyrus Alexander's gristmill. In between, there's a fountain and palm, pine, and redwood trees.

❺ ★ **Hand Fan Museum.** Take a break from sampling wine in this tiny room, which displays a multicultural collection of beautiful hand fans, some dating back to the 1700s. *327A Healdsburg Ave.* ☎ *707/431-2500. www.handfan museum.com. Wed–Sun 11am–4pm, or by appointment. Free.*

❻Ⓐ ★ **Thumbprint Cellars.** A tasting lounge with sleek furnishings, a youthful vibe, and handcrafted small-lot wines, Thumbprint holds occasional events like blending seminars and winemakers' dinners, so call (or go online) in advance to find out what's going on and whether you need a reservation. *36 North St.* ☎ *707/433-2393. www.thumbprintcellars.com. Daily 11am–6pm. Free tastings.*

The sidewalks of Healdsburg are perfect for a stroll.

OR:

6B ★ **Toad Hollow Vineyards.** This tasting room is a playful place to start your day. Frog-themed everything is everywhere, but the wines served over a river-stone bar focus attention into your glass. A few food items, such as balsamic vinegar, are also available. *409A Healdsburg Ave.* ☎ *707/431-8667. www.toadhollow.com. Daily 10:30am–5:30pm. Free tastings.*

7 ★★ **Costeaux French Bakery.** If the wine's leaving you in need of a midday coffee or pastry, you're in luck: Healdsburg has excellent cafes and bakeries. Costeaux, a sunny spot beloved by locals, has been a Healdsburg tradition since 1923, with its breads, soups, salads, and desserts. Fun fact: Costeaux claims the record for having baked the world's largest pumpkin pie. Look for the 6-foot-3-inch (1.9m) pie tin. *417 Healdsburg Ave.* ☎ *707/433-1913. $.* Devotees consider **8** ★ **Flying Goat Coffee** California's best java; they'll drive miles for a cup. *324 Center St. & 419 Center St.* ☎ *707/433-3599. $.* Aromatic **9** **Downtown Bakery & Creamery** sells fantastic sticky buns, fruity pastries, and fresh breads. *308A Center St.* ☎ *707/431-2719. $.*

How often do you get to walk to several tasting rooms all within blocks of each other?

10 ★★★ **kids** **Healdsburg Museum.** From Center Street, turn right onto Matheson Street, and as you pass St. Paul's Episcopal Church, admire its stained-glass windows. A few steps farther and you're at Healdsburg's museum. Andrew Carnegie donated $10,000 in 1909 to make this neoclassical revival–style building a public library, so its entryway still bears his name. Inside, artifacts document local history, from Pomo Indian times to the town's former life as Rancho Sotoyome, to the squatter squabbles known as the "Westside Wars." One man who emerged victorious after the land conflicts became Healdsburg's founder in 1857: Ohio entrepreneur Harmon Heald. The museum also recounts the period after Healdsburg's incorporation with photos, period costumes, and even 19th-century shoes. Since it's also a historical society, hands-on research facilities with microfilmed newspapers and official county records are available. *221 Matheson St.* ☎ *707/431-3325. www.healdsburgmuseum.org. Tues–Sun 11am–4pm (research by appointment). Free.*

11 ★★ **Cellar 360 World Wine Estates.** It's a rare tasting room in which you can taste wines from around the world, but World Wine, due to its global family of brands, represents 150 labels from over 40 international regions. Overwhelming? Nah—savvy staffers guide you through tasting whichever five wines are featured on a given day. That might include big names like Beringer (p 136) and Chateau Souverain or lesser-known ones like Matua Valley (New Zealand) or Castello di Gabbiano (Italy). *308B Center St.* ☎ *707/ 433-2822. www.worldwineestates. com. Daily 11am–6pm. Tastings $5; refundable with purchase.*

Healdsburg's Best Shopping

Though they're not explicit stops on this tour, Healdsburg is packed with inspired shops; among the best are alluring **Evans Designs Gallery** (☎ 707/473-0963), exotic **Baksheesh** (☎ 707/473-8008) and **Spirits in Stone** (☎ 707/723-1723), haven-like **Toyon Books** (☎ 707/433-9270), and sleek **Lime Stone** (☎ 707/433-3080). For specialty wines, try **The Wine Shop** (☎ 707/433-0433) or **Thirty-Four North** (☎ 707/473-0808).

⓬ ★★ Gallo Family Vineyards. At this new tasting room, try a three-wine flight or enjoy individual tastes while eager employees explain what you're sipping. If you're tired of standing over a bar, there are sit-down tables. *320 Center St. ☎ 707/433-2458. www.gallofamily.com. Daily 10am–6pm. Tastings free–$12. Also see p 146.*

⓭ ★★ kids Powell's Sweet Shoppe. Even grown-ups will feel like a kid in this neon-bright candy store. The term "sweet memories" turns literal here, since Powell's sells candies that haven't been seen since the 1950s. While nostalgic confections define the merchandise, they're interspersed with enduring favorites like bubble-gum cigars,

jump-rope-length licorice ropes, and, of course, ice cream. The 1971 version of *Willy Wonka & the Chocolate Factory* plays continuously in the back. *322 Center St. ☎ 707/431-2784. www.powells sweetshoppe.com. Daily 10am–9pm (Sun until 8pm)*

⓮ ★★ Chateau Felice. A newcomer, this funky tasting room presents Chalk Hill wines made in the French tradition. The boutique winery makes only 3,000 cases per year; taste their contents over the copper bar (check out the collection of antique bottle openers) or settle in with a glass on the patio. *223 Center St. ☎ 707/431-9010. www.chateau felice.com. Daily 11am–7pm. Free tastings; wines by the glass $3–$8.*

Where **to Dine**

★★ Barndiva *CALIFORNIA* The philosophy here is "eat the view." Barndiva's deep-red exterior looks like a tidy barn; inside is a flower-and-art-filled space with modern decor. Out back is a walled dining garden. The restaurant insists on using only sustainably produced, seasonally available ingredients from local sources. Potpies are good, but save room for the spicy, out-of-this-world chocolate orbit cake. *231 Center St.*

☎ *707/431-0100. Entrees $8.50–$25. AE, MC, V. Wed–Sat noon–11pm (Fri & Sat until midnight), Sun 11am–11pm. Map p 86.*

★ kids Bear Republic Brewing Co. *AMERICAN* A lively, casual brewpub with appetizers galore, creative sandwiches, and a huge selection of handcrafted ale. Decor includes old bicycles hanging from the ceiling and a California-themed

Thai marinated lobster, avocado, melon, and fresh hearts of palm at Cyrus.

agricultural mural. *345 Healdsburg Ave.* ☎ *707/433-2337. Entrees $7.75–$15. MC, V. Sun–Thurs 11:30am–9pm (9:30 in summer), Fri–Sat 11am–10pm. Map p 86.*

★ **Bistro Ralph** *FRENCH* In this minimalist white restaurant, the ever-changing menu features globally influenced starters, pricy meat-oriented entrees, and a Healdsburg-based wine list. Reservations recommended. *109 Plaza St.* ☎ *707/433-1380. Entrees $17–$36. MC, V. Mon–Sat 11:30am–2:30pm, 5:30–approx. 9pm. Map p 86.*

★ **Bovolo** *BREAKFAST & ITALIAN* A cute 24-seat spot in Plaza Farms (p 87) makes everything, including gelato, from scratch. Breakfast options are unique—try the lavender-buttermilk waffle—as are antipasti (like quinoa caponata), sandwiches, pasta, and pizza. No escargot, although Bovolo is Italian for "snail." *106 Matheson St.* ☎ *707/431-2962. Entrees $6.50–$10.50. MC, V. Mon–Thurs 8am–6pm, Fri–Sun 8am–9pm. Map p 86.*

★★ **Cena Luna** *ITALIAN* Classy with dark-wood furnishings, Cena Luna changes its menu weekly, but fresh homemade pasta is always amazing. The husband-and-wife

chefs know what they're doing. *241 Healdsburg Ave.* ☎ *707/433-6000. Entrees $14–$22. AE, DC, MC, V. Mon–Sat 5pm–close (approx. 8–10pm). Map p 86.*

★ **kids** **Center Street Café & Deli** *AMERICAN* Step in here and be swept back to the 1950s; whimsical knickknacks and nostalgic what-have-yous are playfully placed all over this big, fun dining room. Breakfasts are delish, deli lunches are made to order, and an old-fashioned soda fountain serves luscious shakes. *304 Center St.* ☎ *707/433-7224. Entrees $4.50–$12. AE, DISC, MC, V. Daily 7am–4pm (until 7pm in summer). Map p 86.*

★★★ **Cyrus** *CALIFORNIA-FRENCH* The county's latest shining-star chef, young Douglas Keane, formerly of SF's lauded Gary Danko, is making a loudly heard splash in his new kitchen; there are whispers that he may be giving French Laundry—and Napa—a run for their money. In beautiful Les Mars Hotel this sophisticated restaurant named for pioneer Cyrus Alexander offers prix-fixe cuisine, but you can mix and match the amount and kinds of courses you order. Order wine; the food pairs exceptionally well. Reservations recommended. *29 North St.* ☎ *707/433-3311. Tasting menus $58–$95. AE, MC, V. Daily 5:30–9:30pm. Map p 86.*

★★★ **Dry Creek Kitchen** *CALIFORNIA* Celeb chef Charlie Palmer's only California venture is a successful melding of splendid cuisine and excellent service. Within hip Hotel Healdsburg, the kitchen turns out inspired, well-presented dishes based on what's seasonally relevant and available. *317 Healdsburg Ave.* ☎ *707/431-0330. Entrees $24–$34. AE, MC, V. Fri–Sun noon–2:30pm, Sun–Thurs 5–9:30pm, Fri–Sat 5–10pm. Map p 86.*

kids Healdsburg Bar & Grill
AMERICAN This all-American restaurant has a thorough menu for kids and a refreshing on-tap selection (Guinness and Sierra Nevada included) for parents. There's a strong do-it-yourself vibe, from ordering at the kitchen to making your own Bloody Mary (Sat & Sun). Sporadic live music really gets the place going. *245 Healdsburg Ave. ☎ 707/433-3333. Entrees $10–$25. MC, V. Daily 11:30am–10pm. Map p 86.*

★★ Manzanita CALIFORNIA Named after a type of tree and accented with woodsy elements amid stylish modernity, the mood's set as soon as you walk in. Once seated, an inspired menu (which changes weekly) and gracious owners take care of the rest. Try anything wood-fired. *336 Healdsburg Ave. ☎ 707/433-8111. Entrees $13–$28. AE, DISC, MC, V. Wed–Sun 11:30am–2:30pm, 5:30–9:30pm. Map p 86.*

★★ Oakville Grocery CALIFORNIA One of four stores bearing this name (p 34), this outpost has an al fresco eating area that's always packed on sunny days. Before settling on your order, browse in awe at the fascinating gamut of colorful gourmet options in this small but impressive market. Try a sandwich or pizza with wine from the tasting bar. *124 Matheson St. ☎ 707/433-3200. Entrees $5–$16. AE, MC, V. Daily 8am–7pm. Map p 86.*

★ Restaurant Charcuterie
FRENCH-MEDITERRANEAN A small restaurant whose offerings center around cured pork. Decor consists of hundreds of cute piggy figurines, which is slightly disconcerting. Still, service is friendly and there are enough options if pig's not your preference. *335 Healdsburg Ave. ☎ 707/431-7213. Entrees $9–$25.*

AE, MC, V. Daily 11:30am–3pm (Sat–Sun noon–3:30pm), 5–8:30pm (Fri–Sun until 9:30pm). Map p 86.

★ Taqueria El Sombrero
MEXICAN This low-key joint, popular with locals, has all the expected Mexican fare, plus breakfast and seafood. *245 Center St. ☎ 707/433-3818. Entrees $2–$10. DISC, MC, V. Daily 9am–9pm. Map p 86.*

★ Willi's Seafood & Raw Bar
SMALL PLATES An energetic vibe permeates Willi's dining room, bar, and outdoor patio. If you want to hunker down with your own big meal, this isn't the place—but if you want to swap tastes of fancily prepared seafood like miso-glazed sturgeon, Willi's fits the bill. *403 Healdsburg Ave. ☎ 707/433-9191. Small plates $7–$29. DISC, MC, V. Mon, Wed, Thurs, Sun 11:30am–9pm, Fri–Sat 11.30am–10pm. Map p 86.*

★★ Zin NEW AMERICAN With exposed concrete walls hung with big semi-abstract vineyard paintings, Zin is a stylish place to eat. Chef Jeff Mall trained under Bradley Ogden, a fact reflected in his culinary creations. Ask about blue-plate specials or try staples like beer-battered green beans and egg-noodle pappardelle. To go with your meal, order—you guessed it—zin. *344 Center St. ☎ 707/473-0946. Entrees $15–$29. AE, MC, V. Mon–Fri 11:30am–2pm, daily 5:30pm–close. Map p 86.*

After Dark: Raven Theater

The 500-seat pulse point of the town's performing arts scene stages uproarious theatric and stirring music performances. Check the website for show times. *115 North St. ☎ 707/433-6335. www.raventheater. org & www.ravenplayers.org.*

Guerneville

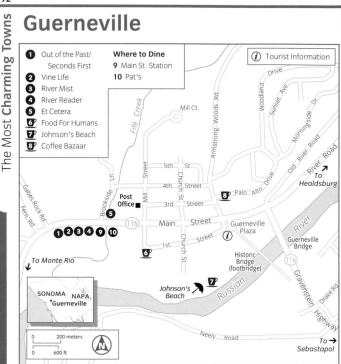

1 Out of the Past/
Seconds First
2 Vine Life
3 River Mist
4 River Reader
5 Et Cetera
6 Food For Humans
7 Johnson's Beach
8 Coffee Bazaar

Where to Dine
9 Main St. Station
10 Pat's

(i) Tourist Information

A **mystical redwood forest enchants visitors** as they make the winding drive into Guerneville. The town itself (say "*Gurn*-ville," or risk identifying yourself as an out-of-towner by elongating the middle "e") is a throwback to everything small-town America used to be—except for its progressive orientation. Rainbow flags and signs proclaiming "This is a hate-free zone" adorn many businesses—a testament to the village's largely gay and lesbian population. Many storekeepers keep their pets beside them as they regale tourists with little-known facts about the area. This half-day walking tour, rather than a hyper-structured itinerary, is more a leisurely stroll down Main Street; part of your fun should be wandering into boutiques that appeal directly to you in addition to the ones listed here. START: **Where Highway 116 becomes Main Street, just after the Safeway grocery store. Walk east. Trip Length: Less than a half-mile (.8km).**

---

1 **Out of the Past** and **Seconds First** are two businesses housed in one incense-scented storefront. You'll find oddities like Betty Boop

light-switch covers and hilarious fridge magnets, plus peculiar posters and vintage clothes. *16365 Main St.* ☎ *707/869-2211. Daily 11am–6pm.*

Guerneville is a small town with a big, open mind.

2 ★★ Vine Life. A haven for interior decorating fanatics, oenophiles, and foodies, this shabby-chic boutique sells specialty food items, hand-printed stationery, local wines, and other little surprises. *16359 Main St. ☎ 707/869-1234. www.vinelifegifts. com. Daily 11am–5pm (6pm during summer).*

3 River Mist. Wares here include artsy jewelry and decorative collectibles. Even if you don't intend to buy, step inside to see the mural depicting the town and to pat Yip, the resident Pomeranian. *16357 Main St. ☎ 707/869-0475. Summer hours Mon–Thurs 11am–5pm, Fri–Sun 11am–7pm. Winter hours Wed–Mon 11am–5pm.*

4 ★ River Reader. This simple, straightforward bookshop has an excellent collection of progressive and alternative literature, a small kids' section, a local-author shelf, and a newsstand with gay-themed magazines front and center. A few ethnic gifts, too. Be sure to give Callie the calico cat some attention; she basks in it. *16355 Main St. ☎ 707/869-2240. Daily 10am–6pm (5pm on Sun).*

5 ★ Et Cetera. Et Cetera showcases an inspired mix of ethereal Asian-inspired homewares and earthy furnishings. *16270 Main St. ☎ 707/869-5808. www.etcetc1.com. Daily 10am–6pm.*

Veer off Main Street to find **6 Food For Humans,** a natural foods market that stocks organic produce, snacks, and eco-friendly merchandise. *16385 1st St. ☎ 707/869-3612. $.* Buy a sandwich or a wrap, crackers, cheese, and fruit, then tote your picnic down to **7 kids Johnson's Beach** on the Russian River, where you can take a dip or admire Guerneville Bridge. There's a kiddie pool, so bring the little ones. *16241 1st St. www.johnsons beach.com. Daily 10am–6pm, mid-May to early Oct.* For a pick-me-up after your riverside picnic, try the java or ice cream at eclectic **8 Coffee Bazaar.** *14045 Armstrong Woods Rd. ☎ 707/869-9706.*

Where **to Dine**

Main Street Station *ITALAN*
This corner restaurant is undeniably upbeat. Menu options include pizza, sandwiches, salads, and pasta. Don't miss the evening jazz performances. *16280 Main St. ☎ 707/869-0501. Entrees $6–$16. AE, MC, V. Daily 10am–10pm. Map p 92.*

Pat's Restaurant & Bar *AMERICAN* This basic down-home diner has an adjoining woodsy bar. Don't let the tough-looking staff fool you; they're as sweet and professional as can be. *16236 Main St. ☎ 707/869-9904. Entrees $4–$11. Cash only. Daily 10am–3pm. Map p 92.*

Yountville

1 Bouchon Bakery
2 Beard Plaza
3 Vintage 1870
4 Antique Fair
5 Bell Wine Cellars

Where to Dine
6 Bistro Jeanty
7 Bouchon
8 Compadres
9 French Laundry
10 Gordon's
11 Hurley's
12 Napa Valley Grille
13 Redd
14 Domaine Chandon

Pioneer George C. Yount, known for having planted the valley's first grapevine, is this town's namesake and founder. Since before its 1855 inception, Yountville (say "*Yont*-ville") has been a premier winemaking region. In 1973, prestigious French champagne house Moët et Chandon chose Yountville as the site for its U.S. expansion, and Domaine Chandon was born. About 20 years later, chef Thomas Keller bought a small restaurant called The French Laundry. Much of the sophistication that now defines Yountville sprang up around these two institutions; since their establishment, other prominent winemakers and chefs have moved in so that the mile-long walking town is now an unparalleled dining destination. When visiting, notice the locals; there are about 3,000 of them, and they range from world-famous chefs to immigrant grape pickers to young skateboarders to patriotic veterans who live at America's largest veterans home, right here in town. After dark, bars become lively. This tour is relatively short, because tiny Yountville's main attractions are unarguably its restaurants. (See "Where to Dine," below, to plan your dining experiences.) **START: Bouchon Bakery, 6528 Washington St. Distance: Less than a mile (1.6km) of walking.**

Yountville is tiny, but worth a visit and a stroll.

Grab a morning pastry at Thomas Keller's ★ **Bouchon Bakery.** Buying from the small, usually packed *boulangerie* is an affordable way to sample the creations of America's most famous chef. The confections here are as much a treat for the eyes as they are for the palate, even if you don't partake, at least gaze at the perfectly laid-out sweets in the glass case. There's no inside seating, so sit outside on a bench or stroll while savoring a buttery croissant, a signature chocolate *bouchon,* or impossibly fresh bread. *6528 Washington St.* ☎ *707/944-2253. $.*

❷ **Beard Plaza.** As you walk out of Bouchon Bakery, turn right to explore the myriad art galleries in this courtyard complex built in the late 1980s by the Beard family. The works for sale in these intimate exhibition spaces (like **RAS** and **Images**) are the creations of talented glass artists, painters, sculptors, jewelers, and ceramicists. Much of the art is modern or wine-inspired. *6540 Washington St.*

❸ **Vintage 1870.** Walk southward down Washington and on your left, you'll soon see this swap-meet-style shopping center in a historic brick building; the onetime Groezinger Winery was built in 1870 and at its height was California's largest winery. Foodies will want to check out **Cravings,** which offers an array of food items, including many mustard varieties. Among the other shopping options: several art galleries, a fun shoe shop, a kids' clothing store, and a wine room. *6525 Washington St., 707/944-2451 www vintage1870.com. Daily 10am–5:30pm.*

Continue down Washington and you'll hit ❹ **Antique Fair,** a gem of an antiques store showcasing nostalgic artifacts from bygone eras. Though pricey, seeing these fascinating items that look like they could have come out of a wealthy 19th-century manor is worth stepping in for. *6512 Washington St.* ☎ *707/944-8440. www.antique fair.com. Daily 10am–5pm.*

❺ ★ **Bell Wine Cellars.** Somewhat of a walk farther down Washington and a bit off the beaten path (consider driving) is Bell, a small artisanal winery where the tasting bar is in a warehouselike room among casks and barrels. But the wine's excellent, and so's the company: South African owner/winemaker Anthony Bell is quite liable to come out and converse about the ardent passion he has for crafting each wine he'll have you taste. Reservations recommended. *6200 Washington St.* ☎ *707/944-1673. www. bellwine.com. Daily 10:30am–4pm.*

Where **to Dine**

★ **Bistro Jeanty** FRENCH This casual, warm bistro, with muted buttercup walls and a patio area, serves seriously rich French comfort food for legions of fans. Think tomato soup in a puff pastry, crème brûlée (made with a thin layer of chocolate cream), and rib-gripping free-for-alls including coq au vin, cassoulet, and a thick-cut pork chop with jus. Quality has suffered since Jeanty has branched out to three restaurants, but when the kitchen is on, it's still a fine place to sup. *6510 Washington St.* 707/944-0103. *Entrees $14.50–$29. AE, MC, V. Daily 11:30am–10:30pm. Map p 94.*

★★ **Bouchon** FRENCH Dark and rich surroundings complement attentive service and a refined menu developed by Thomas Keller. The *gnocchi a la parisienne,* made with wheat instead of potato, melt in your mouth. Don't neglect the superlative wine list. A bonus, especially for restless residents and off-duty restaurant staff, is the late hours, although the menu becomes more limited when the crowds dwindle. *6534 Washington St.* 707/944-8037. *Entrees $16–$29. AE, MC, V. Daily 11:30am–1am. Map p 94.*

★ **Compadres Bar & Grill** MEXICAN A casual spot to enjoy a margarita or local microbrew on the outdoor patio with Adirondack chairs and two wood-burning fire pits. Bonus: nightly marshmallow roasts (free!). *6539 Washington St.* 707/944-2406. *Entrees $8–$20. AE, DC, DISC, MC, V. Sun–Wed 8am–10pm, Thurs–Sat 8am–11pm. Map p 94.*

★★★ **The French Laundry** AMERICAN-FRENCH Not much has been left unsaid about what's often called the world's best restaurant. The interior is small and fancy, service is unparalleled, and the food—well, let's just say it can be described in two words: Thomas Keller. The chef's signature nine-course degustation or vegetarian tasting menu changes daily based on his ingenious whims; **plan well in advance**—the waiting list to dine here is months long. *6640 Washington St.* 707/944-2380. *Typical dinner for 2: $420. AE, MC, V. Dinner daily 5:30–9:15pm, lunch Fri–Sun 11am–1pm. Closed on holidays and the first 2 weeks of Jan. Dress code enforced. Map p 94.*

Gordon's CALIFORNIA Part country store, part deli, and part casual

Bouchon is a bread heaven straight from Thomas Keller.

Bistro Jeanty is an Yountville staple.

restaurant. One wall is lined with an intriguing collection of jams, mustards, olive oils, wines, and other gourmet goods for sale. Breakfast (oatmeal, omelets, and homemade pastries), lunch (soup, salads, and sandwiches), and real homemade flavor come from an open kitchen. Perfect if you want to escape the town's high-falutin' restaurants for an intimate brush with locals. *6770 Washington St., Yountville.* ☎ *707/944-8246. Entrees $5–$15. MC, V. Daily 7:30am–3pm. Map p 94.*

★★ **Hurley's Restaurant and Bar** *CALIFORNIA* Chef Bob Hurley is passionate about presenting balanced cuisine that pairs well with wine. Here, you get elite food without the matching attitude. The bar, which serves cocktails and snacks until midnight, is a local favorite. *6518 Washington St.* ☎ *707/944-2345. Entrees $18–$29. AE, DISC, MC, V. Daily 11:30am–10pm. Bar menu available until midnight. Map p 94.*

★ **Napa Valley Grille** *CALIFORNIA* The theme at this chain restaurant is, well, Napa Valley. Entrees are listed on the lunch menu according to their Napa town of origin (Calistoga, St. Helena, and so forth). Try the pastas or items off the "Oakwood Grille." *6795 Washington St.* ☎ *707/944-8686. Entrees $14–$34.50. AE, DC, DISC, MC, V.* Daily 11:30am–9:30pm (Fri–Sat until 10pm). Map p 94.

★★ **Redd** *CALIFORNIA* Richard Reddington, an alumnus of NY's Daniel and Beverly Hills's Spago, incorporates ethnic influences into his regionally inspired seasonal menu. The dining space is clean and modern with chic accoutrements. *6480 Washington St.* ☎ *707/944-2222. Entrees $13–$29. Tasting menus $75–$160. AE, DC, DISC, MC, V. Mon–Sat 11:30am–2:30pm. Sun 10am–3pm. Daily 5:30–9:30pm (Fri–Sat until 10pm). Map p 94.*

★★ **Restaurant at Domaine Chandon** *CALIFORNIA FRENCH* Domaine Chandon, one of very few wineries that offers on-site fine dining, maintains a classy, conservative dining room as well as a gorgeous outdoor space. The vanilla-scented kabocha squash ravioli, paired with 1997 Chandon Vintage Brut, is unlike anything you've ever tasted. Cap off your meal with a chocolate crepe made with coconut cream and caramelized bananas—pair it with Chandon Riche bubbly, and you'll leave walking on air. *1 California Dr.* ☎ *707/204-7529. Entrees $26–$36. AE, DC, DISC, MC, V. Thurs–Mon 11:30am–2pm, 6–9pm. Days & hours may vary by season; call ahead. Map p 94.*

Glen Ellen

Downtown Glen Ellen

	Where to Dine
1 Navillus Birney	**8** fig café
2 Downtown	**9** Garden Court
3 Glen Ellen	**10** Glen Ellen Inn
Village Market	**11** Jacks' Bistro,
4 Benziger Family Winery	La Estancia,
5 Jack London Village	Olive & Vine
6 The Olive Press	**12** Saffron
7 Sonoma Valley	**13** Wolf House
Regional Park	

Glen Ellen, a small and sweet unincorporated Sonoma town, is home to fewer than 5,000 people, which makes it a tight-knit community. Local characters are many, from earthquake predictor Jim Berkland to Pixar's John Lasseter (often called today's Walt Disney) to Jack London's relatives—and, indeed, Jack London himself. Yes, the man is dead and gone (you can see his gravesite at the state park dedicated to him), but he's still very much present—not in a woo-woo kind of way, but in the form of extreme local reverence bordering on obsession. Case in point: There's a Jack London State Historical Park, a Jack London Village, a Jack London Lodge, a Jack's Bistro & Wine Bar—all within a 5-mile (8.1km) radius. Anyhow, Glen Ellen's living residents—artists, authors, winemakers, historians, and entrepreneurs of all sorts—are as spirited and passionate about their little hamlet as London was. They're quick and eager to share, with a complete lack of pretension, insider tips of what to see and do here. Though some would argue that Glen Ellen's too spread-out for a proper walking tour (unlike other Sonoma towns, there's no true town center), it's doable if you're not averse to occasionally walking about a mile along scenic byways. Otherwise, consider driving.

This tour, depending on your pace, can be done in a half- or a full day. *Tip:* There's not much in the way of streetlights, so if you're going out after dark, several local inns supply flashlights to guests upon request. START: **Navillus Birney Tasting Room, 13647 Arnold Dr. Distance: About 1.5 miles (2.4km).**

❶ ★ Navillus Birney Tasting Room. At the town's first intersection (Arnold Dr. and Warm Springs Rd.) in the 1920s mercantile Glen Ellen Square structure is this small country-style tasting room showcasing Navillus Birney's wines. Though the wines are good and tastings are free, history buffs may be more interested in the exhibit documenting Glen Ellen's rich past; look for the photos of Jack London and M. F. K. Fisher. *13647 Arnold Dr.* ☎ *707/933-8511. See p 153.*

Jack London's Saloon in downtown Glen Ellen.

❷ ★ "Downtown." What locals call "downtown" is really just a 2-block stretch of Arnold Drive that runs from Warm Springs Road to London Ranch Road. It has about 20 buildings (many of them historic), a few old bridges, a Civil War cannon, and the convergence of the Sonoma and Calabasas creeks. The heyday here was about a century ago when trains brought in tourists. Still, the town hasn't changed much since the days when Jack London lived, wrote, and farmed nearby—it received its first traffic light in 2006 and still has virtually no sidewalks.

❸ ★ Glen Ellen Village Market. This very gourmet market (without

the gourmet attitude) has hot and cold cases, delicious panini, a fabulous salad bar alongside an impressive produce section, and an excellent wine and cheese selection. A great place to stock up on picnic supplies for your picnic at **Sonoma Valley Regional Park ❼**. *13751 Arnold Dr.* ☎ *707/996-6728. Daily 6am–9pm.*

Walk about a mile (1.6km) uphill on London Ranch Rd.

❹ ★★ kids Benziger Family Winery. Known for having the valley's best tour (it draws tourists around by a tractor, for heaven's sake), this biodynamic winery is one of the region's most welcoming. *1883 London Ranch Rd.* ☎ *888/490-2739. See p 135.*

The fog rolls over the vineyards at Benziger.

Walk or drive another half-mile (.8km) up London Ranch Rd.

❺ ★ Jack London Village. This quaint little shopping spot houses an eclectic selection of restaurants and small shops, including a brand-new chocolate shop and cheesemonger, the **Eric Ross Winery** tasting room, as well as the **Olive Press** (see bullet ❻). *14301 Arnold Dr.*

❻ The Olive Press. At this cooperative press, locals come to mill their own oil in the hopper (this is where Beltane Ranch makes its gourmet batches) and tourists come to taste the freshest extra-virgin flavor-infused blends they've ever tried—for free. But it's not as socialist as it sounds: Even if you bring your own bottle, a gallon of oil can go for $128. A better deal, perhaps, are the olive-themed gift items, foods, and books. *14301*

Arnold Dr. No. 1. ☎ *707/939-8900. www.theolivepress.com. Daily 10am–5pm.*

Just past the Jack London Village and across Calabasas Creek is an entrance to:

❼ Sonoma Valley Regional Park. This 162-acre (65-hectare) park has beautiful biking and walking paths, numerous easy hiking trails (some paved and some dirt), and a fenced dog park. It's most beautiful in spring, when the wildflowers bloom, but fall's magnificent colors, just before the oaks shed their leaves, rank a close second. There's a pretty picnic and lawn area at the trail head. *13630 Sonoma Hwy.* ☎ *707/565-2041. www.sonoma-county.org/parks. Open daily from sunrise to sunset. Parking $5.*

Where **to** Dine

★★★ the fig café & winebar
CALIFORNIA-MEDITERRANEAN the girl and the fig's (p 81) sister restaurant (which also refuses to capitalize its name) is more casual than its Sonoma Plaza sibling, but don't let the rustic neighborhood vibe fool you. The plates that come out of the open kitchen represent the kind of sophistication more commonly associated with urban restaurants. Start with a thin-crust pizza, a cheese plate, or the signature fig and arugula salad; end with the lavender crème brûlée. A huge perk here is the lack of a corkage fee, so bring along a bottle. If you didn't bring your own, wine is available by the flight, glass, or bottle—and there's a nice list to choose from. Reservations not accepted. *13690 Arnold Dr.* ☎ *707/938-2130. Entrees $10–$19. AE, DISC, MC, V. Daily 5:30–close (around 9pm). Sat–Sun 9:30am–2:30pm. Map p 98.*

kids Garden Court Café *AMERICAN* A sunny, friendly place with savory breakfasts and lunches, as well as Sonoma wines and occasional special Friday-night dinners. At breakfast, order eggs done any which way. Lunch offerings consist mostly of sandwiches and salads. There's a pet-friendly umbrella-shaded terrace outside; owners can order meals for their dogs off a three-option menu. *13647 Arnold Dr.* ☎ *707/935-1565. Entrees $6–$13. MC, V. Wed–Mon 7:30am–2pm. Map p 98.*

★★ Glen Ellen Inn Restaurant
CALIFORNIA-FRENCH A locals' favorite for its warm, romantic atmosphere. The beautiful presentations that emerge from the open kitchen here change with the seasons. Garden seating is the favorable choice on sunny days, but the covered patio is also welcoming. The

Glen Ellen's fig café is the casual version of the famous Sonoma restaurant, the girl and the fig (p 81).

550-selection wine list offers numerous bottles from Sonoma, and more than a dozen wines by the glass. For dessert, don't miss the fabulous house-made sundae: Coconut-encrusted French-vanilla ice cream floats in bittersweet caramel sauce. Reservations recommended. *Tip:* There's a small parking lot behind the restaurant. *13670 Arnold Dr. ☎ 707/ 996-6409. Main courses $9–$25. AE, DISC, MC, V. Fri–Tues 11:30am–9pm, Wed–Thurs 5:30–9pm. Map p 98.*

★★ Jack's Bistro & Wine Bar

FRENCH This earnest little restaurant and bar in Jack London Village is a true find. Classy and white, yet rustic and in an old winery building, this bistro's entree options are as French as they come. Start with the *trois fromages* salad and be sure to ask which of the French wines goes best with your meal—staffers here are wine-pairing experts. On summer weekends, musicians perform jazz and blues from 6-8:30pm. *14301 Arnold Dr. ☎ 707/933-3043. Entrees $8–$25. AE, DISC, MC, V. Tues-Sun 11:30am-10pm. Map p 98.*

★★ La Estancia Argentine Grill

ARGENTINE Glen Ellen's brand-new, bright-yellow restaurant serves a rarity in wine country: classic Argentinean cuisine. That means lots of beef and some Italian-inspired choices, which pair well with the friendly service. In Jack London

Village. *14301 Arnold Dr. ☎ 707/933-0118. Entrees $9–$29. AE, DISC, MC, V. Tues–Sun 11am–10pm. Map p 98.*

Olive & Vine Culinary Adventures

CALIFORNIA This pretty cafe-deli has a small sit-down area, but most of its business comes from its extensive catering offerings, so to-go picnics and box lunches ($14–$16) are superb. Offerings also include simple breakfasts (mostly pastries), coffee options, and wine-tasting. In Jack London Village. *14301 Arnold Dr. ☎ 707/996-9150. Entrees $10–$15. MC, V. Wed–Mon 8am–6pm. Map p 98.*

★★ Saffron

CALIFORNIA This narrow, intimate room beckons you in from the street. Once inside, you'll enjoy creative cuisine and an interesting wine list highlighting Spanish wines, plus an impressive selection of beers and ales (more than 20 selections span the globe). *13648 Arnold Dr. ☎ 707/938-4844. Entrees $16–$27. MC, V. Tues–Sat 5–9pm. Map p 98.*

★★ Wolf House

NEW AMERICAN Glen Ellen's most polished restaurant, in Jack London Lodge, is elegant yet relaxed, whether you're seated in the handsome dining room or out on the terrace, which overlooks a serene creek. The lunch menu adds fancy flourishes to old American favorites, while Chef Jay Veregge's dinners emphasize locally procured ingredients, some even culled from the Lodge's garden. A reasonably priced Sonoma-centric wine list offers many by-the-glass options. Reservations recommended. After dinner, head to the Lodge's fun **saloon,** which is filled with colorful folks, TVs broadcasting sports games, and Jack London photos and memorabilia. *13740 Arnold Dr. ☎ 707/996-4401. Entrees $8.50– $27. AE, MC, V. Daily 11:30am–3pm (open at 11am Sat–Sun), 5:30–9pm. Map p 98.*

Calistoga

1 Railroad Depot
2 Dr. Wilkinson's
3 Evans Designs
4 American Indian
   Trading Co
5 Sharpsteen Museum
6 Napa River
7 Holy Assumption
   Monastery
8 Main Element Gallery
9 Hurd Beeswax Candles
10 Ca'toga Galleria d'Arte
11 Mudd Henns
12 Calistoga Roastery
13 Calistoga Creamery

Where to Dine

14 All Seasons
15 Bosko's
16 Brannan's
17 Checker's
18 Hydro Grill
19 Kitani Sushi
20 Pacifico
21 Stomp
22 Soo Yuan
23 Wappo

Calistoga is an Old Western–style town with more than a touch of California eccentricity. Its people are still obsessed with Sam Brannan, a Maine-born pioneer who became California's first millionaire by selling gold-mining tools after stoking frenzy for the precious metal (he ran through San Francisco shouting of its discovery in the American River). When he came to this formerly Wappo, then Spanish, area, he was so taken with its hot springs that he bought thousands of acres on which to develop a spa resort town similar to what already existed in Saratoga, New York. In 1885, meaning to say that he would transform this into the Saratoga of California, he instead (perhaps due to his demising penchant for alcohol) proclaimed, "I will make this the Calistoga of Sarafornia!" The name stuck, and more than 120 years later, pleasure seekers still come to enjoy the tiny town's therapeutic mineral water and mud baths. The waters here are so coveted that they're bottled and sold for a handsome profit: The next time you see Crystal Geyser or Calistoga Water at your local market, remember your visit here. This tour highlights downtown Calistoga's history and cultural diversity, with stops at the town's best stores and galleries.
START: **The Historic Calistoga Depot, 1458 Lincoln Ave. Distance: Less than a half-mile (.8km) of walking, doable in a half to a full day.**

Calistoga's main drag is Lincoln Avenue.

❶ ★ kids Napa Valley Railroad Depot. In 1868, it became possible to take the train into Calistoga, making it a gateway destination for wine country. This depot, California's second oldest, is on the National Register of Historic Places. Its site now supports six restored rail cars that still look as though they've just docked at the station. Inside the cars is a variety of quirky businesses, including a psychic from India, a florist, a wine store—and the **Calistoga Chamber of Commerce and Visitors Bureau:** Stop in to get insightful advice about the area, including current happenings. *1458 Lincoln Ave.* ☎ *707/942-6333. www.calistogachamber.com. Mon–Fri 10am–5pm, Sat 10am–4pm, Sun 11am–3pm (closed daily from 12:30–1pm).*

❷ ★★ Dr. Wilkinson's Hot Springs Resort. You can get a massage at any old spa, but only at Dr. Wilkinson's, one of Calistoga's

Treat yourself to a mudbath at Dr. Wilkinson's.

many hot-spring resorts, can you detoxify in a volcanic-ash mudbath with a facial mask and cucumbers over your eyes, then soak in a wildly bubbling mineral bath, then get wrapped in a blanket, *then* have a muscle-melting 1-hour massage. It's called "The Works," and it's not for everyone (refrain if you're sensitive to heat or think you might not like being surrounded in mud—though it's better than it sounds), but those who like it *adore* it. Sure, the spa might not win any awards for its decor anytime soon (it's rather bland), but it gets first prize for its ability to relax clients. Named for the late Dr. John Wilkinson, an ahead-of-his-time chiropractor who provided alternative therapies in the 1940s, the resort is now co-managed by his children, Mark and Carolynne. *1507 Lincoln Ave.* ☎ *707/942-4102. http://drwilkinson.com. "The Works" $149.*

❸ Evans Designs. Back on Lincoln Avenue, this gallery is a good place to browse glass art, raku ceramics, and handmade jewelry. *1421 Lincoln Ave.* ☎ *707/942-0453. www.evansdesigns.com. Daily 10am–6pm.*

❹ American Indian Trading Co. Another notable local store is this narrow showcase. The owners, working in conjunction with Native

Learn about Napa's past at the Sharpsteen Museum.

American tribes, sell stunning turquoise-and-silver jewelry, kachinas, dreamcatchers, medicine bags, and other crafts made by descendents of Calistoga's original residents. *1407 Lincoln Ave.* ☎ *707/942-9330 or 877/735-7755. www.spiritfeather.com. Daily 10am–6pm.*

5 **kids** ★★ **Sharpsteen Museum.** The Sharpsteen chronicles northern Napa County's natural and cultural history. The definite highlight is the painstakingly created diorama depicting Brannan's resort as it was in 1868. The 32-foot-long (9.6m) town replica took nearly 3 years to build and sits under the panoramic photo on which it's based. Other exhibits display Wappo artifacts, Robert Louis Stevenson paraphernalia, a geothermal demonstration, a restored stagecoach, and a re-created barn. Ben Sharpsteen, the museum's founder, was an Academy Award–winning Disney filmmaker; the museum also contains one of his Oscars. *1311 Washington St.* ☎ *707/942-5911. www.sharpsteen-museum.org. Daily 11am–4pm. Suggested donation: $3+ for adults.*

Just to the left of the museum is the beautiful **6** **Napa River,** home to a threatened population of steelhead and Chinook salmon. Right here, you can actually cross the river on foot—there's a shallow barrier across which adults and kids can easily wade to get to the playground on the other side.

Back out on Washington Street, pass the mint-green Community Presbyterian Church (3rd and Washington sts.) to find the fairy-tale-like **7** ★★ **Holy Assumption Monastery & Orthodox Religious Center,** founded in the 1940s by Russian and Chinese refugee nuns. They transformed a hotel into this peaceful religious center and built one of its woodsy chapels to replicate the one at Fort Ross. Surrounding the quaint buildings are fountains, a koi pond, and Asian-inspired gardens. If you keep your eyes peeled, you may spot the friendly resident one-eyed cat. The parish welcomes visitors of all backgrounds. *1519 Washington St.* ☎ *707/942-6244. Hours vary; call ahead. Free, but donations accepted.*

Turn right to get back on Lincoln Avenue, cross a bridge over the river, and enter **8** **Main Element Gallery,** a store with exquisite artworks and upbeat staff. *1333A Lincoln Ave.* ☎ *707/942-6347. Daily 10am–6pm (5pm on Fri).*

At **9** ★ **kids** **Hurd Beeswax Candles,** the store's fast-talking owner, Mary Sue Frediani, explains her various wares; she stocks hand-rolled, honeycomb, and long-burning candles for all occasions. For a real treat, though, ask to see the observation beehive through a hidden window in the wall. Frediani points out the queen bee, who lays 1,500 eggs each day. In the same retail space is **OnThEdge Winery**'s tasting bar, where fourth-generation vintners pour you a free taste of their heritage Charbono. If you want more, pay \$2 per taste or buy a bottle for about \$30. *1255A Lincoln Ave.* ☎ *707/942-7410. www.hurdbees waxcandles.com. Daily 10am–5:30pm (8pm Fri–Sat).*

In the same shopping complex is ➓ **Ca'toga Galleria d'Arte,** a gorgeous space showcasing the works of Venice-born artist Carlo Marchiori. His Renaissance, baroque, and neoclassical styles are evidenced here in the form of porcelain plates, acrylic paintings, original furniture—and a fantastic cosmological ceiling mural that you can marvel at by merely looking up. Look down, and you'll see a glittering terrazzo floor that charts the pre-Copernicus universe. Find the Latin inscription "Hic Es" ("You are here"), and you'll know you've found Earth. *1206 Cedar St.*

☎ *707/942-3900. www.catoga.com. Thurs–Mon 11am–6pm (opens 10am on Sat).*

➒ **Mudd Henns.** End your tour by buying an only-in-Calistoga souvenir: mud. Yes, you can actually purchase the therapeutic local muck pre-packaged and ready to take home. A favorite is the detoxifying Fango Mud bath powder, made with volcanic ash, salicylic powder, and pine needle extract, to relieve achy muscles and joints. *1348C Lincoln Ave.* ☎ *707/942-0210. www.mudd hens.com. Daily 10am–9pm.*

Calistoga's not exactly a high-stress place, but take time anyway to unwind at either of the town's best coffee shops: ➓ **Calistoga Roastery** for its fresh single-bean varietal coffees *1426 Lincoln Ave.* ☎ *707/942-5757. \$.* or ➓ **Calistoga Creamery & Bakery** for rich brownies and good old-fashioned ice cream. *1353 Lincoln Ave. 707/942-0777. \$.*

Where **to Dine**

★★ **All Seasons Bistro** *AMERICAN* This cleanly decorated bistro is very white, save for a red ceiling accented with Art Deco–style fans. As the name might imply, the menu changes seasonally; order from it or ask about Chef Thomas Halligan's tasting menus. *1400 Lincoln Ave.* ☎ *707/942-9111. Entrees \$19–\$29. DISC, MC, V. Lunch Fri–Sun noon–close, dinner Wed–Sun 5:30pm–close. Map p 102.*

★ **Bosko's** *ITALIAN* This trattoria with rock walls, wood-fired pizza,

and fresh homemade pasta has a relaxing atmosphere. Save room for dessert; the tiramisu is stupendous. *1364 Lincoln Ave.* ☎ *707/942-9088. Entrees \$8.75–\$20. AE, MC, V. Daily 11am–10pm. Map p 102.*

★ **Brannan's** *NEW AMERICAN* A large Arts and Crafts–style restaurant with a classy fireplace dining room for chilly evenings and *al fresco* seating for warm days. Big salads, substantial sandwiches, and well-spiced specialties. *1374 Lincoln Ave.* ☎ *707/942-2233. Entrees \$10–\$32. AE, MC, V.*

Daily 11:30am–3pm, 4:30–9pm (9:30pm Fri–Sat). Map p 102.

kids Checkers *ITALIAN* Though entrees are mostly Italian (think pastas, pizzas, and calzones), the menu also lists unexpected options like Thai noodle salad. Start with a hot, garlicky appetizer like spinach and artichoke dip. *1414 Lincoln Ave.* ☎ *707/942-9300. Entrees $8–$15. AE, DISC, MC, V. 11:30am–9:30pm (10pm Fri–Sat). Map p 102.*

★ **Hydro Grill** *AMERICAN* The more casual counterpart of All Seasons Bistro (see above), Hydro Grill has brick walls, lots of mirrors, and a great bar scene. Twenty on-tap beers make the Friday and Saturday evening entertainment more fun: Live music encompasses genres from blues to rock 'n' roll to swing. *1403 Lincoln Ave.* ☎ *707/942-9777. Entrees $8–$17. DISC, MC, V. Daily 9am–11pm. Map p 102.*

★ **Kitani Sushi** *JAPANESE* A selection of Japanese specialties (udon, tempura, and the like) complement a long sushi list in this small, traditionally decorated restaurant. *1631 Lincoln Ave.* ☎ *707/942-6857.*

Stomp offers a fabulous prix-fixe meal.

Entrees $4–$23. MC, V. Wed–Mon noon–2:30pm (opens at 11:30am weekdays), 5–9:30pm. Map p 102.

★ **kids Pacifico** *MEXICAN* At this festive *restaurante,* try a grilled fajita or one of the many traditional dishes with a pitcher of bright-blue Cabo Waborita. Friday nights, a mariachi band plays; on Saturdays, it's live Latin jazz. *1237 Lincoln Ave.* ☎ *707/ 942-4400. Entrees $10–$18. MC, V. Daily 10am–close (usually around 10pm). Map p 102.*

Soo Yuan *CHINESE* This low-key joint with a long MSG-free menu offers Mandarin and Szechwan soups, platters, and moo-shu. *1354 Lincoln Ave.* ☎ *707/942-9404. Entrees $4.25–$14.50. AE, DISC, MC, V. Daily 11:30am–10pm (summer until 11pm Fri–Sat). Map p 102.*

★★ **Stomp** *NEW AMERICAN* With decor that manages to be simultaneously earthy and sophisticated, Mount View Hotel's (p 123) superb restaurant has memorable small plates and entrees, plus a notable wine list. Tuesday through Thursday, Chef Chris Aken presents a $35 prix-fixe menu. ***Note:*** At press time, there were rumors that Stomp might soon relocate to St. Helena under a different name. No word about whether the hotel would replace it with another restaurant. *1457 Lincoln Ave.* ☎ *707/942-8272. Entrees $15–$30. AE, DC, DISC, MC, V. Wed–Fri 6–9pm, Sat 5:30–10pm, Sun 5:30–9pm. Map p 102.*

★ **Wappo Bar & Bistro** *CONTI-NENTAL* This nook has an extensive wine list accompanying creative concoctions like chile relleno stuffed with currants and pine nuts and accented with walnut-pomegranate sauce. If it's warm out, dine on the brick patio. *1226 Washington St.* ☎ *707/942-4712. Entrees $13.75– $24. AE, MC, V. Wed–Mon 11:30am– 2:30pm, 6–9:30pm. Map p 102.* ●

The Wine Country **by Bike**

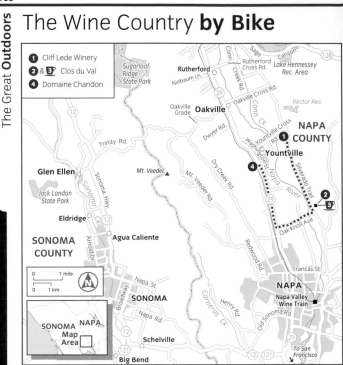

1 Cliff Lede Winery
2 & 3 Clos du Val
4 Domaine Chandon

With incomparable scenery and relatively flat terrain, Napa and Sonoma are consummate bikers' destinations. Touring on two wheels while inhaling fresh country air is by far the most exhilarating way to appreciate wine country. This route, appropriate for those in moderate physical condition, cycles through Napa Valley and stops at some of its best wineries. *Tip:* Temper your intake and eat well, since biking under the influence is illegal. If you only want to imbibe at two wineries, picnic but don't taste at Clos du Val. START: **Yountville's Washington Street. Trip Length: Half a day (allow a full day if you like lingering at wineries). For where to rent bikes (they'll deliver the bikes to you) see p 200.**

Head north on Washington, then turn right on Yount St., then right again on Yountville Crossroad. After 3 miles (4.8km), look for the first stop on your right.

1 ★★ **Cliff Lede Winery** is the northernmost winery in the famous

Stag's Leap District. In the tasting room, young, energetic staffers will eagerly tell all about their rich Bordeaux-focused varietals. After tasting, relax and examine works by famous artists at an outdoor terrace with views of vineyards and the Vaca Mountains. *1473 Yountville*

Cross Rd. ☎ 707/944-8642. See p 140.

Turn right out of Cliff Lede's parking lot; after a fifth of a mile (.3km), Yountville Crossroad will end. Turn right on historic Silverado Trail and pedal the 3.7 stunning miles (6km) to glamorous

❷ ★ Clos du Val. Be sure to try this French-influenced winery's signature cabernet. A peek at Clos du Val's rose garden and a game in its lovely *pétanque* (French bocce) court will round out your visit; this is also your picnic stop (see below). 5330 Silverado Trail, Napa. ☎ 707/259-2200. See p 141.

Enjoy lunch at ❸ Clos du Val, which has two picnic areas. For the prettiest surroundings, choose the olive grove.

Continue south on Silverado Trail. Turn right on Oak Knoll, cross Hwy. 29 and the railroad tracks, turn right on Solano Ave., and follow it north 4 miles (6.4km) until it ends in an intersection, where you'll find your next stop.

Bike your way through the wine country.

Cycle up ❹ ★★ Domaine Chandon's long vineyard-flanked driveway and across a creek bridge to the winery's entrance. Since Domaine Chandon was founded by French champagne house Moët & Chandon, there are many luxurious amenities here. Enjoy an educational presentation in a 28-seat theater before tasting the valley's most renowned bubbly. 1 California Dr., Yountville. ☎ 707/944-2280. See p 143.

To get back to this tour's starting point, bike to the end of Domaine Chandon's driveway to take a left onto California Dr. Cross the railroad tracks, go under a bridge, and ride until California Dr. ends. Take a left on Washington St.

Food & Safety along the Way

You'll want to eat sometime along the ride; to assemble your own picnic, stop at Yountville's family-owned **Ranch Market Too** (6498 Washington St.; ☎ 707/944-2662) beforehand to buy food (bring a backpack if you do this). Alternatively, book with ★★ **Napa Valley Bike Tours** (6488 Washington St.; ☎ 800/707-BIKE or 707/944-2953), a company that will cater lunch at any local winery with picnic grounds. Another benefit of going with Napa Valley Bike Tours: Its experts, who helped us devise this tour, follow clients with a van. That way, if you want to buy wine as you taste, **you don't have to haul bottles (or cases) around.** Vans also contain first-aid kits and bicycle maintenance tools. Not least of all, NVBT provides a knowledgeable accompanying guide, so you won't have to worry about looking down to read directions as you ride.

The Best Wine Country **Hike**

0 — 1 Mile
0 — 1 Km

1. Visitor Center
2. Pioneer Trail
3. Parson Jones Tree
4. Burbank Circle
5. Icicle Tree
6. East Ridge Trail
7. Bullfrog Pond
8. Pool Ridge Trail
9. Redwood Forest Theater
10. Colonel Armstrong Tree
11. Discovery Trail

Manning Flat Trail

Inset

Austin Creek State Rec. Area

Bullfrog Pond Trail

McCray Mtn.

Gilliam Creek

Gilliam Creek Trail

Map Area
SONOMA NAPA

See inset

Armstrong Redwoods State Res.

Restroom
Picnic Area
Campground
---- Riding & Hiking Trail
==== Hiking Trail Only
xxxx Service Road

To Guerneville ↓

The Armstrong Redwoods State Reserve is the natural California you always see in photos: Think majestic, millennia-old redwoods through which only slivers of sunlight break through. The adjacent **Austin Creek State Recreation Area,** by contrast, is more of an open forest with a greater variety of indigenous trees and wildlife. This loop hike highlights the park's biology and history, and takes you for a walk among the giant redwoods. It is suitable for those in moderate physical condition. Purchase your picnic the day before. **17000 Armstrong Woods Rd., Guerneville. ☎ 707/869-2015. www.parks.ca.gov. Trip Length: About 4 miles (6.4km). ⏱ ½ day.**

Travel Tip

Stock up (the night before) on picnic supplies at **Oakville Grocery** (in Healdsburg and Oakville; see p 91).

Park in front of the ❶ **Visitor Center** and follow signs to ❷ **Pioneer**

Trail, a mulch path surrounded by first-generation redwoods. Notice the green carpeting flanking the trail. That's not clover, but oxalis—identifiable by its compound leaves with three leaflets and colored flowers. After passing a number of downed trees swept over by strong winds (redwood has a surprisingly shallow root system), you'll find the still-sturdy ❸ **Parson Jones Tree.** This is a prime example of the Coastal Redwood, the tallest of the tree species—and at 310 feet/93m, Parson Jones is the reserve's tallest tree. In shady, cool conditions, redwoods can grow 3 feet (.9m) per year, but once their top is exposed to sunlight, that rate gets slashed to only an inch. This impressive organism, more than 1,300 years old, was named for Rev. William Ladd Jones, an ardent supporter of saving the grove from logging. He was also the husband of Lizzie Armstrong Jones (see below).

Where the trail splits at the creek, take the right fork and look for ❹ **Burbank Circle,** a perfect circle of centuries-old trees—it's a mystery how they got that way.

Stay on Pioneer Trail and on your left, you'll see the ❺ **Icicle Tree,** so named because of the massive icicle-like burls that used to hang off it. Burls occur when a tree repeatedly buds over in the same spot. Unfortunately, vandals have sheared the tree of most of its protrusions; redwood is highly valued for furniture-making and can fetch a pretty penny—a sad example of how short-term commercial gain can trump long-term sustainability.

Take a rest and savor the goodies you picked up from **Oakville Grocery.**

With a renewed sense of energy following your meal, veer right onto the ❻ **East Ridge Trail.** Foliage becomes more diverse here: You'll notice that cool shadiness changes to open forestry highlighted by a serene mix of redwoods, oaks, firs, and madrones. If it's springtime, wildflowers like buttercups, iris, lupines, and—yes, this *is* California—poppies

will enhance your hike. At the paved road, turn right and you'll encounter ❼ **Bullfrog Pond** (listen for the singing bullfrogs).

Walk back down the way you came, but make a right onto ❽ **Pool Ridge Trail,** which ends in a paved loop with a parking area. Veer right here and go down a short path to ❾ **Redwood Forest Theater,** a natural amphitheater that used to seat more than 2,000 people for outdoor concerts and weddings (they no longer use it because the ecosystem is too delicate).

On the other side of the paved loop is the enormous ❿ **Colonel Armstrong Tree,** which has stood for about 1,400 years, making it the preserve's oldest tree. It's 308 feet (92m) high and has a diameter approaching 15 feet (4.5m; stand in front of it for a picture—its size versus yours will make you gasp). Colonel James B. Armstrong was an Ohio-born lumberman with ironically conservationist instincts—it was his efforts that kept this reserve preserved. He bought the land in 1875 and fought to make it a state park. He died before that happened, but his daughter, Lizzie Armstrong Jones, saw to it that a county initiative was passed to ensure her father's dream.

Last, take the short ⓫ **Discovery Trail.** It'll merge with the Pioneer Trail to lead you back to your car.

Ponder the tall trees at Armstrong Redwoods State Reserve.

The Great Outdoors

From the **Russian River** to the **Pacific Coast**

Map legend:

- Picnic Area
- Campground

Map Area: SONOMA NAPA

1. Bodega Bay
2. Seaweed Café
3. Hwy 1
4. Fort Ross
5. Roshambo
6. River's Edge
7. Russian River

Sonoma's **dazzling Pacific coastline** and tranquil Russian River never fail to remind me why I live in California, and why Sonoma is a hydrophile's haven. Spend the morning at a breathtaking beach and the afternoon floating on a freshwater river, and you'll find yourself wondering whether life can get much better. This tour also takes you for a drive along the famously rugged, cliff-hugging Pacific Coast Highway 1 ("PCH" to locals). Start the day early (8:30am) so you can comfortably fit everything in. ***Tips:*** Dress in layers for the ever-changing coastal weather, and wear shoes in which you'd be comfortable walking on wet ground. **START: Bodega Bay. Trip Length: 1 day.**

1 ★★ **Bodega Bay's** seascapes and breezes are a refreshing escape from everyday life. Stroll around for about 10 minutes to get a feel for this fishing village's permeating coastal culture. Hitchcock fans will be particularly intrigued by **Potter Schoolhouse.** Hitchcock's eye for so-innocent-they're-creepy locations must have been on high alert when he spotted this 1873 building—he gave it a significant role in *The Birds*. This house is worth simply strolling by (it is a private residence). *17110*

The Pacific Coast is an awesome sight.

Bodega Lane. ☎ *707/876-3257.*
www.bodegaschool.com. **Note:** The
tiny town of Bodega Bay is not to be
confused with the town of Bodega,
which is a bit farther southeast.
www.bodegabay.com.

2 ★★ **Seaweed Café.** Seaweed's recently expanded dining
room is art-filled space with a fireplace and handcrafted furnishings—
but as nice as the interior is, the real
highlight is the view of the bay paired
with the global menu, which focuses
on organic coastal cuisine. The
seasonal dishes are made "slow
food"–style with ingredients from
Sonoma ranches and farms, and a
rotating selection of specials comple-
ments a la carte entrees. As for wine,
you won't be able to order anything
made west of Highway 101, a result
of local pride. However, there's a
wide selection of whole-leaf teas
from around the world. *1580 East-
shore Rd., Bodega Bay.* ☎ *707/875-
2700.*

3 ★★★ **kids** **Hwy. 1 along
Sonoma Coast State Beach.**
This 21-mile (34km) drive is some of
Sonoma's most dramatic coastal
land. You'll pass rugged shale bluffs,
coves, headlands, and offshore

reefs. More than 300 bird species
populate this stretch of land. If it's
spring, look for capacious sprays of
wildflowers like blue lupine and ver-
bena. There are plenty of pullouts
for photo ops, and beaches—many
of which have tide pools teeming
with invertebrate life—are accessible from more than a dozen points.
Veer left when you reach Goat Rock
Road to visit the peninsula's tip,
Whale Point, so named because
the annual grey whale migration
passes through here from December to April (humpbacks are here
year-round). Whale Point is also the
site of **Goat Rock Beach,** the Russian River's mouth and home to hundreds of harbor seals (pups are born
here from Mar–June). *Sonoma
Coast State Beach.* ☎ *707/875-3483.*
www.parks.ca.gov.

4 ★★ **kids** **Fort Ross State
Historic Park.** On a wave-cut
marine terrace, Fort Ross has steep
bluffs, old-growth redwoods, and
many points at which you can see
impact of the San Andreas Fault,
which comes ashore 2 miles south of
the fort and through the old Russian
orchard—look for sag ponds, escarp-
ments, damaged trees, off-kilter

Kayak your way along the Russian River.

A picnic, Sonoma style.

fences, all evidence of the massive 1906 earthquake. *19005 Hwy. 1, Jenner.* ☎ *707/847-3286. www.parks. ca.gov. Park grounds open daily a half-hour before sunrise & close a half-hour after sunset. Historical buildings, the visitor center & the bookstore are open daily 10am–4:30pm. Parking fee: $6.*

Travel Tip: Rain

If the day turns out to be rainy, gray, and cold (and kayaking is the last thing you want to do), consider stopping at funky Guerneville on your way back from the coast. For a detailed tour of Guerneville, see p 92.

5 Roshambo Winery. Stop off for a quick sip at Roshambo. The free tastes come with a view of the Russian River Valley. *3000 Westside Rd., Healdsburg.* ☎ *888/525-WINE.* See p 155.

Rent a canoe or kayak from **6 River's Edge** in Healdsburg, and buy a box lunch here for later. Choose from a basic $12 lunch (with a choice of sandwiches, chips, a cookie, and a fruit) or the $25 gourmet option (a locally procured affair of cheese, fruit, crackers, cold cuts, and dessert). *13840 Healdsburg Ave., Healdsburg.* ☎ *800/345-0869. www.riversedgekayakandcanoe.com. Canoes & double kayaks $15 per hour, single kayaks $10 per hour. Reservations recommended. Rentals include paddles, life vests & shuttle rides. Guided trips are available upon request.*

7 ★★★ kids The Russian River. Take a relatively leisurely float on this rain-fed river—this fun ride is appropriate for those in moderate physical condition, as well as children. Glide through the lush Alexander Valley past vineyards and arboreal private property interspersed with unnamed-but-inviting beaches on which you can break out your picnic. Keep an eye out for glimpses of wildlife like river otters, turtles, great blue heron, osprey, and egrets. Finish at either Rio Nido (a shorter, 11-mile/18km journey) or the Healdsburg beach (longer at 15 miles/24km)—you'll recognize Rio Nido by the congregation of River's Edge boats, and the Healdsburg beach is a dead end, so it's impossible to miss. River's Edge will shuttle you back to your car from either finishing point. *Allow 4–5 hours.* ●

Where to Stay in Wine Country

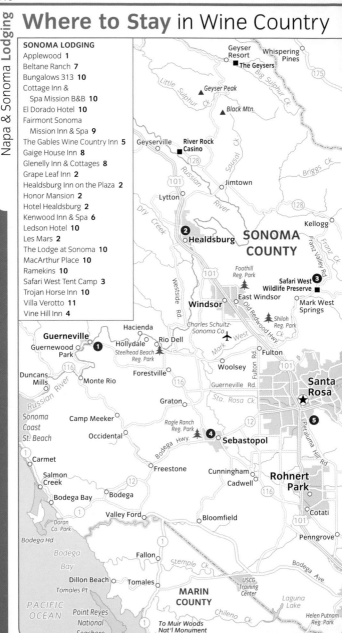

SONOMA LODGING

Applewood **1**
Beltane Ranch **7**
Bungalows 313 **10**
Cottage Inn &
  Spa Mission B&B **10**
El Dorado Hotel **10**
Fairmont Sonoma
  Mission Inn & Spa **9**
The Gables Wine Country Inn **5**
Gaige House Inn **8**
Glenelly Inn & Cottages **8**
Grape Leaf Inn **2**
Healdsburg Inn on the Plaza **2**
Honor Mansion **2**
Hotel Healdsburg **2**
Kenwood Inn & Spa **6**
Ledson Hotel **10**
Les Mars **2**
The Lodge at Sonoma **10**
MacArthur Place **10**
Ramekins **10**
Safari West Tent Camp **3**
Trojan Horse Inn **10**
Villa Verotto **11**
Vine Hill Inn **4**

NAPA LODGING

1801 First Inn **15**
Adagio Inn **24**
Ambrose Bierce House **15**
Auberge du Soleil **23**
Aurora Park Cottages **28**
Beazley House **15**
Best Western
  Stevenson Manor **28**
Blackbird Inn **15**
Calistoga Ranch **28**
Candlelight Inn **15**
Carneros Inn **12**
Casalana **28**
Castle in the Clouds **21**
Cedar Gables Inn **15**
Chateau de Vie **28**
Churchill Manor **15**
Cottage Grove Inn **28**
The Cottages of
  Napa Valley **17**
Dr. Wilkinsons **28**

Embassy Suites **15**
Harvest Inn **24**
Hennessey House **15**
Indian Springs **28**
La Belle Epoque **15**
Lavender **19**
Maison Fleurie **19**
Meadowood **27**
The Meritage Resort **13**
Milliken **15**
Mount View Hotel **28**
Napa River Inn **15**
Poetry Inn **20**
Rancho Caymus **22**
Roman Spa Hot
  Springs Resort **28**
Silverado **16**
Villagio Inn & Spa **18**
Vintage Inn **19**
White Sulphur Springs
  Inn & Spa **25**

Napa Lodging A to Z

★ **Adagio Inn.** ST. HELENA
Rooms in this quiet Edwardian B&B
feature stained-glass windows and
reading nooks. Amenities include a
decadent breakfast, king beds,
Wi-Fi, and evening wine and cheese.
1417 Kearny St. ☎ *707/963-2238.*
www.adagioinn.com. 3 units.
$275–$340. MC, V. Map p 116.

★ **Ambrose Bierce House** ST.
HELENA   Once the home of author
Ambrose Bierce, this 1872 Victorian
offers comfortable rooms with
canopied beds, Jacuzzi tubs, fireplaces, and a champagne breakfast.
Walking distance from downtown.
1515 Main St. ☎ *707/963-3003.*
www.ambrosebiercehouse.com. 4
units. $209–$299. MC, V. Map p 116.

★★★ **Auberge du Soleil**
RUTHERFORD   With interior decor
that's nearly unsurpassed in wine
country (it's contemporary Spanish-
Mediterranean), Auberge is upscale
enough to belong to Relais &
Châteaux. Rooms feature sublime
linens on oversized beds, outdoor
terraces, flat-screen TVs, and Wi-Fi.
Visit the superb restaurant, the luxu-
riant spa, and the open-air art gallery.
180 Rutherford Hill Rd. ☎ *707/963-
1211. www.aubergedusoleil.com. 50*
units. Doubles $600–$3,500. AE, DC,
DISC, MC, V. Map p 116.

★ **Aurora Park Cottages** CALIS-
TOGA   This retreat's homey cottages have outside decks where you
can savor a basket of pastries and
fruit. Innkeepers are local experts,
so ask them to customize a tour
plan. *1807 Foothill Blvd.* ☎ *707/
942-6733. www.aurorapark.com.*
6 units. $205–$295. AE, MC, V.
Map p 116.

★★ **Beazley House** NAPA   Open
since 1981 and still run by its original
owners, this pet-friendly, wood-
shingled property stakes its claim as
Napa's first B&B. Offerings include
country-style rooms (no TV), gardens,
Wi-Fi, and Friday wine tastings.
910 1st St. ☎ *800/559-1649. www.*
beazleyhouse.com. 11 units. Doubles
$169–$309. MC, V. Map p 116.

**Best Western Stevenson
Manor Inn** CALISTOGA   Close to
town center, this value-oriented inn
has large rooms with a fireplace,
kitchenette, or balcony. Amenities
include breakfast, a pool, a hot tub, a
sauna, and a steam room. Check the
website for deals. *1830 Lincoln Ave.*
☎ *707/942-1112. www.stevenson*
manor.com. 34 units. Doubles $110–
$239. AE, DC, DISC, MC, V. Map p 116.

★★ **Blackbird Inn** NAPA   A stay
at this well-located B&B includes

The Auberge du Soleil is THE luxury lodging choice in Napa.

Sublime scenery surrounds Calistoga Ranch.

afternoon wine tastings, Wi-Fi, and DVDs to borrow. Craftsman elements give the exterior a lodge feel, while rooms are country-style with spa tubs and fireplaces. *1755 1st St.* ☎ *707/226-2450. www.blackbird Innnapa.com. 8 units. $145–$285. AE, DC, DISC, MC, V. Map p 116.*

★★★ **Calistoga Ranch** CALISTOGA   Run by the prestigious Auberge brand, this quiet, airy ranch amidst the pines combines modern luxury with natural woodsiness. Freestanding, pet-friendly lodges display elegant decor and a setup blurring the line between indoor and outdoor. A superior spa and restaurant impress. *580 Lommel Rd.* ☎ *707/254-2800. www.calistoga ranch.com. 46 units. Doubles $475–$1,225. AE, DC, DISC, MC, V. Map p 116.*

★★ **Candlelight Inn** NAPA   A Tudor mansion on Napa Creek, this B&B in the redwoods (2 miles/3.2km from downtown) is a perennial favorite. Country-style rooms have a private balcony, marble fireplace, or two-person Jacuzzi tub. Enjoy the three-course breakfast. *1045 Easum Dr.* ☎ *707/257-3717. www.candle lightinn.com. 10 units. Doubles $149–$329. AE, DISC, MC, V. Map p 116.*

★★ **The Carneros Inn** NAPA   This cluster of private residences epitomizes clean design. Delve into 27 acres (11 hectares) of vineyards, a spa, restaurants (p 76), and an infinity pool. *4048 Sonoma Hwy. (Hwy. 12).* ☎ *707/299-4900. www. thecarnerosinn.com. 104 units. Doubles $435–$475. AE, DC, DISC, MC, V. Map p 116.*

★ **CasaLana** CALISTOGA   If you're a gourmet, you'll be enticed by hands-on cooking classes. Even if you're not, you'll be minutes from downtown in a country-style room with a private entrance and Wi-Fi. *1316 S. Oak St.* ☎ *707/942-0615. www.casalana.com. 2 units. $175–$250. AE, DISC, MC, V. Map p 116.*

The Embarcadero suite comes with a fireplace at the Napa River Inn.

Tips for Choosing Lodging

Wine country differs from other tourist destinations in that its lodging options don't consist mainly of huge corporate hotel chains. In fact, many of the region's resorts, hotels, inns, B&Bs, and vacation rentals are family-owned and have surprising personal touches accenting that fact. How to choose where to stay should depend on your personal preferences; if you're social and interested in a personal experience that involves meeting your innkeepers and mingling with other guests, go for a B&B. If you prefer more anonymity and upscale amenities, choose a resort or larger hotel. If you're looking for complete seclusion or are planning something like a small family reunion, a vacation rental is the best bet. Bear in mind that while wine country is home to many hundreds of wonderful lodging facilities, this book's limited space precludes listing each and every one—these, however, are either very prominent or highly recommended.

★ Castle in the Clouds

YOUNTVILLE This B&B's name is accurate; see if you can spot Mondavi or Opus One from your 400-foot-high (120m) perch. The property is gated and includes old-fashioned furnishings, a vineyard, a hot tub, and Wi-Fi. *7400 St. Helena Hwy. (Hwy. 29).* ☎ *707/944-2785. www.castleintheclouds.com. 4 units. $275–$395. AE, MC, V. Map p 116.*

★★ Cedar Gables Inn NAPA

This Shakespeare-inspired 1892 manor's Renaissance-era artifacts mix with rich textures and colors. Rooms have whirlpool baths and fireplaces, and come with a three-course breakfast and an evening wine reception. Ask owners Ken and Susie Pope for a tour of the secret staircases. Three blocks from downtown. *486 Coombs St.* ☎ *800/309-7969. www.cedargablesinn.com. 9 units. $199–$319. AE, DISC, MC, V. Map p 116.*

★ Chateau de Vie CALISTOGA

The "house of life" is a B&B on a small working winery (try the cabernet). Highlights include a generous breakfast, refined rooms, a pool, and a view of Mt. St. Helena. *3250 Hwy. 128.* ☎ *877/558-2513. www.cdvnapavalley.com. 4 units. $209–$329. AE, MC, V. Map p 116.*

★★ Churchill Manor NAPA

This B&B a few blocks from downtown is a beautiful 1889 Victorian mansion bolstered by columns. Intricately decorated rooms feature vintage tubs and huge showers; outside, there's a fountain courtyard, rose gardens, and a generous veranda. Borrow a tandem bike before heading out. *485 Brown St.* ☎ *800/799-7733. www.churchillmanor.com. 10 units. Doubles $155–$305. AE, DISC, MC, V. Map p 116.*

★★ Cottage Grove Inn CALIS-

TOGA Calm permeates these cottages set in an elm grove at the end of Calistoga's main strip. Relax by a fireplace or under a skylight in a two-person Jacuzzi tub. Furnishings are homey and cozy, and a stay includes breakfast and evening wine. *1711 Lincoln Ave.* ☎ *800/799-2284. www.cottagegrove.com. 16 units. Doubles $225–$350. AE, DC, DISC, MC, V. Map p 116.*

★★★ The Cottages of Napa Valley NAPA

Originally a 1929 motel, this sheltered complex was remodeled to embody country-style chic. A stay here is utterly gratifying, in part because of the amenities: a breakfast basket with delights from Bouchon, Wi-Fi, and weekend wine receptions. Each exceptionally comfortable cottage features a king bed, fireplace, kitchenette, Jacuzzi tub, and front and back patios. *1012 Darms Lane.* ☎ *707/252-7810. www.napacottages.com. 8 units. $255–$475. AE, MC, V. Map p 116.*

★ Dr. Wilkinson's Hot Springs Resort CALISTOGA

Calistoga's longest family-owned business (established 1952) still has character. A mud bath here is a must; equally enjoyable are massages, facials, and mineral pools (p 103). Easy access to shops and restaurants. *1507 Lincoln Ave.* ☎ *707/942-4879. www.drwilkinson. com. 42 units. Doubles $109–$209. AE, MC, V. Map p 116.*

★★ 1801 First Inn NAPA

Named for its downtown address, this Queen Anne Victorian blends contemporary touches with classic European decor. An in-house chef prepares delectable three-course breakfasts and gourmet hors d'oeuvres for evening wine tastings. *1801 1st St.* ☎ *707/224-3739. www.1801first.com. 8 units. $325–$475. AE, DISC, MC, V. Map p 116.*

Embassy Suites NAPA

Effort went into giving this chain a local feel. Touches include a swan pond with a wooden mill, a pool, and a large atrium where breakfast (included) is cooked to order and cocktails (also included) are served each evening. Suites' layout is such that the bedroom closes off from the living room. *1075 California Blvd.* ☎ *707/253-9540. www.napavalley. embassysuites.com. 205 units. Doubles $159–$299. AE, DC, DISC, MC, V. Map p 116.*

★★ Harvest Inn ST. HELENA

This upscale property offers rustic country charm, daily wine tastings, and gorgeous gardens. Breakfast is included, and many suites feature fireplaces, spa tubs, Wi-Fi, and private terraces. Try a treatment at the spa. *1 Main St.* ☎ *800/950-8466. www.harvestinn.com. 74 units. Doubles $400–$600. AE, DISC, MC, V. Map p 116.*

★ Hennessey House NAPA

This downtown B&B has flowery Wi-Fi–equipped rooms. The main house is an 1889 Victorian and its six units are less pricey than the four in the Carriage House. A stay includes a sumptuous breakfast, afternoon tea, and evening wine. *1727 Main St.* ☎ *707/226-3774. www.hennesseyhouse.com. 10 units. Doubles $135–$319. AE, DC, DISC, MC, V. Map p 116.*

★★ Indian Springs CALISTOGA

Deriving its name from Calistoga's

Don't be put off by the MOTEL sign: Dr. Wilkinson's is a fine place to stay.

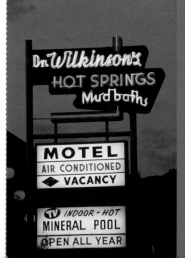

previous life as a Native American healing ground, this resort with comfortable bungalows is where you can detoxify in a volcanic-ash mudbath and soak in a naturally heated 1913 Olympic-size thermal-geyser-fed mineral pool. *1712 Lincoln Ave.* ☎ *707/942-4913. www.indianspringscalistoga.com. 16 units. Doubles $175–$285. DISC, MC, V. Map p 116.*

★ **La Belle Epoque** NAPA This plush B&B and its two-unit sister property across the street, the Buckley House, are century-old Queen Anne Victorians standing as stately testament to Napa's architectural history. Rooms boast elegant antiques and excellent linens. Indulge in the candlelit breakfast and the nightly wine-and-cheese reception. *1386 Calistoga Ave.* ☎ *800/238-8070. www.napabelle.com. 7 units. $229–$429. AE, DISC, MC, V. Map p 116.*

★ **Lavender** YOUNTVILLE A homey 1870 B&B with wooden floors and French-tinged country furnishings, Lavender's small touches include lavender sachets, chocolate upon turndown, Wi-Fi, and afternoon snacks. Borrowing the inn's bicycles makes exploring fun (although local attractions are walking distance). *2020 Webber Ave.* ☎ *707/944-1388. www.foursisters.com. 8 units. $150–$250. AE, DC, DISC, MC, V. Map p 116.*

★ **Maison Fleurie** YOUNTVILLE The "flowering house" certainly is. This garden property offers rooms with country-style decor and stone fireplaces, breakfast each morning, and wine and hors d'oeuvres each afternoon. *6529 Yount St.* ☎ *800/788-0369. www.maisonfleurienapa.com. 13 units. Doubles $130–$285. AE, DC, DISC, MC, V. Map p 116.*

★★★ **Meadowood Napa Valley** ST. HELENA That President Bush stayed here during his most recent Napa visit says it all. This exclusive Relais & Châteaux property, also a private club for local leaders, is reminiscent of a grand country estate; it has personalized service, a luxury spa, tennis courts, croquet lawns, pools, and a golf course. Lodging is amid oaks in a private 250-acre (100-hectare) valley. *900 Meadowood Lane.* ☎ *800/458-8080. www.meadowood.com. 85 units. Doubles $525–$2,275. AE, DISC, MC, V. Map p 116.*

★ **The Meritage Resort** NAPA The new Meritage, 4 miles (6.4km) from downtown in the Carneros

The sprawling Meadowood Napa Valley has something for anyone who is willing to shell out a pretty penny.

region, claims the world's only underground cave spa. Also on-site are wine caves, vineyards, and tastings. Siena restaurant's Tuscan cuisine accompanies a comprehensive wine list. Rooms offer Wi-Fi, plasma TVs, and fireplaces. *875 Bordeaux Way.* ☎ *866/370-6272. www.themeritage hotel.com. 338 units. Doubles $329–$399. AE, DC, DISC, MC, V. Map p 116.*

★★★ Milliken Creek Inn & Spa

NAPA   This garden property is known for luxury and detail-orientedness. Earth-toned rooms have king canopy beds, fireplaces, fresh orchids, and private decks with river views. Marble bathrooms feature hydrotherapy tubs and rain showers. Breakfast is gourmet, and an evening wine-and-cheese reception is attended by vintners. Don't forego an aromatherapy massage at the spa. *1815 Silverado Trail.* ☎ *707/255-1197. www.millikencreek inn.com. 12 units. Doubles $325–$675. AE, DC, DISC, MC, V. Map p 116.*

★★ Mount View Hotel

CALISTOGA   Smallish, romantic rooms with European-style antiques are set in a downtown 1917 building. Highlights include a pool and Jacuzzi, a lobby fireplace, Stomp Restaurant (p 106), and Wi-Fi. Breakfast snacks are delivered each morning, and there's an on-site spa. *1457 Lincoln Ave.* ☎ *800/816-6877. www. mountviewhotel.com. 32 units. Doubles $169–$339. AE, DISC, MC, V. Map p 116.*

★ Napa River Inn

NAPA   In the 1884 Napa Mill complex, this downtown inn overlooks the Napa River. Pet-friendly rooms feature Wi-Fi and historical, nautical, and country stylings. In-room breakfast service and two restaurants, Celadon and Angèle, are superb. *500 Main St.* ☎ *707/251-8500. www.napariver inn.com. 66 units. Doubles $199–$499. AE, DC, DISC, MC, V. Map p 116.*

★★★ Poetry Inn

YOUNTVILLE   Cliff Lede Vineyards (p 140) opened Stags Leap District's only public lodging in 2005—and what lodging! Ultraluxurious rooms sit 500 feet (150m) above the valley; vineyard views are spectacular. Decor is classy and private outdoor showers add uniqueness. At breakfast (included), try the brie-and-strawberry French toast, then enjoy an open-air massage, lounge by the pool, or marvel at the wine cellar's rarities. *6380 Silverado Trail.* ☎ *707/944-0646. www.poetryinn.com. 3 units. $575–$1,250. AE, DC, MC, V. Map p 116.*

★ Rancho Caymus Inn

RUTHERFORD   This Spanish hacienda–style inn has a rich history, cozy-funky decor, and architecture featuring adobe fireplaces, 100-year-old timber, stucco walls, and clay tile. Amenities include Wi-Fi, breakfast, and a romantic garden courtyard. Some rooms have kitchenettes, whirlpool tubs, or private balconies. A new addition is La Toque restaurant. *1140 Rutherford Rd.* ☎ *707/963-1777. www.rancho caymus.com. 26 units. Doubles $155–$430. AE, MC, V. Map p 116.*

Roman Spa Hot Springs Resort

CALISTOGA   Though this is a spa resort, rooms are modest. The property contains three mineral-water pools (two are on-site) and two Finnish saunas. *1300 Washington St.* ☎ *707/942-4441. www.romanspahot springs.com. 60 units. Doubles $115–$205. AE, DISC, MC, V. Map p 116.*

Silverado Resort

NAPA   This resort is a country club, so it's great for golf (two courses) but lacks the intimacy of many other wine-country inns. Suites have kitchenettes and undersized bathrooms. Decor is low-key—more practical than aesthetic. Highlights include the spa and The Grill. *1600 Atlas Peak Rd.* ☎ *707/257-0200. www.silveradoresort.com. 280 units. Doubles $170–$365. AE, DC, DISC, MC, V. Map p 116.*

You may find it hard to leave the palatial grounds at Villagio Inn & Spa.

★★★ Villagio Inn & Spa

YOUNTVILLE   Yountville's fanciest lodging has a distinctly Mediterranean feel, from the water features to the Roman-style "ruins." Rooms are luxurious, and a stay comes with a bottle of Beringer and a superb breakfast buffet. Staffers are hospitable, and the spa's river-stone massage may well be Napa's best treatment. *6481 Washington St.* ☎ *707/944-8877. www.villagio.com. 138 units. Doubles $207–$585. AE, DISC, MC, V. Map p 116.*

Vintage Inn & Spa YOUNTVILLE   Villagio's older downtown sister property has spacious rooms with generous tubs and balconies. Amenities like free wine and breakfast make guests feel welcome. Ask for a room overlooking Domaine Chandon. *6541 Washington St.* ☎ *707/944-1112. www.vintageinn. com. 92 units. Doubles $230–$585. AE, DISC, MC, V. Map p 116.*

★ White Sulphur Springs Inn & Spa

ST. HELENA   Founded in 1852, White Sulphur claims to be California's oldest spa resort. Its serenity comes from its natural surroundings: a creek, redwood grove, and waterfall, plus sulphur springs feeding a soaking pool. Reasonably priced rooms are simple (no phone or TV) and it's a drive to restaurants, but breakfast is included. *3100 White Sulphur Springs Rd.* ☎ *707/299-4900. www.whitesulphursprings.com. 38 units. Doubles $95–$210. AE, DISC, MC, V. Map p 116.*

Sonoma Lodging A to Z

★ Applewood Inn

GUERNEVILLE   This sweet 1922 mission revival–style mansion's individually decorated rooms are Wi-Fi equipped. Outside, there's a pool, hot tub, and organic herb garden for the on-site restaurant (a stay includes breakfast). A 2-minute drive to Main Street, but feels forested and remote. *13555 Hwy. 116.* ☎ *707/869-9093. www.applewoodinn.com. 19 units. Doubles $185–$345. AE, MC, V. Map p 116.*

★★ Beltane Ranch

GLEN ELLEN   This B&B in a pastel-yellow 1892 manor has everything a country ranch should: clean, antiques-furnished rooms with private entrances (no TV or phone); a big, delectable breakfast; a wraparound porch; hiking trails; a tennis court; and lots of greenery. Enjoy the drive up from the highway and request an upstairs room with a view. *11775 Sonoma Hwy. (Hwy. 12).* ☎ *707/996-6501. www.beltaneranch.com. 6 units.*

$140–$220. Check or cash only. Map p 116.

★ **Bungalows 313** SONOMA These private, spacious downtown cottages have kitchens, though a tasty breakfast is provided. There's also a fountain courtyard and the option of staying in the romantic 1906 brick house. Attention to detail reveals itself in small and large touches like fresh flowers and inviting interiors. *313 1st St.* ☎ *707/996-8091. www.bungalows313.com. 5 units. $160 and up. DISC, MC, V. Map p 116.*

★★ **The Cottage Inn & Spa Mission B&B** SONOMA This well-loved retreat proximal to Sonoma's mission incorporates Cal-Med architecture and gardens. Individually decorated rooms have private entrances, fireplaces, spa tubs, and big comfy beds. Included: a pastries-and-fruit breakfast and access to a fitness club. *302 1st St.* ☎ *800/944-1490. www.cottage innandspa.com. 8 units. $188–$347. DISC, MC, V. Map p 116.*

★★ **El Dorado Hotel** SONOMA El Dorado's strong points are its chic decor—more town than country—and excellent plaza location. Small but sunny rooms, all recently renovated, feature four-poster beds, fine linens, and small balconies. Outside, there's a heated lap pool. The hip El Dorado Kitchen (p 81) is a must-try; chef Ryan Fancher was formerly at French Laundry. *405 1st St.* ☎ *707/996-3030. www.eldoradosonoma. com. 27 units. Doubles $145–$190. AE, DC, MC, V. Map p 116.*

★★★ **Fairmont Sonoma Mission Inn & Spa** BOYES HOT SPRINGS Established in 1927, this recently restored Sonoma institution gets better with age. Rooms are charming; many have fireplaces. The mineral-water-fed spa is divine, as is the cuisine at upscale Santé.

Though it's in a drab area 3 miles (4.8km) from Sonoma, guests don't want to leave; free wine tastings add to the desire to stay. The resort offers excursions like free hiking and biking tours and access to a nearby 18-hole golf course. *100 Boyes Blvd.* ☎ *707/938-9000. www.fairmont. com/sonoma. 226 units. Doubles $209–$1,500. AE, DC, DISC, MC, V. Map p 116.*

★ **The Gables Wine Country Inn** SANTA ROSA This cozy B&B looks like a dollhouse from the outside and, inside, a Victorian manor. Rooms feature claw-foot tubs and historical appointments. Enjoy the lavender garden and sample wine in the evening. Splurge on the quiet creekside cottage, which has a hot tub. *4257 Petaluma Hill Rd.* ☎ *800/422-5376. www.thegablesinn.com. 8 units. $175–$250. AE, DISC, MC, V. Map p 116.*

★★★ **Gaige House Inn** GLEN ELLEN Though this creekside inn was originally built in 1890, it's been entirely remodeled, including an addition of eight Asian-themed suites with decor rivaling that of five-star hotels. The superb breakfast is served in a light-filled space by friendly attendants. There's also an in-house spa, plus a pool and hot tubs. *13540 Arnold Dr.* ☎ *800/935-0237. www.gaige.com. 23 units. Doubles $295–$590. AE, DISC, MC, V. Map p 116.*

A tempting pool is only one of the features that makes the Fairmont an oasis in Boyes Hot Springs.

Relax in the pool at the Honor Mansion.

★ Glenelly Inn & Cottages

GLEN ELLEN   At this 1916 inn, try to stay in the cute country cottages in a wooded oak niche as opposed to the suites, which are also nice but a bit darker and smaller. Breakfast is included. *5131 Warm Springs Rd.* ☎ *707/996-6720. www.glenelly.com. 9 units. $165–$295. AE, DISC, MC, V. Map p 116.*

★★ Grape Leaf Inn HEALDSBURG

Country chic (very chic) with stained-glass touches, this refined B&B is a century-old Queen Anne Victorian offering luxury amenities, soothing gardens, an exceptional four-course breakfast, and cozy rooms with skylights, fireplaces, and spa tubs. The speak-easy tasting room (hidden behind a bookcase!) hosts nightly wine-and-cheese tastings. *539 Johnson St.* ☎ *707/433-8140. www.grape leafinn.com. 12 units. Doubles $225–$395. MC, V. Map p 116.*

★ Healdsburg Inn on the Plaza

HEALDSBURG   Clean, comfortable rooms have high ceilings, fireplaces, and flourishes hearkening back to when the inn was built: 1901. A stay includes breakfast and afternoon wine. Since the inn is in the middle of town, request a room in the quieter back. *112 Matheson St.* ☎ *800/ 431-8663. www.healdsburginn.com. 12 units. Doubles $200–$325. AE, DISC, MC, V. Map p 116.*

★★★ Honor Mansion HEALDS-

BURG $1.5+ million went into developing this property, resulting in an indulgent retreat. Plush suites in an Italianate Victorian building are surrounded by more than 120 rosebushes and a quarter-acre (.1-hectare) vineyard. A talented chef culls herbs from on-site gardens to create magnificent breakfasts. Also outdoors are a lap pool; jogging trail; croquet lawn; putting green; and tennis, bocce, and basketball courts. *14891 Grove St.* ☎ *707/433-4277. www.honor mansion.com. 13 units. Doubles $220–$550. AE, MC, V. Map p 116.*

Many of the Gaige House Inn's rooms come with a fireplace.

The perfect spot to curl up after a long, arduous day of wine tasting: a room with a fireplace at Les Mars Hotel.

★★★ Hotel Healdsburg HEALDS-
BURG A modern option amid Healdsburg's more traditional properties, this $21-million hotel offers rooms with hardwood floors and Tibetan rugs, private balconies, deep bathtubs, and Frette linens. Outside, there's a pool and green lounging spaces. Cuisine is divine throughout, from breakfast to dinner at Charlie Palmer's inspired Dry Creek Kitchen (p 90). At the small spa, try the Combination Massage. *25 Matheson St.* ☎ *707/431-2800. www.hotel healdsburg.com. 55 units. Doubles $260–$790. MC, V. Map p 116.*

★★ The Kenwood Inn & Spa
KENWOOD Gorgeous mission-style architecture houses rooms with textured decor. Other features include fountain courtyards, a tasting room, three Jacuzzis, and a pool. Try a bath or facial at the "vinotherapy" spa. A bit close to Highway 12, but maintains romance and privacy. Breakfast included. *10400 Sonoma Hwy. (Hwy. 12).* ☎ *707/833-1293. www. kenwoodinn.com. 30 units. Doubles $325–$650. AE, MC, V. Map p 116.*

★★ Ledson Hotel SONOMA
This perfectly located hotel built by a fifth-generation winemaker transports guests to a time when antiques were new. Grand decor and modern amenities accent excellent service. Luxuriate by the fireplace while listening to live music at the hotel's Harmony Restaurant (p 81). *480 1st St.* ☎ *707/996-9779. www.*

ledsonhotel.com. 6 units. $350–$395. AE, DISC, MC, V. Map p 116.

★★★ Les Mars Hotel HEALDS-
BURG This newish hotel presents the ultimate in old-Europe-style luxury. Gracious service awaits each guest, as do inspired touches like Louis XV armoires, lavish four-poster beds, and Bain Ultra soaking tubs. A gourmet three-course breakfast and nightly cheese tastings are included, and dinner at the hotel's Cyrus—Healdsburg's new "it" restaurant—is a real treat (p 90). *27 North St.* ☎ *707/433-4211. www. lesmarshotel.com. 16 units. Doubles $445–$1,025. AE, MC, V. Map p 116.*

★★ The Lodge at Sonoma
SONOMA At this comfortable resort, an inviting lobby welcomes guests before they retreat to a well-appointed room, suite, or cottage. A treatment at Raindance Spa invigorates, while a meal at Carneros surpasses even high expectations.

The lobby at The Lodge at Sonoma.

1325 Broadway. ☎ 707/935-6600. www.thelodgeatsonoma.com. 182 units. Doubles $169–$389. AE, DC, MC, V. Map p 116.

★★ **MacArthur Place** SONOMA On one of Sonoma's main thoroughfares (so factor in some noise) is this country-style inn with pretty grounds. Breakfast is included, as is a wine-and-cheese reception in the library, where you can borrow a movie or book. Rooms are flowery and, if you upgrade to a suite, spacious. *29 E. MacArthur St.* ☎ *707/ 933-2929. www.macarthurplace. com. 64 units. Doubles $199–$475. MC, V. Map p 116.*

★ **Ramekins** SONOMA This B&B and culinary school is the perfect stay for foodies. Packages include a bottle of wine and discounts on cooking classes that take place downstairs. Individually decorated rooms are Wi-Fi-equipped and have antique pine furniture and oversized bathrooms. Breakfast features homemade granola and pastries. *450 W. Spain St.* ☎ *707/933-0452. www. innatramekins.com. 6 units. $125– $235. AE, DISC, MC, V. Map p 116.*

★★ **Safari West Tent Camp** SANTA ROSA Central to both valleys is this ultimate family getaway. The 400-acre (160-hectare) preserve, home to hundreds of African animals, maintains a cluster of safari tents with hardwood floors. From each accommodation, guests can watch giraffes, zebras, and cheetahs.

Breakfast is included, and the safari drive is a must-do (p 24). *3115 Porter Creek Rd.* ☎ *707/579-2551. www.safariwest.com. 32 units. $225–$350. AE, MC, V. Map p 116.*

★ **Trojan Horse Inn** SONOMA This recently redone 1887 Victorian farmhouse is romantic and comfortable. Rooms feature antique furnishings and memory-foam mattresses sheathed in Frette. Pleasantries include a multi-course breakfast, a hot tub, bikes to borrow, and wine receptions. *19455 Sonoma Hwy. (Hwy. 12).* ☎ *707/996-2430. www. trojanhorseinn.com. 6 units. $190– $245. AE, DISC, MC, V. Map p 116.*

★ **Villa Verotto** CARNEROS Elusive, exclusive, and exquisite, this freshly remodeled vineyard estate has a pool, a hot tub, and three smartly decorated bedrooms. The owners of the gated property keep its address confidential until booking to ensure guests' privacy—but it's about 5 miles (8km) from Sonoma Plaza. ☎ *415/ 225-3027. www.verotto.com. 1 unit. $650–$1,200. MC, V. Map p 116.*

Vine Hill Inn SEBASTOPOL Once an 1897 farmhouse, this romantic B&B still keeps a barn with chickens, goats, and a blind pony. Rooms have private decks, Jacuzzi tubs, hardwood floors, and warm decor. A tasty breakfast, swimming pool, and vineyards add to the appeal. *3949 Vine Hill Rd.* ☎ *707/823-8832. www.vine-hill-inn.com. 4 units. $150. AE, DISC, MC, V. Map p 116.* ●

The décor at MacArthur Place is reminiscent of the Wild West.

The Best **Wineries**

Napa Valley Wineries

To Robert Louis Stevenson Mem. St. Pk.

Pope Valley

Calistoga

To Petrified Forest

Diamond Mountain Rd.

Angwin

Bell Canyon Res.

Bothe-Napa Valley St. Park

SONOMA   NAPA
Map Area

Acacia Vineyard **2**
Andretti Winery **8**
Artesa Vineyards & Winery **5**
Baldacci Family Vineyard **15**
Beaulieu Vineyards **33**
Benessere Vineyards **50**
Beringer **46**
Bouchaine Vineyards **1**
Burgess Cellars **49**
Cakebread Cellars **27**
Carneros Creek Winery **4**
Chapellet Vineyards & Winery **22**
Chateau Montelena **58**
Charles Krug Winery-Peter Mondavi Family **45**

St. Helena

Lake Hennessey Rec. Area

Sage Canyon

Cliff Lede Vineyards **16**
Clos du Val **12**
Clos Pegase **57**
Conn Creek Napa Valley **30**
Corison Winery **38**
Cosentino Winery **19**
Cuvaison Winery **55**
Darioush **11**
Domaine Carneros **3**
Domaine Chandon **14**
Duckhorn Vineyards **52**
Far Niente **20**
Flora Springs **41**
Franciscan Oakville Estate **37**
Frank Family Vineyards **53**
Freemark Abbey Winery **51**
Grgich Hills Cellars **35**
Hagafen **10**
Hall Winery **42**
The Hess Collection **6**
Honig Vineyards & Winery **32**
Joseph Phelps Winery **40**
Ladera Vineyards **59**
Louis M. Martini Winery **44**
Monticello Vineyards/
  Corley Family Napa Valley **9**
Mumm Napa **24**
Opus One **26**
Paraduxx Winery **18**
Peju Province Winery **29**
Plumpjack Winery **22**
Provenance Vineyards **36**
Raymond Vineyards **31**
Robert Craig Wine Cellars **7**
Robert Mondavi Winery **25**
Rubicon Estate **34**
St. Clement Vineyards **47**
St. Supéry Winery **28**
Schramsberg Vineyards **56**
Shafer Vineyards **17**
Sterling Vineyards **54**
Sutter Home Winery **43**
Trefethen Vineyards **13**
V. Sattui **39**
Viader **48**
ZD **23**

Rutherford

Oakville Grade

Oakville

Oakville Cross Rd.

Rector Res.

Yountville Cross Rd.

Dwyer Rd.

Yountville

Mt. Veeder

NAPA COUNTY

Mt. Veeder Rd.

Oak Knoll Ave.

Silverado Trail

SONOMA COUNTY

Redwood Rd.

SONOMA

Carneros Ck.

Henry Rd.

Trancas St.

NAPA

Napa Valley Wine Train

Old Sonoma Rd.

Cutting Wharf Rd.

To San Francisco

0   1 mile
0   1 km

Northern Sonoma Wineries

Alderbrook **13**
Alexander Valley Vineyards **19**
Arista Winery **10**
Bella Vineyards & Wine Cave **23**
Chalk Hill Estate Vineyards
  Winery **6**
Clos du Bois **20**
De La Montanya Winery
  & Vineyards **12**
DeLoach Vineyards **2**
Ferrari-Carano Vineyards
  & Winery **24**
Foppiano Vineyards **14**
Gallo of Sonoma **16**
Gary Farrell Vineyards & Winery **8**
Geyser Peak Winery **22**
Harvest Moon Estate & Winery **3**
Hop Kiln Winery **9**
Huntington **15**
Jordan Winery **18**
Kendall-Jackson Wine Center **5**
Korbel Champagne Cellars **7**
Paradise Ridge Winery **1**
Roshambo Winery **11**
Sebastopol Vineyards/
  Dutton Estate **4**
Simi Winery **17**
Stryker Sonoma **20**

Sonoma Valley Wineries

Arrowood Vineyards & Winery **12**
B.R. Cohn Winery **14**
Bartholomew Park Winery **10**
Benziger Family Winery **16**
Blackstone Winery **20**
Buena Vista Carneros **9**
Charles Creek **7**
Chateau St. Jean **19**
Cline Cellars **2**
Gloria Ferrer Champagne Caves **3**
Gundlach Bundschu **6**
Imagery Estate Winery **13**
Kaz Vineyards & Winery **21**
Kenwood Vineyards **18**
Kunde Estate Winery & Vineyards **17**
Ledson Winery & Vineyards **23**
Navillus Birney Winery & Vineyards **15**
Ravenswood Winery **11**
St. Francis Winery & Vineyards **22**
Schug Carneros Estate Winery **4**
Sebastiani **8**
Tin Barn Vineyards **5**
Viansa Winery **1**

Wineries A to Z

Wine Tip

Do you need help clarifying what cabernet tastes like, where merlot fits in, and what makes a California chardonnay distinctive? See Savvy Traveler, "A Quick Guide to Wine Varietals" (p 207).

Acacia Vineyard NAPA

Founded in 1979 in the famous Carneros region, Acacia specializes in dark pinot noir and chardonnay. Bring your camera into the tasting room: Because it's 2 miles (3.2km) from San Francisco's San Pablo Bay, you'll want to snap photos of the

water views. *2750 Las Amigas Rd., Napa.* ☎ *877/226-1700. www.acacia vineyard.com. By appointment Mon–Sat 10am–4pm, Sun noon–4pm. Tours ($10–$15, including tastings) by appointment Mon–Fri 11am or 2pm. Tastings $10–$15. North on Calif. 121, then right on Duhig Rd., left on Las Amigas Rd. Map p 130.*

Alderbrook SONOMA

For a rural winery, Alderbrook is remarkably close to Healdsburg Plaza, so it's a great place for a serene wine-accented picnic away from the throngs—especially if you want a view to remember. Visitors can buy wine and specialty food items (think

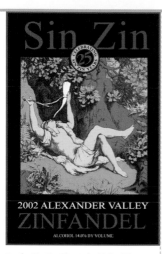

Try the Sin Zin, Alexander Valley Vineyards' cult wine.

fruity chardonnay or dark, dry Carignane paired with fresh French bread) in the laid-back tasting room. If it's windy out, stay in the tasting room to absorb the fireplace's heat. *2306 Magnolia Dr., Healdsburg.* ☎ *800/ 405-5987. www.alderbrook.com. Daily 10am–5pm (closed major holidays). No tours. Tastings free–$5, refunded with purchase. Hwy. 101 S, exit Westside, turn right. Map p 131.*

Alexander Valley Vineyards

SONOMA   This estate, now owned by the Wetzel family, was once the property of Cyrus Alexander (yes, as in Alexander Valley). The Wetzels bought the land from the Alexanders and, in 1975, "AVV" was born. The winery is on the Russian River and makes for a perfect picnic spot— views of Sonoma Valley are superb from here. Try their award-winning Cyrus (a cab-dominated blend) or their zinfandels, Redemption Zin and Sin Zin; the latter was an instant sensation and is considered their cult wine. *8644 Hwy. 128, Healdsburg.* ☎ *800/888-7209. www.avvwine. com. Daily 10am–5pm. Free tours of*

wine caves by appointment. Tastings free–$2. 6 miles (9.7km) northeast of Healdsburg. Map p 131.*

Andretti Winery NAPA   Andretti is a Northern Italian–style winery founded by race-car driving champion Mario Andretti in 1996. Despite the celebrity cachet, the staff here couldn't be more down-to-earth. Ask them anything about Napa; they're likely to be able to answer. Tastings take place in a Tuscan villa, adjacent to which is an outdoor patio where visitors take in views of vineyards and mountains while sipping a light, zesty chardonnay or a richer cabernet sauvignon. *4162 Big Ranch Rd., Napa.* ☎ *888/460-8463. www.andretti winery.com. Daily 10am–5pm (closed major holidays). No tours available for groups smaller than 10 people. Tastings: $8 for 4 wines. Hwy. 29 north, then right onto Oak Knoll Rd., then right on Big Ranch Rd. Map p 130.*

Arista Winery SONOMA   Known for their small lots of pinot noir and bone-dry gewürztraminer, this family-owned boutique winery recently opened a hospitality center. There, visitors stroll through beautiful Japanese water gardens and gaze at hundred-year-old oaks while tasting wine. Picnic spots are available, and a midweek visit is best to avoid crowds. *7015 Westside Rd., Healdsburg.* ☎ *707/473-0606. www. aristawinery.com. Thurs–Mon 10am–5pm, Tues & Wed by appointment. No tours. Tastings free for appellation wines, $5 for single-vineyard pinot noirs (fee refunded with wine purchase). From Healdsburg, take Westside Rd. west for about 8 miles (13km). Map p 131.*

★ Arrowood Vineyards & Winery

SONOMA   More than 20 years ago, a married couple founded Arrowood on a hillside overlooking Sonoma. Today, visitors savor samples of the handcrafted cabernets Arrowood is known for in their newish Hospitality House. The sun-dappled tasting room has a spacious balcony from which sippers can see Sonoma Mountain. Choose between two tours: the 40-minute overview or the in-depth 90-minute vineyard and cellar tour. Both end with tastings. *14347 Sonoma Hwy. (Hwy. 12), Glen Ellen.* ☎ *800/ 938-5170. www.arrowoodvineyards. com. Daily 10am–4:30pm. Tours ($20–$30, including tastings) daily at 10:30am & 2:30pm, by appointment. Tastings: $5–$10. Map p 132.*

★★ Artesa Vineyards & Winery NAPA

Art and architecture strike first when encountering this winery; its modern semi-pyramid structure and stakelike sculptures impress, as do arching fountains, a water-centric courtyard, and a stark tasting room. But do the wines live up to the arresting visuals? Oh, yes, especially the chardonnay and pinot noir. Peruse the Carneros Center, which documents the region's history—or the museum, which displays ancient winemaking tools. *1345 Henry Rd., Napa.* ☎ *707/224-1668. www.artesawinery.com. Daily 10am–5pm. Tours (free) daily 11am & 2pm. Tastings: $10–$15 for 6 tastes. From Hwy. 12, turn left on Old Sonoma Rd., then left on Dealy Lane, which becomes Henry Rd. Map p 130.*

The Lower fountain at Artesa Winery.

Baldacci Family Vineyards

NAPA Tom and Brenda Baldacci founded their winery in 1998 with the notion of sharing wine with friends and family; hence the reason many of their hand-farmed creations are named after relatives. Try Elizabeth, a pinot noir that shares a name with Tom's mother—but don't miss the winery's signature cabernet. *6236 Silverado Trail, Napa.* ☎ *707/944-9261. www.baldaccivineyards.com. Sat–Sun 11am–4pm & Mon–Fri by appointment. Tours (free) by appointment (book several weeks in advance). Tastings: $5 (refunded with wine purchase). Map p 130.*

Bartholomew Park Winery

SONOMA "Bart Park" is more than a winery; it's a full destination with a museum, memorial park, picnic grounds, and hiking trails. If you're here solely for tasting, you'll be satisfied with the limited-production single-vineyard wines, particularly the much-honored 2001 cabernet sauvignon (it took gold in two major competitions). If you're in a learning mood, check out Bartholomew Park Museum, which chronicles the property's whimsical history. But if you're feeling energetic, hit the trails. All 3 miles (4.8km) of them are well marked and beautiful. On a clear day, you can see all the way to San Francisco. *1000 Vineyard Lane, Sonoma.* ☎ *707/935-9511. www.bartholomewparkwinery.com. Daily 11am–4:30pm (closed major holidays). Tours offered onlu on weekends, every hour starting at noon; price included with tasting. Tastings: $5. From Hwy. 12, turn right on E. Napa St., then left on 7th St. E., then slight right on Castle Rd. & follow it around to the winery's gates. Map p 132.*

★★ Beaulieu Vineyard NAPA

This renowned winery was founded in 1900 by Frenchman and Napa pioneer Georges de Latour. Today,

Beaulieu Vineyard (otherwise known as B.V.).

the vintage named in his honor—Georges de Latour Private Reserve Cabernet—is the company's benchmark and resides in every serious collector's cellar. In the recently opened Reserve Room, guests sample this and older selections. For a more pedestrian (and crowded) experience, the understated main tasting room offers a flight of five of the winery's staple wines. Fun fact: Beaulieu's wines have been served by every American president since FDR. *1960 St. Helena Hwy., Rutherford.* ☎ *707/967-5233. www.bvwines.com. Mon–Fri 10am–5pm (closed major holidays). No tours. Tastings: $10–$35. Hwy. 101 N. Exit at Hwy. 37, then north on Calif. 121. Map p 130.*

★★ Bella Vineyards Do yourself a favor—call ahead for a cave tour at Bella. No, not a vineyard tour, a cave tour. Why? Because you'll see mysterious arched doors built into the hillside when you pull up to the unassuming, barnlike tasting room, and after a few sips of hearty, spicy old vine zinfandel you'll ask the staff about the doors. They tell you the doors, flanked by old olive trees, are caves housing barrels and underground functions rooms. During your tour, you'll feel warm and cozy thanks to well-placed mood lighting and big, sturdy wood tables filling the winding caverns. You'll be so happy you stopped by this small family-run winery (named Bella as an ode to the owners' two young daughters) located in the heart of Dry Creek Valley that you'll leave plotting a way to schedule your next underground party at the Bella wine caves. *9711 W. Dry Creek Rd. Healdsburg.* ☎ *866/572-3552 or 707/473-9171. www.bella winery.com. Daily 10am–5pm. Tours by appt. Map p 131.*

Benessere Vineyards NAPA *Benessere* is the Italian word for well-being, and that's certainly the feeling one gets from being here. This 42-acre (17-hectare) country estate is known for its small lots of Italian-inspired wines, many of which come from sangiovese grapes; try Phenom-enon—its makers deem it "the pinnacle of winemaking at Benessere." Visit Monday through Wednesday, when the tasting room is least crowded. *1010 Big Tree Rd., St. Helena.* ☎ *707/963-5853. www. benesserevineyards.com. Daily 10am–5pm by appointment. Tours ($7.50 including tastings) daily by appointment. Tastings: $7.50 (refunded with wine purchase). Hwy. 29 N., then right on Big Tree Rd. Map p 130.*

★ Benziger Family Winery SONOMA A highlight here is the 45-minute tractor-drawn tram tour. Sit back as a knowledgeable driver maneuvers through the estate's hilly vineyards and discusses how vines get turned into wines. (Tours are first-come, first-served, so stop by in the morning to buy afternoon tickets.) The winery also has a peacock aviary, rose gardens, picnic grounds, and an educational

Benziger's rolling hills of vines.

The main building at Beringer Vineyards.

Vineyard Discovery Center. The tasting room, where visitors taste current and special releases, is in a German-style mansion. Particularly worthy of trying, if available: 2003 Sonoma Mountain Red; and, if you like dessert wines, the 2004 Port. *1883 London Ranch Rd., Glen Ellen. ☎ 888/490-2739. www.benziger.com. 10am–5pm. Tram tours ($10) daily; call for schedule. Tastings: $5 (includes logo glass). Calif. 121 N. becomes Arnold Dr., then left onto London Ranch Rd. Map p 132.*

★★ Beringer Vineyards NAPA
Whoever knows Napa knows Beringer. Established in 1876 by German brothers Jacob and Frederick Beringer, it's Napa's oldest continually operating winery (the Beringers finagled survival during

Prohibition by making sacramental wine). That distinction earned it a spot on the National Register of Historic Places. In 1934, the Beringers pioneered the idea of public winery tours and have since perfected their brainchild. Now there are four tour options ranging from a basic introduction to a thorough exploration of Beringer's vintage legacy. In summer, try a seasonal white, but the 2002 Knights Valley Cabernet Sauvignon is sublime on any day of the year. *2000 Main St., St. Helena. ☎ 707/963-4812. www.beringer. com. Daily 10am–5pm (June 1–Oct 1 until 6pm). Tours ($10–$35) daily 10:45am–3:45pm. Tastings: $5–$30. Hwy. 101 N. Hwy. 29 N. through St. Helena. Turn left into Beringer Vineyards. Map p 130.*

Blackstone Winery SONOMA
Blackstone has a charming, clean tasting room with lively visitors. But if the weather's nice, opt for the outdoor bar where friendly staff pour reserve wines and guests can practically reach out and touch the vines. There's also a gourmet shop where you can put together a picnic to enjoy on the grounds. For kicks, try the winery's flagship merlot—surprisingly, it's America's best-selling domestic red wine. *8450 Sonoma Hwy. (Hwy. 12), Kenwood. ☎ 800/ 955-9585. www.blackstonewinery. com. Daily 10:30am–4:30pm. Tours $15; 1-week advance reservation*

The vines and vistas at B.R. Cohn.

The Buena Vista Winery's tasting room is a landmark.

required. Tastings: $5. Hwy. 101 N. Exit at Hwy. 37, then north on Calif. 121. Map p 132.

Bouchaine Vineyards NAPA Carneros' oldest continuously operated winery offers tastings of its Burgundy-inspired creations in its Wine Visitor Center. Try the pinot noir and chardonnay, as well as the more exclusive wines sold only here. After tasting, step out onto the terrace, where an endless view of vineyards awaits. *1075 Buchli Station Rd., Napa.* ☎ *707/252-9065. www.bouchaine.com. Daily 10:30am–4pm (closed some Sun in winter; call to verify). Free tours by appointment. Tastings free–$5. Hwy. 101 N. Exit at Hwy. 37, then north on Calif. 121. Map p 130.*

B.R. Cohn Winery SONOMA Founded in 1984 by Bruce Cohn, this estate winery specializes in fine cabernet and merlot. And since there are olive trees all over the property, the winery also produces gourmet olive oils and vinegars. The tasting room may be small, but the flavors are big, especially if you're trying the 2001 or 2003 Sonoma Valley Merlot. Cohn, interestingly, is the Doobie Brothers' longtime band manager. His other career inspired a Doobie Red wine series, as well as many musical events at the winery (check the website for schedule). *15000 Sonoma Hwy. (Hwy. 12), Glen Ellen.* ☎ *800/*

330-4064. www.brcohn.com. Daily 10am–5pm. Seasonal picnic tours ($25) by appointment. Tastings: $5–$10 (fee waived with wine purchase). Hwy. 121 N. to Hwy. 12 N., winery is 5 miles (8km) north of Sonoma Plaza. Map p 132.

★★★ Buena Vista Carneros SONOMA Not many wineries can boast that their tasting room is a California Historical Landmark—but then again, Buena Vista *is* America's oldest continuously operating winery and where California's wine industry was born. Founded in 1857 by Hungarian colonel **Agoston Haraszthy,** it still has that delightful old-world feel: ivy-covered buildings, antique fountains, and a restored 1862 press house, which houses the tasting room. Try the highly rated Estate Vineyard Series, a near-perfect selection of chardonnay and pinot noir. Picnic grounds are gorgeous here, too. *18000 Old Winery Rd., Sonoma.* ☎ *800/926-1266. www.buenavistacarneros. com. Daily 10am–5pm (closed major holidays). Free self-guided tours all day; reservations recommended for the daily guided tours ($15–$50). Tastings: $5 & up. Calif. 121 N. to Napa St. & turn right. Take Napa St. to Old Winery Rd. Map p 132.*

Cakebread Cellars NAPA A small, independent winery with handcrafted wines, Cakebread is

Peter Mondavi Sr., owner of Charles Krug Winery, takes in the aroma of a red wine.

known for its chardonnay and cabernet. When Jack and Dolores Cakebread founded it with $2,500 in 1973, they wanted to encourage people to incorporate wine and food into a healthy lifestyle. They've stuck to that goal and now offer a variety of wine and culinary education programs. The tasting area shares space with immense fermenting tanks. *8300 St. Helena Hwy. (Hwy. 29), Rutherford.* ☎ *800/588-0298. www.cakebread.com. Daily 10am–4:30pm. Tours (free) 10:30am daily (reservations required). Tastings: $10 (by appointment; includes souvenir glass). Map p 130.*

Chalk Hill Estate Vineyards and Winery

SONOMA Of the estate's 1,200 acres (480 hectares), only 350 (140 hectares) are vineyards. The rest encompass winery buildings and a wilderness preserve—but that doesn't mean the wines aren't great. Selections include rich chardonnay, cabernet, merlot, sauvignon blanc, and pinot gris. Embark on the culinary tour and tasting, which turns out to be an educational ramble through chef Didier Ageorges' organic culinary garden. *10300 Chalk Hill Rd., Healdsburg.* ☎ *707/838-4306. www. chalkhill.com. Mon–Fri 10am–4pm. $15 estate tour daily at various times from 10am–3pm; culinary tour $40 on Mon, Thurs. & Fri. Tastings: $10. Appointment recommended. Hwy. 101 N. Exit at Shiloh, turn right. Then left on Old Redwood Hwy., right on Pleasant, left on Chalk Hill Rd. Map p 131.*

Chappellet Vineyard & Winery

NAPA For an up-close winery experience, head toward Pritchard Hill. Atop it, you'll find Chappellet and its stellar view of vineyards, mountains, and a lake. After an intimate tour that delves into Chappellet's sustainable farming practices, head to the cellar to taste the winery's signatures: cabernet, merlot, and chenin blanc. Just be sure you've made

Chateau Montalena's ivy-covered chateau.

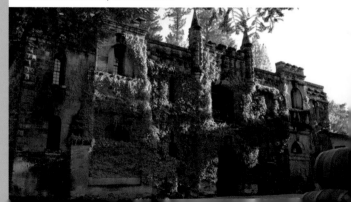

reservations. *1581 Sage Canyon Rd. (Hwy. 128), St. Helena.* ☎ *707/ 963-7136. www.chappellet.com. Tour & tasting ($15) Mon–Sat 10:30am & 2pm by appointment. Silverado Trail to Hwy. 128 E. Map p 130.*

Charles Creek SONOMA   Though its vineyards are scattered through wine country, the winery's tasting room is a storefront on Sonoma Plaza. Can't decide which of the handcrafted wines to taste? Charles Creek is known for its chardonnay, cabernet, and merlot. There's always local art on display and the room's *pièce de résistance*—aside from its artisan wines—is a cow sculpture made entirely of wine corks. *483 1st St. W., Sonoma.* ☎ *707/935-3848. www.charlescreek.com. Daily 10am–5:30pm. From Jan 1 to Apr 1, closed on Tues & Wed. No tours. Tastings: $3 (waived with purchase). Hwy. 12 to Sonoma Plaza. Map p 132.*

★ **Charles Krug Winery— Peter Mondavi Family** NAPA One of only three Napa wineries deemed a California Historical Landmark (the others are Beringer and Schramsberg), this is the county's oldest working winery. It was founded in 1861 by Prussian immigrant Charles Krug, the first to make commercial wine in Napa. The Mondavi family bought the estate in 1943 and has operated it since. They opened the valley's first tasting room, where, over a bar made of redwood wine tanks, visitors taste the winery's signature Bordeaux varietals. There's also opportunity to try rare ports and 20-plus-year-old wines. *2800 Main St. (Hwy. 29), St. Helena.* ☎ *707/ 967-2229. www.charleskrug.com. Daily 10:30am–5pm (closed major holidays). Tours currently unavailable during winery redevelopment. Tastings: $10–$15 (free for Napa County residents with ID & 4 guests). Hwy. 101 N. to Hwy. 37 E., then north on Calif. 12 to Hwy. 29 N. Map p 130.*

★ **Chateau Montelena** NAPA This place really is a château, complete with an immense 1882 stone castle. At the base of Mount St. Helena, it overlooks wildlife-laden Jade Lake and a Chinese garden. The entertaining tour starts with a video introduction, includes the vineyard and cellar, and ends up in the Estate Room for vintage tasting. On the edifice's highest floor is another cavernous tasting room where non-tour visitors sample less rare wines. The chardonnay is the most acclaimed, but there's also cabernet and Riesling. *1429 Tubbs Lane, Calistoga.* ☎ *707/942-5105. www.montelena.com. Daily 9:30am–4pm (except major holidays & 3rd Sat in May). Tours ($25) daily at 2pm, by prepaid reservation. Tastings: $10–$25. Hwy. 29 to Tubbs Lane (hard to find, so call for specific directions). Map p 130.*

★ **Chateau St. Jean** SONOMA At Sugarloaf State Park's edge, these elegant grounds include European-style gardens with colorful flora and a 19th-century fountain that's a sculpture of St. John himself. There's also a gourmet food shop, picnic space, and a welcoming visitor center. Taste winemaker Margo van Staaveren's chardonnay, cabernet, and gewürztraminer before exploring the 1920 château—it's so precisely

Chateau St. Jean really looks like a French château.

restored that it made the National Trust for Historic Preservation. See if you can spot the fish-filled ponds shaped like lakes Michigan and Huron (the original owners got rich mining iron in Michigan). Oh, and if you've ever dismissed merlot as being too passé for you, this is the place in which to fall in love with it again. *8555 Sonoma Hwy. (Hwy. 12), Kenwood.* ☎ *707/833-4134. www.chateaustjean.com. Daily 10am–5pm. Tours (free) daily at 11am & 3pm, or private tour & reserve tasting ($25) by appointment. Tastings: $5–$10. Hwy. 101 N. Exit at Hwy. 12 E. & follow for 12 miles (19km). Map p 132.*

★ **Cliff Lede Vineyards** NAPA This art-rich winery was born when Canadian Cliff Lede bought S. Anderson Vineyard in 2002. The tasting room, in a century-old stone pump house, is where to try Lede's Bordeaux-focused varietals and the sparkling wines that still bear the S. Anderson name. Meticulously landscaped gardens are graced with rosebushes and sculptures by artists like Keith Haring. A new winemaking facility opened in 2005, and the former winery is now a modern art gallery. Cliff Lede also offers Stags Leap District's only public lodging: the lovely Poetry Inn. *1473 Yountville Cross Rd., Yountville.* ☎ *707/944-8642. www.clifflede vineyards.com. Daily 10am–5pm.*

The tasting room at Cline Cellars.

Tours ($25) daily at 10:30am & 2:30pm (reservations required). Tastings: $10. Silverado Trail north, then left on Yountville Cross Rd. Map p 130.*

Cline Cellars SONOMA   This family-owned winery in the Carneros district has its tasting room in an 1850s farmhouse. With six ponds and more than 5,000 rosebushes, it's a beautiful place to try a variety of zinfandel and Rhone-style wines, such as the Marsanne-Roussanne blend. *24737 Hwy. 121, Sonoma.* ☎ *707/940-4000. www.clinecellars. com. Daily 10am–6pm (closed Christmas). Free tours daily 11am, 1 & 3pm. Tastings free (or for reserves, $1 per taste). Hwy. 101 N. Exit at Hwy. 37, then north on Calif. 121. Map p 132.*

★ **Clos du Bois** SONOMA   Clos du Bois—French for "enclosure in the woods" or "vineyard of drink," depending on the translation—produces France-style varietals. On campus are *pétanque* courts (bocce ball for Francophiles) and a picnic area with gazebos. The educational 45-minute tour shows winemaking in progress, demonstration vineyards, and examples of Clos du Bois' sustainable farming. The best part: wine samples right from barrels. The tour ends with a reserve tasting, during which you may be lucky enough to sample the wine under the Marlstone label—though it's just Clos du Bois' fancy way of saying "meritage," these are still some of the most complex flavors around. No matter how you translate it, that's one good deal. *19410 Geyserville Ave., Geyserville.* ☎ *800/222-3189. www.closdubois. com. Daily 10am–4:30pm (closed major holidays). Tours ($10, includes souvenir glass & wine tasting) daily at 11am & 2pm by appointment. Tastings free, or $5 for reserve tasting (includes souvenir glass). Hwy. 101 N. Exit at Independence Lane, then left on Geyserville Ave. Map p 131.*

★ **Clos du Val** NAPA Co-founded in 1972 by a Frenchman who scoured the world for the best winery spot, Clos du Val is known for its cabernet, so try it in the rustic tasting room. A onetime fermentation chamber, it has a high, vaulted ceiling and terra-cotta walls. Double doors in the back allow guests to see steel tanks fermenting the pinot noir this establishment's known for (try the 2004 Carneros Pinot Noir, if you can). Outside, there's a rose garden, two picnic areas, and a pétanque court. *5330 Silverado Trail, Napa.* ☎ *707/259-2200. www. closduval.com. Daily 10am–5pm. Customized tours (about $10) by 24-hour advance appointment (includes tasting). Tastings: $5 for regular tasting (waived with purchase), $20 for reserve tasting (includes souvenir glass). Map p 130.*

Clos du Val is a Napa favorite.

★★ **Clos Pegase** NAPA Book publisher Jan Shrem bought these vineyards in 1983 and named his winery after Pegasus, the mythological winged horse that created a spring that fed divine grapevines. Then, Shrem held an architects' competition. Michael Graves, the winner, designed the winery's stunning structures. They house a world-class fine-art collection, including a huge painting behind the tasting bar, where informed pourers dole out specialties like Mitsuko's Vineyard chardonnay and pinot noir. There's also a remarkable sculpture

garden and a vineyard-adjacent picnic facility (call to reserve a table). *1060 Dunaweal Lane, Calistoga.* ☎ *707/942-4981. www.clospegase. com. Daily 10:30am–5pm. Tours (free) daily 11am & 2pm. Tastings: $5–$10. Hwy. 101 N. Exit at Hwy. 37, then north on Calif. 121. Left on Hwy. 29 N., then right on Dunaweal Lane. Map p 130.*

Conn Creek Napa Valley NAPA This winery focuses on limited-production cabernets and Bordeaux blends. Also try the sauvignon blanc—it's only available here. Taking its name from the stream running alongside the vineyard, Conn Creek has a Mediterranean-style building with a pleasant garden. It's just below Rutherford Hill, in the shadow of the renowned Auberge du Soleil resort and spa. *8711 Silverado Trail, St. Helena.* ☎ *707/963-9100. www.conncreek.com. Daily 10am–4pm. Tours of AVA blending room available by joining wine club. Tastings: $5, including reserve*

The sculptures and the architecture at Clos Pegase are one-of-a-kind.

tasting (waived if you join the winery's mailing list or refunded with purchase). Hwy. 29 N., turn right on Oakville Cross Rd., then left on Silverado Trail. Map p 130.

Corison Winery NAPA Tastings here are conducted the old-fashioned way: in the barrel cellar. Winemaker Cathy Corison specializes in handcrafted cabernets and her bottle labels bear ancient symbols. One depicts rain; the other, a sprouting seed. Tours include a visit to the winery's organically farmed Kronos Vineyard. *987 St. Helena Hwy. (Hwy. 29), St. Helena. ☎ 707/963-0826. www.corison.com. Daily 10am–5pm. Free tours daily by appointment. Tastings: $10 (deducted from purchase). Map p 130.*

Cosentino Winery NAPA Founder and winemaker Mitch Cosentino offers more than 30 hand-harvested, small-lot wines, including some rich, sweet ones, like the romantically named Francesca d'Amore Vin Santo. Though this is fine and artistic wine, the staff is friendly. *7415 St. Helena*

If you visit Napa and Sonoma during the fall harvest, you'll see plenty of heavy vines, like these pristine cabernet grapes in Napa Valley.

Hwy. (Hwy. 29), Yountville. ☎ 707/ 944-1220. www.cosentinowinery. com. Daily 10am–5pm. Tours (free) daily 11am–4pm. Tastings: $5–$10 (includes souvenir glass). Map p 130.

Cuvaison Winery NAPA This mission-style winery on the Silverado Trail was founded in 1969 by Silicon Valley techies. Since then, Cuvaison, a French word roughly meaning "fermentation of grape skins," has proved that its wines are award-worthy—praise has been especially heaped on the 2003 and 2004 Estate Selection chardonnays, so try them if you can. From the tasting room site, there are great views of northern Napa. Picnic grounds are noteworthy for their 350-year-old oak trees. *4550 Silverado Trail, Calistoga. ☎ 707/ 942-2468. www.cuvaison.com. Daily 10am–5pm. Tours ($15) by appointment. Tastings: $8–$10 (includes souvenir glass). Map p 130.*

★★ Darioush NAPA "Impressive" is hardly an adequate word to describe this new winery. Inspired by the ancient Persian city of Persepolis, Darioush Khaledi, a native of Iran's Shiraz region, founded this epic complex in 1997. Rows of Greco columns and scalloped rooflines greet visitors outside. Inside, a blend of modern and ancient decor commingles with the effects of the strong Bordeaux-style wines Darioush is known for. To splurge, try the "Private Tasting with Cheese Pairing Experience." In addition to a private tour of the visitor center and amphitheatre, a personal host leads you to the classy six-seat Barrel Chai (say "shay") Private Tasting Room, where flights of Darioush's finest wines are expertly paired with local cheeses. *4240 Silverado Trail, Napa. ☎ 707/257-2345. www. darioush.com. Daily 10:30am–5pm. Private tasting & cheese pairing tours ($35) daily 11am & 3pm by appointment. Tastings: $20. Map p 130.*

The grounds of Domaine Carneros are fit for a queen.

De La Montaña Winery and Vineyards SONOMA

This upbeat country-style winery has a tasting room surrounded by beauty: Apple orchards, golden poppies, and Felta Creek set the ambience. Most days, owner Dennis De La Montaña is behind the counter pouring. Best to try are the primitivo, pinot noir, Viognier, and zinfandel. Book the short walking tour of the small winery; you'll see the vineyards and the barrel room. Bring lunch—there's a vineyard patio on which visitors can eat *al fresco*. And if you want to stay overnight, the winery's cozy Little Yellow Cottage sleeps four people. *999 Foreman Lane, Healdsburg.* ☎ *707/433-3711. www.dlmwine. com. Sat & Sun 11am–4:30pm. Mon–Fri by appointment. Tours (free) by appointment. Tastings free. Hwy. 101 N. to central Healdsburg exit. Left on Mill St., which turns into Westside Rd. Right onto Felta Rd. & go under the bridge. Map p 131.*

DeLoach Vineyards SONOMA

Guided tours at this Russian River winery include the organic biody-namic garden and wine samples straight from the barrel. In DLV's tasting room, recently remodeled by sought-after local architect Howard Backen, sample single-vineyard pinot noir, chardonnay, and zinfandel. Fresh bread is served with the wine to appease the moderately hungry. For a bigger meal, bring lunch and savor it in the outdoor courtyard with a refreshing bottle of, say, the winery's 2004 O.F.S. Sauvignon Blanc. Afterward, toss a game of horseshoes. *1791 Olivet Rd., Santa Rosa.* ☎ *707/526-9111. www.deloach vineyards.com. Daily 10am–4:30pm. Tours ($10) daily 10am, noon & 2pm by appointment. Tastings: $5–$7 (fee waived with wine purchase). Hwy. 101 N. Exit at River Rd., then left on Olivet Rd. Map p 131.*

★ Domaine Carneros NAPA

Owned by French champagne magnate Claude Taittinger, this is the only sparkling-wine producer to use only Carneros grapes. Domaine Carneros also offers a sophisticated welcome: Visitors ascend to the imposing Louis XV–style château via a grand staircase flanked by vineyards. In the tasting room and on the sunny veranda, sampler courses pair with cheese, and tastings come with free hors d'oeuvres. Try a light wine called Le Reve—it's a dream. Come at twilight, since hours are later than other wineries. *1240 Duhig Rd., Napa.* ☎ *707/257-0101, ext.108. www.domainecarneros.com. Daily 10am–6pm. Tours (free–$30) daily 10:15am–4pm. Tastings: $6.25–$11 by the glass; $13–$14 for flights. Hwy. 12 N. to Duhig Rd. Map p 130.*

★ Domaine Chandon NAPA

French champagne house Moët et Chandon founded this prominent winery in 1973. Enjoy bubbly-and-food pairing—the Chandon Blanc de Noirs is highly recommended—while taking in fine art and even better views. Domaine Chandon also has an exceptional fine-dining restaurant. *1 California Dr. (at Hwy. 29), Yountville.* ☎ *707/944-2280. www.chandon.com. Call ahead; hours vary by season. Tours (free–$25) daily. Tastings: $9–$14. Map p 130.*

Duckhorn Vineyards NAPA At Duckhorn's high-end Estate House, taste smooth Bordeaux varietals, such as the 2002 Estate Grown Napa Valley Cabernet Sauvignon, at the O-shaped bar. Prior to the 1pm estate tasting (make reservations), take the intimate winery tour and be sure to see the waterfowl art collection and the handsome gardens. Owners Dan and Margaret Duckhorn are known for their hospitality. *1000 Lodi Lane, St. Helena.* ☎ *888/354-8885. www.duckhornvineyards.com. Daily 10am–4pm. Tours (free) daily noon. Tastings: $10–$25. Hwy. 29 N., then right on Lodi Lane. Map p 130.*

★★ Ferrari-Carano Vineyards and Winery SONOMA Ferrari-Carano is one of wine country's most beautiful wineries. Villa Fiore, its Tuscan-style hospitality center, has a tasting bar overlooking the estate's impressive fountains. Limited releases are seasonally available, but the winery's classics, like the Italian-influenced 2003 Siena, are more likely to be behind the bar. On the tour, experience behind-the-scenes winemaking, an underground cellar, and an eye-popping ramble through 5 acres (2 hectares) of verdant gardens laced with streams and waterfalls. *8761 Dry Creek Rd., Healdsburg.* ☎ *800/831-0381. www.ferrari-carano.com. Daily 10am–5pm (closed major holidays). Tours (free) daily at 10am (reservations required). Tastings: $5 (refundable with $25 wine purchase). Hwy. 101 N. Exit & left on Dry Creek Rd. Map p 131.*

Flora Springs Winery NAPA Forsake the crowds and get off the beaten path at this small, tucked-away estate in the Rutherford appellation. The Komes family specializes in bold reds, so try the Meritage blend and the cabernet—but don't miss the smooth sauvignon blanc, either. Tours include hillside caves and barrel samples of not-yet-released wines. Flora Springs also has a tasting room at 677 Hwy. 29, next to Dean & Deluca. *677 S. St. Helena Hwy., St. Helena.* ☎ *707/967-6723. www.florasprings.com. Daily 10am–5pm. Tours ($20) Mon–Fri 10am & 2pm by appointment. Tastings: $5–$12 by appointment. On Hwy. 29 just south of St. Helena. Map p 130.*

Foppiano Vineyards SONOMA The self-guided tour is a highlight at Sonoma County's oldest continually

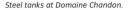
Steel tanks at Domaine Chandon.

The Ferrari-Carano estate comes with a grand pool.

owned family winery (founded 1896); visitors can walk through the petite sirah, chardonnay, cabernet, and merlot vines and learn about the recycled pumice pile (a sustainable way to feed vines). This low-key winery also has picnic tables, so bring lunch *12707 Old Redwood Hwy., Healdsburg.* ☎ *707/433 7272. www.foppiano.com. Daily 10am–4:30pm. Self-guided tours (free) all day. Tastings free. Hwy. 101 S., exit Old Redwood Hwy. Map p 131.*

★ **Franciscan Oakville Estate**
NAPA   This high-end property, with sunny patios and a visitor center offering a range of tastings, is known for its merlot and cabernet, though its best wine is the Magnificat, a deep, round blend named after Bach's music. Also interesting is the Cuvée Sauvage, a chardonnay made from fermented wild yeast. To try blending your own wine, book "Mastering Magnificat," one of the estate's educational seminars. *1178 Galleron Rd., Rutherford.* ☎ *707/ 963-7111, ext. 73830. www.franciscan. com. Daily 10am–5pm (closed major holidays). No tours. Tastings: $5–$50 (personalized tastings require reservations). At Hwy. 29. Map p 130.*

Frank Family Vineyards NAPA
Originally known for its sparking wine, this winery now specializes in still ones: cabernet and chardonnay in

particular (try the smoky 2002 Rutherford Reserve Cabernet Sauvignon). But it maintains a separate tasting space for its five versions of *méthode champenoise* bubbly—festive Champagne Rouge is worth trying. The winery's staff is known for its friendliness, and the entertaining tour includes all the lore that comes with being old enough for the National Register of Historic Places (it was built in 1884). Outside, a picnic area with vineyard views and centuries-old oak trees awaits. *1091 Larkmead Lane, Calistoga.* ☎ *800/574-9463. www.frankfamilyvineyards.com. Daily 10am–4pm. No tours. Tastings free. Hwy. 29 N., then right on Larkmead Lane. Map p 130.*

Freemark Abbey Winery NAPA
Established in 1886, Freemark Abbey was founded by California's first female winery owner, Josephine Tychson. In 1939, the estate got its name from three partners who bought it: Charles *Free*man, *Mark* Foster, and *Abbey* Ahern. The tour goes to a century-old cellar, the crushing area, and an adjacent vineyard. The tasting room, once a candle factory, has a fireplace and live piano music on weekends. Winemaker Tim Bell's Cabernet Bosché is a must-try, as is the limited-production dessert Riesling. *3022 St. Helena Hwy. (Hwy. 29), St. Helena.* ☎ *800/963-9698. www.freemarkabbey.com. Daily*

The champagne caves at Gloria Ferrer.

10am–5pm (May–Oct open until 6pm). Tours (free) weekdays by appointment. Tastings: $5–$15 (includes souvenir glass). Map p 130.

Gallo of Sonoma SONOMA

Gallo has a new tasting room on Healdsburg Square with a country atmosphere. Try the pinot gris or pinot noir for free, or splurge and try the chardonnay or cabernet. Shell out a bit more money (provided you've made reservations), and you'll be whisked away to Barrelli Creek Vineyard in northwestern Alexander Valley for an educational vineyard-farming experience. Then, by a lake, you'll sample wines and local cheeses. *320 Center St., Healdsburg.* ☎ *707/433-2458. www.galloofsonoma.com. Daily 10am–6pm. Tours ($45, includes transportation to vineyard & tasting; reservations required) daily 10am. Tastings free–$12. Hwy. 101 N. Exit at Central Healdsburg, left on Plaza St., right on Center St. Map p 131.*

Gary Farrell Vineyards & Winery SONOMA

At this boutique producer of premium Russian River Valley pinot noir, sauvignon blanc, and chardonnay, there's a great view from the hilltop tasting room. The tour shows off the state-of-the-art winemaking facility and includes four wine tastes. *10701 Westside Rd., Healdsburg.* ☎ *707/473-2900. www.garyfarrellwines.com. Daily 11am–4pm. Tours ($10) daily 10am (reservations required). Tastings:*

$5–$10. Hwy. 101 N. Exit & left at River Rd., then right on Wohler Rd., then left on Westside Rd. Map p 131.

Geyser Peak Winery SONOMA

Two levels of wine tasting occur here: The sunlit downstairs tasting offers free tastes of 10 popular wines (sauvignon blanc stands out). Upstairs, the classy Reserve Tasting Room offers table service for those who pay the nominal fee for reserve wines (don't miss the unusual sparkling shiraz) while viewing the barrel cellar below. Both rooms are stocked with knowledgeable, welcoming staff. Bring a picnic to enjoy on the flagstone patio; in summer, there's live music on Saturday afternoons. *22281 Chianti Rd., Geyserville.* ☎ *707/857-9400. www.geyserpeak winery.com. Daily 10am–5pm (closed major holidays). No tours. Tastings free–$10. Hwy. 101 N. Exit & left at Canyon Rd. Exit, then right on Chianti Rd. Map p 131.*

★ Gloria Ferrer Champagne Caves SONOMA

The so-called "first lady of Sonoma," Gloria Ferrer is the culmination of seven generations of winemaking. The winery is known for its sparklers, though it also makes chardonnay, pinot noir, merlot, and syrah. Its large hacienda-style tasting room, where wine is served with spiced almonds, opens onto an outdoor terrace overlooking the vineyards. Take the free tour of the fermenting tanks, bottling line, and underground aging caves. *23555*

Carneros Hwy. (Calif. 121), Sonoma. ☎ 707/996-7256. www.gloriaferrer. com. Daily 10:30am–5:30pm. Daily guided underground cave tours (free) noon, 2 & 4pm. Tastings: $2–$10. Hwy. 101 N. Exit at Hwy. 37, then north on Calif. 121. Map p 132.

Grgich Hills Cellar NAPA Ever since Croatian immigrant Miljenko "Mike" Grgich founded **Grgich Hills** in 1977, his winery has won acclaim. The new Hospitality Center begins serving wine earlier than most tasting rooms, so if you want an early start, come here. At the dark-wood bar, taste handcrafted cabernets and chardonnays made from sustainably farmed organic grapes. On Friday afternoons, the $5 tasting fee includes barrel tasting—a before-the-bottle preview of new releases. 1829 St. Helena Hwy. (Hwy. 29), Rutherford. ☎ 800/532-3057. www.grgich.com. Daily 9:30am–4:30pm. Tours ($10) daily 11am & 2pm by appointment. Tastings: $5 (includes souvenir glass). Map p 130.

★★ Gundlach Bundschu Winery SONOMA Outdoorsy as opposed to stuffy, Gundlach Bundschu's cavernous tasting room is built right into the hillside. In it, winemaker Linda Trotta's creations—mostly red wines—are poured for eager guests as they enjoy light snacks. If it's available, try the Kleinberger; it's the only one made in America. An informative tour includes the caves and vineyard, and colorful tales about the winery's illustrious past; it has been around since 1858, after all, and is America's oldest family-owned winery. A variety of excellent picnic grounds overlook the valley. 2000 Denmark St., Sonoma. ☎ 707/938-5277. www.gunbun.com. Daily 11am–4:30pm (closed major holidays). Free tours on weekends noon–3pm; weekdays by appointment. Tastings: $5–$10. Hwy. 101 N. Exit at Hwy. 37, then north on Calif.

121. Right on Napa St., then right on 8th St. Left on Denmark St. Map p 132.

Hagafen Cellars NAPA In Hebrew, **hagafen** means "the vine," and there are plenty of them at this small kosher winery—Napa's only one. Banish thoughts of Manischewitz, though. Sure, Hagafen's wines might be made according to Jewish law and blessed by an in-house rabbi, but these wines are as premium and flavorful as any other on the Silverado Trail—the award party on the tasting room wall attests to that. The most bedecked vintage offered is the white Riesling, so don't decline a taste. Hagafen wines have even been served at the White House. 4160 Silverado Trail, Napa. ☎ 707/252-0781. www.hagafen.com. Daily 10am–5:30pm. Free tour daily 11am by appointment. Tastings: $5–$10. Map p 130.

★ Hall Winery NAPA Hall Winery is actually two wineries: one in St. Helena and one in Rutherford. They're both owned by Kathryn Hall, the former U.S. Ambassador to Austria, and Craig Hall, her husband. The St. Helena location dates back to 1885—though Frank O. Gehry is in the process of modernizing the architecture. The courtyard works well for

Gundlach Bundschu is a friendly, warm place to taste wine and learn about the winery's long family history.

picnics, and tours include the original 1885 building. At the smaller, newer Rutherford location in the eastern hills, visitors see underground caves and modern art—plus, they're treated like VIPs as they taste premium cabernet in the chandeliered tasting room. *ST. HELENA: 401 St. Helena Hwy. (Hwy. 29), St. Helena.* ☎ *707/967-2620. Daily 10am–5:30pm. Free tours all day. Tastings: $10. RUTHERFORD: 56 Auberge Rd., Rutherford.* ☎ *707/967-0700. www.hallwines.com. Tours & tasting ($30) daily 10am–5pm by appointment. Silverado Trail north, left on Rutherford Hill Rd., left on Auberge Rd. Map p 130.*

Harvest Moon Estate & Winery SONOMA
Harvest Moon is a little family-owned winery with welcoming servers in the small but nice tasting room. Though they focus on zinfandel, the gewürztraminer is more tasteworthy. *2192 Olivet Rd., Santa Rosa.* ☎ *707/573-8711. www.harvestmoonwinery.com. Daily 10:30am–4:30pm. Tours (free) daily 11am–4pm. Tastings: $2–$7.50. Hwy. 101 N. Exit at River Rd. & go west, then left on Olivet. Map p 131.*

★★★ The Hess Collection Winery NAPA
This winery might be remote, but the drive up Mt. Veeder is an attraction unto itself. Inside, design is contemporary to match Donald Hess' museum-quality art collection on the upper levels of the 1903 stone winery (formerly Christian Brothers). Downstairs is a dramatic tasting room with a maple bar, over which patrons taste internationally influenced wines, like the ones in the New World collection, produced with sustainable farming methods. In the wine store, French oak barrels line the walls. The concierge room provides tourist info and a phone for reservations. *4411 Redwood Rd., Napa.* ☎ *877/707-4377. www.hesscollection.com. Daily 10am–4pm (closed major holidays). Free self-guided art tours all day. Tastings: $10–$25. Hwy. 101 N. to Hwy. 29 N. Exit Trancas St./Redwood Rd. Map p 130.*

Honig Vineyard & Winery NAPA
In addition to its normal winery tours, Honig hosts educational eco-walks through the vineyard to see the winery's sustainable agriculture methods: bat boxes, beehives, row management, and so on. Guides talk about trellising, pruning, growth cycles, and organic pest prevention. It's followed by wine tasting in the tasting room or on the patio. This midsize, family-run winery's award-winning sauvignon blanc and cabernet are handcrafted and blended. *850 Rutherford Rd., Rutherford.* ☎ *707/ 963-5618. www.honigwine.com. Daily 10am–4pm. Tours ($20–$35) by*

The tasting room counter at Hess Collection Winery.

appointment. Tastings: $10–$20 by appointment. Hwy. 29 N., turn right on Rutherford Rd. Map p 130.

★★ Hop Kiln Winery SONOMA

The distinctive and old-fashioned Hop Kiln structure is a California Historical Landmark. Built by Italians in 1905 as a hop-drying barn, its three stone kilns point skyward, making this winery unmistakable. Its ranchlike Western feel permeates the grounds, whether you're savoring free tastings in the rustic tasting room or picnicking at Old Fig Garden or Duck Pond. Notable vintages include the 2005 Thousand Flowers (a citrus-flavored blend) and the 2004 Big Red (a lush confluence of cabernet sauvignon, pinot noir, and Valdiguié). *6050 Westside Rd., Healdsburg.* ☎ *707/433-6491. www.hopkilnwinery.com. Daily 10am–5pm. No tours. Tastings free. Hwy. 101 N. Exit at Central Healdsburg, then left on Mill St./Westside Rd. Map p 131.*

Huntington SONOMA   One of

Healdsburg's newer tasting rooms, Huntington isn't far from the town plaza. Over its wooden bar in a historic building, whites and reds go glass to mouth. Try the gold-winning 2001 Russian River Valley Chardonnay. *53 Front St., Healdsburg.* ☎ *707/433-5215. www.huntington wine.com. Thurs–Sun 11am–5pm. No Tours. Tastings free. Hwy. 101 N. Exit & right on Healdsburg Ave., then right on Front St. Map p 131.*

★ Imagery Estate Winery & Art Gallery SONOMA   This is a

winery for art lovers; each bottle label is a tiny version of an original painting, commissioned specifically for the wine it hugs. Each must somehow include Benziger Estate's Parthenon replica (Imagery is Benziger's sister winery and its winemaker is Joe Benziger). A curated collection of more than 175 artworks hangs in Imagery's gallery, a testament to the variety of small, uncommon lots (like malbec, petite sirah, and Viognier) produced here. There's a patio, a picnic lawn, and a bocce ball court. *14335 Hwy. 12, Glen Ellen.* ☎ *707/935-4515. www. imagerywinery.com. Daily 10am–4:30pm (weekends & Memorial Day to Labor Day open until 5:30pm). No tours. Tastings: $5–$10. Map p 132.*

★ Jordan Vineyard & Winery

For the ultimate in classic, refined wine country opulence—with a serious and stately tour and tasting to match—make a reservation to visit Jordan's stunning estate. Inspired by the grand châteaux of southwestern France, owner and oil magnate Tom Jordan's vine-covered winery was founded in 1972. Only a small portion of the property, which spans more than 1,500 acres (600 hectares), is committed to cabernet sauvignon, merlot, and chardonnay vines. Though you may stop by to purchase wine Monday through Saturday, you must make a reservation to take the tour, during which you'll see that literally every detail is attended to here—from the winery construction to the way the beautiful and shiny stainless steel tanks line the fermentation room, to the seating under great oak trees on the patio, to the manicured grounds. Raucous revelers may want to skip this one, as the vibe here is composed and sophisticated. But those who want to feel a bit of the wine country high life *and* enjoy some darn tasty chardonnay and cabernet sauvignon should detour here and take the complimentary tour, which ends with a tasting in the formal library—where you'll also catch glimpses of Tom's wife Sandra's elegant and expensive home and entertaining products, which are available for sale. *1474 Alexander Valley Rd., Healdsburg.* ☎ *800/654-1213 or 707/431-5250. www.jordanwinery. com. Open Mon–Fri 8am–5pm, Sat 9am–4pm. From Hwy. 101, take Dry Creek Rd. exit & turn left at 2nd traffic*

Spring mustard blooms in the vineyard at Joseph Phelps.

light onto Healdsburg Ave.; go 2 miles and turn right onto Alexander Valley Rd.; go 1½ miles, then turn right to enter the estate. Map p 131.

Joseph Phelps Vineyards NAPA

This state-of-the-art winery is a favorite stop for serious wine lovers. Tastings and seminars include blending, smelling, or a wine history lesson. For a quicker experience, taste Joseph Phelps' fabulous flagship wine, Insignia, on the terrace. *200 Taplin Rd. (off the Silverado Trail), St. Helena.* ☎ *800/707-5789. www.jpv wines.com. Tastings & seminars: $20–$30 by appointment. Mon–Fri 9am–5pm; Sat–Sun 10am–4pm. Map p 130.*

Kaz Vineyard & Winery

SONOMA   The philosophy at quirky Kaz is "no harm in experimenting"— and that venturesome spirit pays off in the form of some innovative wines: Sangiofranc, for example, is a blend of sangiovese and cabernet franc. One of Sonoma's smallest wineries, Kaz is exceedingly family-friendly. Its pumpkin patch, coloring books, koi pond, barnlike building, and croquet lawn ensure that kids will have fun while parents relax. The Little House is the winery's cozy on-site lodging (a stay guarantees free wine). *233 Adobe Canyon Rd., Kenwood.* ☎ *877/833-2536. www. kazwinery.com. Daily 11am–5pm. Tastings: $3. From Sonoma Hwy. N, turn right on Adobe Canyon Rd. Map p 132.*

★ Kendall-Jackson Wine Center SONOMA

There are two Kendall-Jackson hotspots: the Wine Center in Santa Rosa and a tasting room on Healdsburg Square. The Wine Center's picture-perfect manor is surrounded by gardens, including a culinary and sensory garden and a demonstration vineyard. Picnic grounds are in a 100-year-old walnut grove, but if you're hungry, consider the food-and-wine reserve tasting. At the recently remodeled Healdsburg tasting room, visitors can try any Kendall-Jackson offering, including their best: the Stature and Estate wines. *WINE CENTER: 5007 Fulton Rd., Santa Rosa.* ☎ *800/769-3649. www.kj.com. Daily 10am–5pm. Garden tours (free) daily 11am, 1 & 3pm. Tastings: $2–$18. Hwy. 101 N. West on River Rd., right on Fulton Rd. TASTING ROOM: 337 Healdsburg Ave., Healdsburg.* ☎ *707/433-7102. Daily 10am–5pm. Tastings: $2–$10. Hwy. 101 N. Exit Central Healdsburg. Map p 131.*

★ Kenwood Vineyards

SONOMA   Though known for its reds, tastings at Kenwood include an array of varietals; the 2002 Russian River Valley Reserve Chardonnay is one of its better whites. The tasting room is in one of the winery's original 1906 structures—a farmhouse, actually. The interior, of course, has been redone; it's now cozy and welcoming. *9592 Sonoma Hwy. (Hwy. 12), Kenwood.* ☎ *707/833-5891. www.kenwoodvineyards.com. Daily 10am–4:30pm. No tours. Tastings free. Hwy. 101 N. Exit at Hwy. 37, then north on Calif. 121. Map p 132.*

Kendall Jackson is one of many wineries switching to synthetic corks.

★★ Korbel Champagne Cellars

SONOMA   To see the very pretty grounds of America's oldest *méthode champenoise* champagne producer, take the tour. It starts at an old railroad station and includes the cellars and History Museum. There's also a rose garden tour, during which you'll see more than 1,000 flower varieties. The tasting room is humongous, and the sandwiches from the fancy deli are amazing. Of the wines to taste, the brut is the most popular, but the pinot grigio, a zesty cuvée, is more exclusive. Korbel is on the way to Armstrong Redwoods State Reserve, so the winery is surrounded by ancient redwoods. *13250 River Rd., Guerneville.* ☎ *707/824-7000. www.korbel.com. Daily 9am–4:30pm (May–Sept open until 5:30pm). Tours (free) daily 10am–3:45pm (call for schedule). Tastings free. Hwy. 101 N. Exit & left on River Rd. Map p 131.*

★ Kunde Estate Winery & Vineyards

SONOMA   Owned and run by fourth-generation Kundes, this winery produces estate-grown wines; a surefire bottle to take home is the 2002 Reserve Cabernet Sauvignon. The wide tasting room, in a cow-barn replica, overlooks a reflecting pool with a fountain and nicely displays the winery's century-long history on the wall behind the bar. Available to buy are Kunde's popular cabernet chocolate cherries, which are a great dessert after picnicking on the oak-surrounded grounds. *10155 Sonoma Hwy. (Hwy. 12), Kenwood.* ☎ *707/ 833-5501. www.kunde.com. Daily 10:30am–4:30pm. Tours (free) all day Fri–Sun. Tastings: $5–$10 (refunded with purchase). Map p 132.*

Ladera Vineyards

NAPA   This off-the-beaten-path winery, built in 1898 on Howell Mountain, was recently restored as a gravity-flow facility. Owner Anne Stotesbery treats visitors like personal guests and leads tours that begin in the gardens and end with tastes in the fermentation room. Ask to try the low-yield, high-quality malbec, which is tapered by a small quantity of cabernet sauvignon. *150 White Cottage Rd., Angwin.* ☎ *707/965-2445. www.laderavineyards.com. Tours & tastings (free; reservations required) Mon–Sat 10am, noon & 2pm. Call for directions. Map p 130.*

★ Ledson Winery & Vineyards

SONOMA   Known to locals as "The Castle," Ledson is memorable for its fairy-tale-like architecture, complete with regal gates and a hyper-pruned fountain courtyard. In the Gothic Normandy–style behemoth of a structure, taste handcrafted wines made from a wide range of small varietal lots at one of multiple bars. Its library and reserve wines are available only at the winery, so tote home the much-praised 1997 Estate Merlot Reserve (if you can afford it, that is: A 1.5-liter bottle sets you back $425). Hungry? There's picnic space and a gourmet market. *2355 7335 Sonoma Hwy. (Hwy. 12), Kenwood.* ☎ *707/537-3810. www. ledson.com. Daily 10am–5pm. Tours*

The tower at Korbel Champagne Cellars.

Ledson Winery is the perfect place to pull up at in your stretch limo.

(free) given upon request. Tastings: $5–$10. Hwy. 101 N. Exit at Hwy. 37, then north on Calif. 121. Map p 132.

★ Louis M. Martini Winery

NAPA   The winery's circa-1933 name notwithstanding, the drink it's best known for is cabernet sauvignon. Its whites, too, have made a name for themselves and you're likely to find gewürztraminer, pinot gris, and chardonnay among the options. Operated by third-generation Martinis (though it's now owned by Gallo), this tasting room was recently redesigned. Be sure to cap your tasting flight with the winery's 55-year-old tawny port. *254 St. Helena Hwy. (Hwy. 29), St. Helena.* ☎ *800/321-9463. www.louismartini.com. Daily 10am–4:30pm (closed major holidays). Tours daily at 11am and 2pm, $30; book 3 days in advance. Tastings free–$15. Map p 130.*

Mahoney Vineyards NAPA

Mahoney Vineyards founder Francis Mahoney helped to develop innovative ways of making pinot noir hybrids. This small winery (formerly Carneros Creek Winery), then, is known for its selection of—you got it—pinot noir. But the chardonnay and syrah here are not to be dismissed, nor are the rare older wines. The tasting room, built in 2001, has a distinctive 12-foot-high (3.6m) Arts and Crafts stained-glass window. The first Friday of each month, an evening event allows guests to partake in food-and-wine pairing, art viewing, and, most alluringly, tastings of new wine releases.

1285 Dealy Lane, Napa. ☎ *707/ 253-9463. www.mahoneyvineyards. com. Daily 10am–5pm. Tours on weekends by appt $20. Tastings: $10. Hwy. 101 N. Exit at Hwy. 37, then north on Calif. 121.*

★ Monticello Vineyards/Corley Family Napa Valley NAPA   For a

just-off-the-beaten-path experience, choose Monticello. In its grand colonial-style Jefferson House (inspired by oenophile Thomas Jefferson), the Corley family hosts comparative seminars and private tastings featuring wines that have been served in the White House. This limited-production winery is known for its cabernet, chardonnay, pinot noir, and merlot. The sheltered picnic grove is a perfect lunch spot. *4242 Big Ranch Rd., Napa.* ☎ *707/ 253-2802. www.monticellovineyards. com. Daily 10am–4pm. Tours ($15) by appointment. Tastings: $10–$25. Hwy. 29 to Oak Knoll Ave., then south on Big Ranch Rd. Map p 130.*

★★ Mumm Napa NAPA   Known

for its sparkling wines, Mumm's glass-enclosed tasting room and its terrace are the places to sample Brut Prestige, Blanc de Noirs, or Santana DVX (developed with Carlos Santana) while soaking in expansive valley views. Mumm's photography gallery includes many dramatic Ansel Adams works and rotating exhibits in long, Spanish-style hallways. Tours visit the demonstration vineyard and winery, where guides demystify *méthode champenoise. 8445 Silverado Trail,*

Take a break on the terrace at Mumm Napa.

Rows and rows of vines at Opus One.

Rutherford. 📞 *800/686-6272. www.mummnapa.com. Daily 10am–5pm. Tours (free) 10am–3pm. Tastings: $5–$14. Hwy. 101 N. Exit at Hwy. 37, then north on Calif. 121. Map p 130.*

Navillus Birney Winery & Vineyards SONOMA
This small, family-owned operation (formerly Sullivan Birney) runs a cute country-style storefront tasting room 2 miles (3.2km) from the winery. On display are artifacts documenting Glen Ellen's history and photos of authors Jack London and M. F. K. Fisher. Try the chardonnay, pinot noir, and syrah. *13647 Arnold Dr., Glen Ellen.* 📞 *707/933-8514. www.navillus birney.com. Daily 10:30am–5pm. Tastings free. From Sonoma Hwy. N., turn left onto Arnold Dr. Map p 132.*

★★ Opus One NAPA
Opus One is synonymous with sheer luxury—not surprising, given that two huge names founded it: Robert Mondavi and Baron Philip de Rothschild (d. 1988). Today, Baroness Philippine de Rothschild (Philip's daughter) and Robert Mondavi run the place—and what a place. Striking architecture blends Californian and European influences, the salon is plush and opulent, and views from the rooftop deck are unsurpassed. Though the tasting fee is steep, it comes into context when you learn that in 1981, a single case sold for $24,000. Always accessible to the average visitor is the current vintage, usually a preponderance of ripe cabernet sauvignon blended with smaller quantities of merlot, malbec, petit verdot, and cabernet franc. *7900 St. Helena Hwy., Oakville.* 📞 *707/944-9442. www.opusone winery.com. Daily 10am–4pm (closed major holidays). Tours (free, but reservations required) daily 10:30am. Tastings: $25. Hwy. 29 N. becomes Main St., then St. Helena Hwy. Map p 130.*

Paradise Ridge Winery
SONOMA This family-owned boutique winery on a hill devotes itself to art almost as ardently as it does to wine (small lots of cabernet, sauvignon blanc, and chardonnay). Among the oaks is a sculpture grove with abstract metal works. The champagne cellar houses a tribute to Kanaye Nagasawa, who produced the majority of Sonoma County wine in the late 1800s. Come for the spectacular view—you can see Point Reyes from here. *4545 Thomas Lake Harris Dr., Santa Rosa.* 📞 *707/528-9463. www.paradise ridgewinery.com. Daily 11am–5:30pm (Jan–Mar closed on weekends) by appointment. Self-guided tours only. Tastings free. Hwy. 101 N. Exit at Bicentennial Way, then merge onto Fountaingrove Pkwy. Turn left on Thomas Lake Harris Dr. Map p 131.*

★ Paraduxx Winery NAPA
This brand-new winery (opened Sept 2005) has a sunny, chic sit-down tasting room where personable wine educators pour red wine (a zinfandel-cabernet blend) into

The distinctive red at Provenance Vineyards.

stemless glasses. Also provided: local artisan foods to pair with the wine. *7257 Silverado Trail, Yountville.* ☎ *707/945-0890. www.paraduxx. com. Daily 11am–4pm. No tours. Tastings: $10–$15 by appointment. Map p 130.*

Peju Province Winery NAPA
Beautiful gardens and unique architecture are a big draw here; sculptures and fountains are featured throughout the lush grounds, while a 50-foot (15m) tower houses the tasting room. Ask the musically inclined tasting-room staff to pour samples of Peju's artisan red wines, like the summery Carignane, or opt for the food-and-wine pairing, offered only on weekdays. Though this winery stays open later than most, it gets crowded in the late afternoon, especially on weekends. *8466 St. Helena Hwy. (Hwy. 29), Rutherford.* ☎ *707/963-3600. www.peju.com. Daily 10am–6pm (closed major holidays). Self-guided*

The floor at Provenance is made entirely of old barrels.

tours only. Tastings: $7 (refunded with wine purchase). Map p 130.

★ PlumpJack Winery NAPA
This hip winery, founded in a partnership between oil heir Gordon Getty and Gavin Newsom (San Francisco's mayor), has always been progressive in its approach to winemaking: It pretty much started the trend of using screw caps instead of corks on cabernet. The full-bodied, berry-tinged 2003 PlumpJack Estate Cabernet Sauvignon is proof that the system works. The best part? PlumpJack offers reasonably priced bottles to take home. *620 Oakville Cross Rd., Oakville.* ☎ *707/945-1220. www.plumpjack.com. Daily 10am–4pm. No tours. Tastings: $5. Hwy. 101 N. Exit at Hwy. 37, then north on Calif. 121. Right on Oakville Cross Rd. Map p 130.*

Provenance Vineyards NAPA
Provenance's deep-red building matches the wines it's known for (though winemaker Tom Rinaldi does make one white, a heck of a sauvignon blanc). The well-lit, cleanly designed tasting room opened in late 2003. Be sure to look down while sipping these handcrafted wines—the floor is made entirely of recycled oak barrels. Tours include the cellar and vineyard. *1695 St. Helena Hwy. (Hwy. 29), Rutherford.* ☎ *707/968-3633. www.provenancevineyards.com. Daily 10am–4:30pm (closed major holidays). Tours ($10, including*

tasting) by appointment. Tastings: $10–$15. Map p 130.

★ Ravenswood Winery

SONOMA This family-owned winery's "no wimpy wines" slogan holds true—these bold zins pack a punch. The tasting room is less than a mile from Sonoma Plaza and tours include up-close views of the vines and barrel tasting in the cellar. *18701 Gehricke Rd., Sonoma.* ☎ *707/933-2332. www. ravenswood-wine.com. Daily 10am– 4:30pm. Tours ($10) daily at 10:30am. Tastings: $5–$15 (counts toward bottle purchase). Hwy. 101 N. Exit at Hwy. 37, then north on Calif. 121. Map p 132.*

Raymond Vineyards

NAPA The Raymonds are fifth-generation winemakers with lineage tracing them to Jacob Beringer. They founded this estate in 1971 between Rutherford and St. Helena. Taste current releases and library vintages of the winery's cabernet, zinfandel, merlot, and chardonnay. *849 Zinfandel Lane, St. Helena.* ☎ *800/525-2659. www.raymondvineyards.com. Daily 10am–4pm. Tours ($15) daily at 11am (24 hr. advance reservation required). Tastings: $5–$10. Just off Hwy. 29. Map p 130.*

Robert Craig Wine Cellars

NAPA Though Robert Craig's winery isn't open to the public, fans of his upscale mountain cabernet can visit the tasting room in downtown Napa. Call ahead to schedule a personalized sit-down tasting and get ready for wines served in restaurants of French Laundry caliber. The 2002 Mt. Veeder Cabernet Sauvignon, with its enveloping mahogany essence, promises to age uncommonly well. Weekend open houses with barrel tastings happen whenever new vintages are released. *880 Vallejo St., Napa.* ☎ *707/252-2250. www.robertcraigwine.com. Mon–Sat 11am–4pm by appointment. No tours. Tastings: $5 (credited toward wine purchase). Hwy. 29 N. Right on* Lincoln, then right on Soscol, then right on Vallejo St. Map p 130.*

★★ Robert Mondavi Winery

NAPA Robert Mondavi is Napa's most powerful winery in terms of sheer size and strength, perhaps because the man himself (Mondavi, that is) pioneered the concept of public tastings; everyone else followed. Still devoted to wine education, this mission-style complex has three tasting rooms and an array of tours, from one focusing on flavor profiling to another ending with a gourmet three course meal. Try the fumé blanc (Mondavi coined the term) and the reserve cabernet, then enjoy the rotating art exhibit or, if it's summer, a music concert (check website for schedule). *7801 St. Helena Hwy. (Hwy. 29), Oakville.* ☎ *707/226-1395. www.robert mondaviwinery.com. Daily 10am– 5pm (closed major holidays).Call for tour schedule ($20–$105; reservations required). Tastings: $5–$30. Map p 130.*

★★ Roshambo Winery + Gallery

SONOMA Roshambo's übercool tasting lounge has glass walls and great Russian River Valley views. There's also a smooth wooden ceiling and a serious modern-art collection. Roshambo was founded in 1999 by then-28-year-old Naomi Brilliant, a photographer who inherited her grandfather's vineyards. Named after the Japanese rock-paper-scissors game—they actually hold invitational tournaments—there's no

The Robert Mondavi Winery fountain.

Autumn oak trees along the Silverado Trail in Napa Valley.

denying the playful spirit here. Other silly events include Willy Wonka costume parties and Drag Brunches. With all the edgy hipness, it's easy to forget this is a winery—but don't: The inspired artisanal creations here, with names like "The Obvious" and "Imago," are definitely taste-worthy. *3000 Westside Rd., Healdsburg.* ☎ *888/525-WINE. www.roshambo winery.com. Daily 10:30am–4:30pm. No tours. Tastings free–$5. Hwy. 101 N. Exit at Central Healdsburg, then left on Mill St. (turns into Westside Rd.). Map p 131.*

★★★ **Rubicon Estate** NAPA Formerly Niebaum-Coppola, this eminent estate is still owned by the Coppola family of filmmaking fame. Every over-21 visitor pays a $25 admission fee (unless they're Napa residents), but that includes wine tasting within original 1882 sandstone walls, access to the gardens and ivy-covered château, and entry to the Centennial Museum, a loving historical tribute to wine and film. Founded in 1887 by Finnish seaman Gustave Niebaum, this remarkable winery offers five different tours, all of which highlight the property's understated glitziness. Try the winery's classics, like Blancaneaux, a Viognier-Roussanne-Marsanne blend, or Rubicon, a cabernet sauvignon–dominated claret. *1991 St. Helena Hwy., Rutherford.* ☎ *707/968-1100. www.rubiconestate.com. Daily 10am–5pm. Tours $15–$45 (call for schedule). Tastings included in $25 entrance fee. Hwy. 29 N. becomes St. Helena Hwy. Map p 130.*

St. Clement Vineyards SONOMA This winery, once owned by Charles Krug and now part of the Beringer Wine Estates, uses fruit from independent growers to make its reds and whites. The 2002 Howell Mountain Cabernet Sauvignon is among the winery's more exceptional selections, but the less-pricey 2004 Carneros Chardonnay isn't bad, either. Imbibe at the hospitality center in the New England–style Rosenbaum House, built in 1878. Relax afterward on the veranda or at picnic tables. *2867 St. Helena Hwy. (Hwy. 29), St. Helena.* ☎ *800/331-8266. www.stclement.com. Daily 10am–4pm (closed major holidays). Tours ($20) by appointment available daily at 10:30am, 12:30 & 2:30pm. Tastings: $10. Map p 130.*

★ **St. Francis Winery & Vineyards** SONOMA At the foot of Hood Mountain, this mission-style winery offers views as enjoyable as its wine. "The House of Big Reds," as it's known, offers three tasting experiences, the most expensive of which pairs reserve zins, merlots, and cabernets with chef Todd Muir's gourmet hors d'oeuvres. *100 Pythian Rd., Santa Rosa.* ☎ *800/543-7713, ext. 242. www.stfranciswinery.com. Daily 10am–5pm (closed major holidays). No tours. Tastings: $5–$20. Hwy. 12 W., then left on Pythian Rd. Map p 132.*

St. Supéry Winery NAPA Known for its Meritage whites and reds, the emphasis at St. Supéry, besides wine production, is educating visitors. Don't be put off by the Atkinson House's somewhat nondescript exterior; inside is a beautiful art gallery and informative displays (one sprays out smells of different grape varieties). Near the house, there's a demonstration vineyard and family-friendly picnic grounds. *8440 St. Helena Hwy. (Hwy. 29), Rutherford.* ☎ *800/942-0809. www.stsupery.com.*

Daily 10am–5:30pm (5pm Oct–Apr; closed major holidays). Guided wine-maker's tour Mon–Thurs ($45; self-guided tours are free). Tastings: $10–$15. Map p 130.

★★ Schramsberg Vineyards

NAPA   California Historical Landmark No. 561 earned the distinction for its founding date (1862) plus its rich history: Robert Louis Stevenson was so inspired by his 1880 visit that he included Schramsberg in "Silverado Squatters." Today, the sparkling wines are so venerable that U.S. presidents present them to foreign dignitaries. Tours feature hand-carved champagne caves housing two million bottles and culminate at a round table in the wood-paneled tasting room, where seated visitors may try Brut Rosé, J. Schram, or other vintages. *Schramsberg Rd., Calistoga.* ☎ *707/942-2414. www. schramsberg.com. Guided tour & tasting ($25) daily by appointment. End of Schramsberg Rd. on Hwy. 29. Map p 130.*

★ Schug Carneros Estate Winery

SONOMA   Founded in 1980, this family-owned winery's specialty is French-style pinot noir and chardonnay. Try them in the small tasting room, which is in a German-style timber-frame building. Afterward, picnic at tables near an herb garden, visit the duck pond, or

You are now at the House of Sebastiani.

merely take in the view; if it's clear out, try to spot Mt. Diablo in the distance. *602 Bonneau Rd., Sonoma.* ☎ *800/966-9365. www.schug winery.com. Daily 10am–5pm. Free tours by appointment. Tastings free–$5. Hwy. 101 N. Exit at Hwy. 37, then north on Calif. 121. Left on Bonneau Rd. Map p 132.*

★★ Sebastiani Vineyards & Winery

SONOMA   Sonoma's oldest family-owned winery was founded in 1904 by Samuele Sebastiani, though the vineyards have been here since 1825. At the large tasting room, try the winery's specialties: cabernet, merlot, and barbera. The grounds display examples of antique wine-making equipment, including the winery's original press. Cuneo Cottage is the estate's homey vacation rental. *Tip:* Sebastiani is 4 blocks from Sonoma Plaza, so park at the winery and walk into town, since parking can be difficult during high season. *389 4th St. E., Sonoma.* ☎ *707/933-3230. www.sebastiani.com. Daily 10am–5pm. Tours ($5–$7.50; trolley tours Fri & Sat) daily 11am–3pm. Tastings free–$18. From Broadway/Calif. 12 N., turn right on E. Napa St., then left on 4th St. E. Map p 132.*

Sebastopol Vineyards/Dutton Estates

SONOMA   Taste Sebastopol Vineyards' Russian River Valley chardonnay, pinot noir, and syrah in the Spanish-style hospitality center surrounded by palm trees. Picnic grounds available. *8757 Green Valley Rd. (at Hwy. 116), Sebastopol.* ☎ *707/829-9463. www.sebastopol vineyards.com. Thurs–Mon 11am–4pm. No tours. Tastings free–$10. Map p 131.*

★ Shafer Vineyards NAPA

Though you have to make reservations 4 to 6 weeks in advance for this 90-minute visit, it's worth it to see Shafer's cellar, cave, barrel room, and sustainably farmed vineyards and to

The striking white buildings at Sterling Vineyards.

try six Shafer wines, including the spectacular Hillside Select. The bright, intimate tasting room has a fireplace and serene vineyard views. *6154 Silverado Trail, Napa.* ☎ *707/ 944-2877. www.shafervineyards.com. Mon–Fri 9am–4pm. Tours & tasting ($25) 10am & 2pm by appointment (make reservations 4–6 weeks in advance). Map p 130.*

★ **Simi Winery** SONOMA   After encountering a UC Davis enology professor at a wine festival, Steve Reeder transferred colleges to learn how to make wine. His creations (chardonnay, cabernet, and sauvignon blanc) are the focal point of Simi's redwood-paneled tasting room. Tours include stone cellars and discussions on how Italian brothers Giuseppe and Pietro founded Simi Winery in 1876—they'd come for the Gold Rush but discovered another California treasure: grapes. For picnics, there's a grove with 70-year-old redwoods. *6275 Healdsburg Ave., Healdsburg.* ☎ *800/746-4880. www.simiwinery. com. Daily 10am–5pm. Tours ($10 adults; $5 children, includes tasting) daily 11am & 2pm. Tastings: $5–$10 (refunded with purchase). Hwy. 101 N. Exit & right at Dry Creek Rd., then left on Healdsburg Ave. Map p 131.*

★★ **Sterling Vineyards** SONOMA The most distinctive part of this recently renovated winery is the aerial gondola that takes you there, providing far-reaching views of Napa Valley. Just this alone is worth the $20 to get in ($15 if it's a winter weekday, $10 if you're under 21). Admission also includes a self-guided tour that includes wine-related art and artifacts (videos and placards provide info) and sit-down wine sampling in the impressive tasting facility. A reserve tour and tasting is $45 and includes samples of wines like the SVR (a Bordeaux blend) and reserve merlot, cabernet sauvignon, and chardonnay. *1111 Dunaweal Lane, Calistoga.* ☎ *707/ 942-3300. www.sterlingvineyards. com. Daily 10:30am–4:30pm (closed major holidays). Between Hwy. 29 & Silverado Trail. Map p 130.*

Fluffy white clouds frame a sea of Sonoma vines.

★ **Stryker Sonoma** SONOMA
Stryker Sonoma has attitude. A friendly, young attitude. It's an extension of founders Pat Stryker and Craig & Karen McDonald. You'll feel it when you arrive at this boutique winery's slatted-wood walkway, march up to the sleek and polished curved bar, gaze up at the lofted wood ceiling, order a taste of zin, and gaze out at the vines through floor-to-ceiling windows. If you tire from the view, cross the mahogany-stained cement floor and peer through the windows overlooking the barrel room below. *Note:* Stryker only sells out of its tasting room, online, and, per winemaker Tim Hardin, "to a few local restaurants we like." Like many vineyards in the Alexander Valley, you won't pay a tasting fee here. Cheers to that. *5110 Hwy. 128, Geyserville.* ☎ *707/433-1944. Fax 707/433-1948. www.strykersonoma.com. Thurs–Sun 10:30am–5pm; Mon–Wed by appointment; open daily 10:30am–5pm during harvest (Aug–Oct). Map p 131.*

★ **Sutter Home Winery** NAPA
Built in 1874 and founded as a winery in 1890, Sutter Home was bought in 1947 by the Trinchero family, who claim to have invented white zinfandel in 1973. Today, similar blush-colored wines characterize the winery's specialties. The tasting room is in the original 1874 building. The organic White Zinfandel garden, with its handsome gazebo, nurtures 125 rose species while century-old palm trees flank the manor. *277 St. Helena Hwy. (Hwy. 29), St. Helena.* ☎ *707/963-3104, ext. 4208. www.sutterhome.com. Daily 10am–5pm. Free self-guided garden tours all day. Tastings free. Map p 130.*

Tin Barn Vineyards SONOMA
Adding to the trend toward wineries self-contained in warehouses is Tin Barn, which is family-owned and eager to show off its new facility. Book the hands-on tour with

A blanket of fog rests over vineyards in Napa Valley.

winemaker Michael Lancaster, who guides visitors above massive fermenting tanks and lets them sample wines from the barrel. The no-frills, tin-topped tasting room has a metal-and-wood tasting bar, over which small lot zinfandel, cabernet, syrah, and sauvignon blanc are paired with local cheeses. *21692 8th St. No. 340, Sonoma.* ☎ *707/938-5430. www.tinbarnvineyards.com. Tours & tastings (free) daily 11am–5pm by appointment. Tours (free) daily 11am–4pm. Tastings: $2–$7.50. Hwy. 101 N. Exit at Hwy. 37, then north on Calif. 121 to 8th St. E. Map p 132.*

★ **Trefethen Vineyards** NAPA
Trefethen was designed and built in 1886 by Scottish seaman Hamden McIntyre, who also designed Far Niente, Rubicon Estate, and the Culinary Institute of America. An old-fashioned wooden gravity-flow winery helped the winery qualify for the National Register of Historic Places. In the tasting room, try Riesling, Viognier, and chardonnay. *1160 Oak Knoll Ave., Napa.* ☎ *707/255-7700. www.trefethen.com. Daily 10am–4:30pm. Free tours by appointment. Tastings: $10–$20. Hwy. 37 W., then right on Hwy. 29, then right on Oak Knoll Ave. Map p 130.*

★★ **V. Sattui Winery** NAPA   In 1885, Vittorio Sattui established his winery in San Francisco. When Prohibition was enacted, he said, "I'll

The Tuscan feel is prominent at Viansa Winery.

do nothing against the law" and shut the operation down. In 1976, his descendents wisely reopened the winery in St. Helena. In the large, festive tasting room, a fourth-generation Sattui is likely to pour your wine. V. Sattui's wines aren't sold in shops or restaurants, so stock up here on vintages like the 2005 Rosato, an interestingly dry rosé. If you buy food at the gourmet deli (lots of free nibbles to try), you can use the picnic grounds, where giant oaks provide shade and beauty. *1111 White Lane, St. Helena.* ☎ *707/963-7774. www.vsattui.com. Daily 9am–6pm (closes at 5pm Nov–Feb). Free self-guided tours all day. Tastings free. Just off Hwy. 29. Map p 130.*

Viader Vineyards and Winery NAPA   On 1,300-foot-high (390m) Howell Mountain, Delia Viader's winery affords stunning valley views from its terrace. The tasting fee includes all five of her high-end wines, including hard-to-find "V," a blend of Petit Verdot and cabernet. *1120 Deer Park Rd., St. Helena.* ☎ *707/963-3816. www.viader.com. Mon–Fri 9am–5pm. Short tours (free if you pay for a tasting) by appointment. Tastings: $15 (by appointment). From the Silverado Trail, turn east on Deer Park Rd. Map p 130.*

★★ Viansa Winery SONOMA   Founded in 1989 by Vicki and Sam Sebastiani (the winery's moniker is an amalgam of their first names), this Tuscan-style hilltop estate houses a branch of the Sonoma Valley Visitors Bureau. It also has an Italian deli that sells excellent focaccia sandwiches and tours into Viansa's underground cellars. An old-world marketplace offers comprehensive wine tastings and plenty of food samples made fresh in the *cucina*. Plus, you can buy their Italian-style varieties like the berry-flavored 2003 Lorenzo and the Sempre Avanti, a blend of four types of red grapes. *25200 Arnold Dr. (Hwy. 121), Sonoma.* ☎ *800/995-4740. www. viansa.com. Daily 10am–5pm. Tours ($5) daily 11am & 2:15pm. Tastings: $5–$20. Map p 132.*

ZD Wines NAPA   Try Abacus, the winery's best cabernet, at the wood-paneled tasting bar. Weekends offer specialized tasting experiences: On Saturdays, ZD presents a wine-and-cheese seminar, while Sundays are reserved for sensory-component tastings. Be sure to reserve both of these in advance. *8383 Silverado Trail, Rutherford.* ☎ *800/487-7757. www.zdwines.com. Daily 10am– 4:30pm. Tours $5 by appointment. Tastings: $5–$25. Map p 130.* ●

The Best of SF **in One Day**

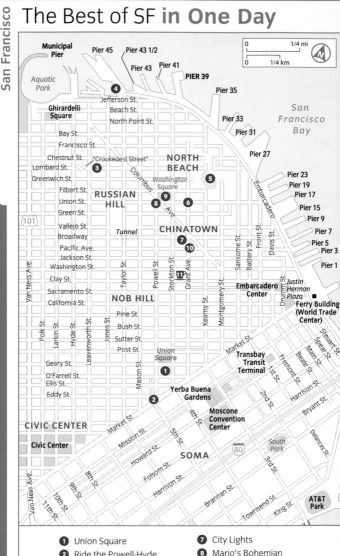

Municipal Pier

Pier 45   Pier 43 1/2

Pier 43   Pier 41

PIER 39

Aquatic Park

Pier 35

Jefferson St.

Ghirardelli Square

Beach St.

North Point St.

Pier 33

San Francisco Bay

Pier 31

Bay St.

Francisco St.

Pier 27

Chestnut St.   "Crookedest Street"

NORTH BEACH

Lombard St.

Greenwich St.

Washington Square

Pier 23

Filbert St.

RUSSIAN HILL

Pier 19

Pier 17

Union St.

Green St.

Pier 15

(101)

Vallejo St.

Tunnel

Pier 9

Broadway

CHINATOWN

Pier 7

Pacific Ave.

Pier 5

Jackson St.

Pier 3

Washington St.

Pier 1

Clay St.

Justin Herman Plaza

Sacramento St.

Embarcadero Center

Ferry Building (World Trade Center)

California St.

NOB HILL

Pine St.

Bush St.

Sutter St.

Post St.

Union Square

Geary St.

Transbay Transit Terminal

O'Farrell St.

Ellis St.

Eddy St.

Yerba Buena Gardens

CIVIC CENTER

Moscone Convention Center

South Park

Civic Center

Market St.

Mission St.

(80)

SOMA

Howard St.

Folsom St.

Harrison St.

Brannan St.

AT&T Park

Townsend St.

King St.

❶ Union Square	❼ City Lights
❷ Ride the Powell-Hyde Cable Car	❽ Mario's Bohemian Cigar Store
❸ Lombard Street	❾ Washington Square Park
❹ Fisherman's Wharf	❿ Chinatown
❺ Coit Tower	🄫 Golden Gate Fortune Cookie Factory
❻ North Beach	

San Francisco has rightly earned its reputation as America's most beautiful city. This first full-day tour introduces you to its best-known neighborhoods: charming Union Square, bustling Fisherman's Wharf, lively North Beach, and fascinating Chinatown. After arriving at Fisherman's Wharf, you can do the rest on foot—but public transportation options are listed just in case. START: **BART/Muni: Powell or Montgomery. Bus: 2, 3, 4, or 38 to Powell St.; 30 or 45 to Geary St. Cable car: Powell lines.**

① ★★ **Union Square.** Start your tour at this hub of San Francisco. The square itself (named for a series of uproarious pro-Union mass demonstrations staged here on the eve of the Civil War) reopened in 2002 after a $25-million restoration that replaced stretches of lawn with a 245-foot-long (74m) granite floor and scattered greenery, turning it into a welcoming and memorable plaza. All that remains from the old square is the 90-foot (27m) Victory Tower, dedicated by Theodore Roosevelt after the Spanish-American War. During the holidays, the square gets decked out with thousands of twinkling adornments, including a colossal Christmas tree. ⏲ *30 min.; best before 9am. Union Sq. is between Post, Geary, Stockton & Powell sts. BART: Powell or Montgomery. Bus: 2, 3, 4, or 38 to Powell St.; 30 or 45 to Geary St. Cable car: Powell lines.*

② ★ kids **Ride the Powell-Hyde Cable Car.** Head to the cable-car turnaround at Powell and Market streets and await the Powell-Hyde line. The first of these engineless cars made its maiden voyage in 1873. As the cable car takes you over Russian Hill, pay attention as you crest Hyde Street at Greenwich Street—you'll catch your first breathtaking glimpse of the San Francisco Bay and Alcatraz Island. ⏲ *30 min.; best before 9:30am. Powell & Market sts. $5 per ride. In winter, wear a jacket; trolleys are open-air.*

③ ★ **Lombard Street.** "The crookedest street in the world" is in fact not even the crookedest street in San Francisco (Vermont St. between 20th and 22nd sts. in Potrero Hill is curvier). Zigzags were added in the 1920s because the street's 27-degree pitch was too steep for automobiles. Cars are permitted only to descend, but pedestrians can take the stairs up or down on either side. The street is loveliest in spring, when the hydrangeas are in bloom. ⏲ *30 min.; best weekday mornings. Lombard St. (between Hyde & Leavenworth sts.). Cable car: Powell-Hyde line.*

Riding a cable car is one of San Francisco's most entertaining activities.

④ ★★ Fisherman's Wharf. San Francisco's most visited destination has history and lots to do. Although much of the wharf is rife with tacky souvenir shops and overpriced restaurants, this is still a must-see. Consider the following mini-tour; it highlights the wharf's most scenic spots and keeps time near the throngs to a minimum. *Hyde & Beach sts. www.fishermanswharf.org. Cable car: Powell-Hyde line to Fisherman's Wharf, Powell-Mason line to Taylor & Bay sts.; F streetcar to Jones & Beach sts. Bus 10, 30, or 47 to Van Ness Ave. & N. Point St.; 19 to Polk & Beach sts.*

④A Victorian Park is where you'll alight from the cable car. You'll see arts and crafts for sale as you walk toward **④B Ghirardelli Square,** built in 1893 as Domingo Ghirardelli's chocolate factory. When the factory relocated in the 1960s, the building became a National Historic Landmark and now houses a shopping center and eateries. **④C The Maritime Museum,** a three-story Art Deco structure shaped like an ocean liner, offers a free look at the city's seafaring past. A walk along the **④D Municipal Pier** affords views of the Golden Gate Bridge. **④E Hyde Street Pier** berths refurbished antique ships, including a 19th-century square-rigger. **④F The Cannery,** once a fruit-canning facility, now houses shops, restaurants, and the National Maritime Visitors Center. **④G Order a crepe** from the cart in the Cannery courtyard. Now fortified, you can brave the crowds at **④H Pier 39.** The vocal sea lions at the end of the pier are a sight to see. ⏱ *2–3 hr.; go in the morning to beat the crowds, and bring a jacket.*

Pier 39's sea lions bathe, bark, and splash about—all around heart-melting fun.

⑤ Coit Tower. The 210-foot (63m) landmark atop Telegraph Hill was erected in 1933 with $125,000 bequeathed by local character Lillie Hitchcock Coit, who wished to add beauty to the city. Inside the tower's base are murals by several artists, many of whom studied under Diego Rivera. Commissioned as part of the New Deal's WPA, the murals have a pro-worker motif that caused a stir in their day. The fee to ascend the tower is worth it: A 360-degree city view awaits. While on Telegraph Hill, look for the flock of wild green parrots, descendents of escapee pets. ⏱ *45 min. From Fisherman's wharf, walk or take bus 39 to Coit Tower.* ☎ *415/362-0808. Admission to the top $3.75, $2.50 seniors, $1.50 kids 6–12. Daily 10am–6pm.*

⑥ ★★ North Beach. Immigrants from Genoa and Sicily who founded the Bay Area's fishing industry settled here in the 1870s, establishing a variety of Italian restaurants, cafes, bakeries, and bars. In the 1950s, these spots became havens for some of the era's most influential writers and artists. Today, the neighborhood is a combination of Mediterranean warmth and lively bohemian spirit. Don't miss the famous **⑦ City Lights Booksellers & Publishers** (at 261 Columbus Ave.), an intimate tribute to Beat literature. ⏱ *1–2 hr. Walk from Coit Tower, or take bus 39 to Washington Sq. Best Mon–Sat from 11am–4pm. Shops are closed Sun and early mornings.*

⑧ Mario's Bohemian Cigar Store Café. Pick up sandwiches and enjoy them in **⑨ Washington Square Park** across the street. *566 Columbus Ave. (at Union St.).* ☎ *415/362-0536. $.*

⑩ ★ Chinatown. San Francisco's most densely populated neighborhood is home to more than 14,000 people. Walk down Grant Street to find shops filled with eclectic knick-knacks. Chinatown locals shop on Stockton Street, which teems with grocery stores, herb shops, and vendors of ceremonial items. At 56 Ross Alley (between Washington and Jackson sts.) is **⑪ ★★ Golden Gate Fortune Cookie Factory,** a delightful hidden treasure where you can sample and buy prophetic confections. ⏱ *1–2 hr.*

Coit Tower crowns Telegraph Hill.

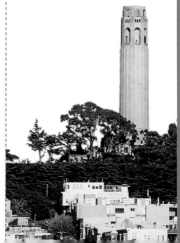

The Best of SF **in Two Days**

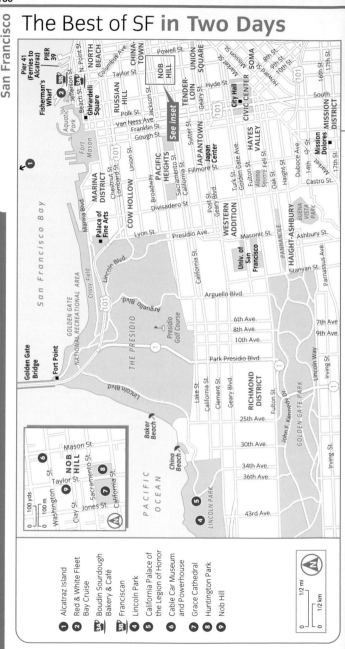

- **1** Alcatraz Island
- **2** Red & White Fleet Bay Cruise
- **3** Boudin Sourdough Bakery & Café
- **4** Franciscan
- **5** Lincoln Park
- **6** California Palace of the Legion of Honor
- **7** Cable Car Museum and Powerhouse
- **8** Grace Cathedral
- **9** Huntington Park
- **9** Nob Hill

If you have 2 days, plan your first day as detailed on p 162. For your second day, start with a major highlight—a visit to Alcatraz. Pre-reserved tickets are required, but if you didn't plan ahead, an alternative bay cruise is listed below. After Alcatraz (or the cruise), visit Lincoln Park, a less-visited but still striking corner of San Francisco, and get a taste of 19th-century San Francisco on Nob Hill.

START: **Pier 41, Fisherman's Wharf. Cable car: Powell-Mason. Bus: 30. Streetcar: F.**

1 ★★★ **Alcatraz Island.** Spanish for "pelican," Alcatraz was so named in 1775 by Juan Manuel Ayala for the birds nesting on its rocky shores. From the 1850s to 1933, the U.S. military used Alcatraz as a fort to protect the bay and its shoreline. In 1934, the government converted the island to a maximum-security prison for the country's most hardened criminals, including Al Capone, "Machine Gun" Kelly, and Robert "The Birdman" Stroud. Given its sheer cliffs, frigid waters, and treacherous currents, Alcatraz was considered inescapable. However, the prison's upkeep cost a fortune; all supplies had to come by boat. After three convicted bank robbers (Frank Lee Morris and brothers Clarence and John Anglin) escaped in 1962 using sharpened spoons and a makeshift raft, the prison closed. The island remained unoccupied until 1969, when Native Americans took it over, bringing their civil rights issues to the forefront. They were removed in 1971, but not before Congress passed more than 50 legislative proposals supporting tribal self-rule. Today, the National Park Service manages Alcatraz. Once inside, you'll receive a headset that plays an audio tour that includes riveting tales from former guards and inmates. From October to mid-February, you can tour the island on a walking path. For an eerie evening experience, take the "Alcatraz After Hours" tour. ⏱ *2–3 hr., including ferry ride. Take the 1st ferry of the day, if possible. Wear a jacket & walking shoes; it's an uphill walk from the ferry landing to the cellblock (motorized carts carry visitors with disabilities). The ferry sells snacks, but there's no food on the island. Pier 41, Fisherman's Wharf.* ☎ *415/773-1188 for information, or 415/705-5555 to reserve tickets. www.nps.gov/alcatraz. Note: It's recommended to buy a ticket that includes the audio tour. Admission (ferry & audio tour): $16.50, $14.75 seniors 62+, $10.75 kids 5–11. Without audio tour: $12, $9.75 seniors,*

Alcatraz Island is in the middle of San Francisco Bay.

Grab a bite of fresh Dungeness crab at the Fisherman's Wharf.

$8.25 kids 5–11. Winter daily 9:30am–2:15pm; summer daily 9:30am–4:15pm. Ferries run every half-hour. Arrive 30 min. before departure in summer (45 min. in winter). After-hours tours depart at 6:15 & 7pm in summer; 4:20 & 5:10pm in winter. Bus: 30. Cable car: Powell-Mason line. Streetcar: F.

2 kids ★ **Red & White Fleet Bay Cruise.** If you were unable to pre-reserve Alcatraz tickets, take this 1-hour bay cruise (named after Stanford University's school colors) with audio narration. You'll travel under the Golden Gate Bridge and around Alcatraz. 🕐 1 hr. Pier 43½. ☎ 415/673-2900. www.redand white.com. Ferry ride & audio tour: $21, $17 seniors 62+ & kids 12–17, $13 kids 5–11, kids under 5 free. Check the website for discount fares. Transport: see bullet **1**.

3A No SF visit's complete without trying the city's famous bread; taste it at ★ kids **Boudin Sourdough Bakery & Café.** 160 Jefferson St. ☎ 415/928-1849. $. For a sit-down meal with a view, opt for **3B** **Franciscan Pier.** 43½. ☎ 415/362-7733. $$$.

4 **Lincoln Park.** This lovely park in San Francisco's northwest corner boasts expansive lawns, eucalyptus trees, an 18-hole golf course, and breathtaking views. Walk north to the Land's End trail head for a closer look at the Marin Headlands and a western profile of the Golden Gate Bridge. 🕐 30 min.; best in the afternoon, when fog has burned off & the sun makes the Marin hills appear golden. Clement Ave. & 33rd Ave. Powell-Hyde cable car to Geary St., transfer to bus 38 to Geary Blvd. & 33rd Ave.; then walk or take bus 18 to Legion of Honor.

5 ★★ **California Palace of the Legion of Honor.** Adding to Lincoln Park's splendor is this neoclassical memorial to Californian soldiers who died in World War I. This exact replica of Paris' Legion of Honor Palace opened on Armistice Day in 1924. Its fine-art collection spans 4,000 years and includes paintings by Monet and Rembrandt, plus international tapestries, prints, and drawings. There's also an excellent collection of Rodin sculptures, including an original cast of *The Thinker*. 🕐 1 hr. Clement St. & 34th Ave. ☎ 415/863-3330. www.thinker.org. Admission $10, $7 seniors 65+, $6 youths 13–17, free for kids 12 and younger, free to all first Tues of each month. Tues–Sun 9:30am–5pm. Transport: see bullet **4**.

6 kids **Cable Car Museum and Powerhouse.** When British-born engineer Andrew Hallidie saw a horse and its heavy carriage fall backward down a steep San Francisco hill, he vowed to create a mechanical transportation device for the city. By 1873, the first cable car had traversed Clay Street. Cable cars have no engines; instead, they're attached to an electrically powered cable that runs at a constant 9½-mph (15kph) rate through an underground rail. When it's time to stop, the car's conductor, or "gripper," pulls a lever to release the car's grip

A view of the Transamerica building from the top of Nob Hill.

on the cable. Inside this free, fascinating museum, you'll see the cables that carry the cars. Though it once ran more than 600 cars, today's system operates only three lines. ⏱ *20 minutes. 1201 Mason St. (at Washington St.).* ☎ *415/474-1887. www.cablecarmuseum.com. Free admission. Daily 10am–5pm; until 6pm Apr–Oct. Closed major holidays. Cable car: Powell lines.*

❼ ★★ Grace Cathedral. After the Crocker mansion was destroyed by the 1906 earthquake and fires, the Crockers donated its site to the Episcopal Church; in 1964, Grace Cathedral was complete. Pay special attention to the main doors—stunning replicas of Ghiberti's bronze Doors of Paradise on the Baptistery of Florence—and the Singing Tower to the right of the main entrance, which has a 44-bell carillon. The cathedral's exterior is made of reinforced concrete beaten to achieve a stonelike effect. Inside, note the 1840 organ and the

impressive stained-glass windows, some of which depict modern figures like Justice Thurgood Marshall, poet Robert Frost (a San Francisco native), and Albert Einstein. ⏱ *25 min. 1100 California St. (at Taylor St.). www.gracecathedral.org.* ☎ *415/749-6300. Free admission. Mon–Fri 7am–6pm, Sat 8am–6pm, Sun 7am–7pm. Bus: 1. Cable car: All lines.*

❽ kids Huntington Park. David Colton, who helped build the Southern Pacific Railroad, had his mansion here until he sold it to Collis Huntington in 1892. The mansion burned as a result of the 1906 quake, and the lot lay empty for 9 years until Huntington donated it to the city. Today, the park is a lovely oasis in an urban section of town. It's still framed by the granite walls that were once part of the Colton estate. ⏱ *15 min. Taylor & California sts. Bus: 1. Cable car: All lines.*

❾ Nob Hill. This famous hillcrest neighborhood is named for its wealthy former residents, or "nabobs," as San Francisco elites were then known. The "Big Four" railroad barons of the Southern Pacific Railroad—Leland Stanford, Mark Hopkins, Charles Crocker, and Collis Huntington—built ostentatious mansions here in the late 1870s, all doomed for destruction by the fires following the 1906 quake. Today, some of the city's most prestigious hotels occupy Nob Hill. ⏱ *20 min. Taylor & Sacramento sts. Bus: 1 from Clement St. & 33rd Ave. to Taylor & Sacramento sts.*

Visit during daylight hours, though the view from the Top of the Mark (p 190), a fancy penthouse lounge, is magnificent at night.

Learn how a cable car actually works at the Cable Car Museum.

The Best of SF **in Three Days**

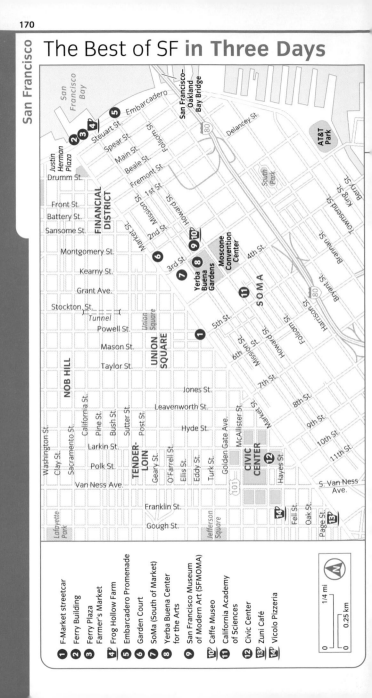

① F-Market streetcar
② Ferry Building
③ Ferry Plaza Farmer's Market
④ Frog Hollow Farm
⑤ Embarcadero Promenade
⑥ Garden Court
⑦ SoMa (South of Market)
⑧ Yerba Buena Center for the Arts
⑨ San Francisco Museum of Modern Art (SFMOMA)
⑩ Caffe Museo
⑪ California Academy of Sciences
⑫ Civic Center
⑬ Zuni Café
⑭ Vicolo Pizzeria

0 ___ 1/4 mi
0 ___ 0.25 km

If you've already made your way through "The Best in Two Days," you'll find that this third full-day tour gives you a taste of the city's epicurean underpinnings, as well as its rich artistic and cultural life. Devote an entire day for this tour. It can be done on foot, although the F-Market streetcar is an attraction unto itself. **Note:** Though the Civic Center is just a few blocks from SoMa, the east-west blocks are quite long. START: From Union Sq., hop on the F-Market streetcar at the Powell St. station; exit at the Ferry Terminal loop.

① kids **★ F-Market streetcar.** Several streetcars travel along Market Street, but the F line heads along the scenic waterfront. Its streetcars were imported from around the world, including vintage cars from Europe and turn-of-the-20th-century trolleys from other U.S. cities. 🕐 *15 min. From Union Sq., enter at the Powell St. station; exit at the Ferry Terminal loop. Fare $1.50, 50¢ seniors & kids 5–17. Free for kids under 5. Avoid rush hour (Mon–Fri, before 9:30am & 4:30–6:30pm).*

② **★★ Ferry Building.** This 1898 building reopened in 2003 after a 4-year, multimillion-dollar renovation. Outside is a 240-foot (72m) clock tower. Inside, a collection of restaurants and gourmet stores offers specialty foods. Make your way to the back of the building for a view of the Bay Bridge. Try to visit on a **Farmer's**

Take a ride on a vintage F-market streetcar.

Market day (see bullet **③** and p 187). 🕐 *1 hr. 1 Ferry Building (at the Embarcadero & Market St.). Minimum hours: Mon–Fri 10am–6pm; Sat 9am–6pm; Sun 11am–5pm (hours for individual businesses may vary). www.ferrybuildingmarketplace.com. F or any Market St. streetcar to the Ferry Bldg. or Embarcadero; bus 2, 7, 14, 21, 66, or 71 to Steuart & Market sts. Also see p 187.*

③ **★★★ Ferry Plaza Farmers Market.** Tuesdays and Saturdays (and from spring to fall, Thurs and Sun too), local farmers and food producers set up booths around the Ferry Building. Saturday mornings are busiest, as locals make their regular trek to stock up on organic fruits and vegetables, fresh-baked goods, and other gustatory delights. Saturdays also feature trailer cars out back, from which city restaurants serve gourmet breakfasts. Given the penchant for using local, organic, and naturally grown produce at many San Francisco restaurants—not to mention homes—this market is a hallmark of city life. 🕐 *1 hr. 1 Ferry Building (at the Embarcadero & Market St.).* ☎ *415/291-3276. Tues & Sun 10am–2pm; Sat 8am–2pm; Thurs 4–8pm. Also see p 187.*

④ **Frog Hollow Farm.** Grab coffee and a fruit-filled pastry here before strolling the scenic waterfront. *Ferry Building Marketplace.* ☎ *415/445-0990. $.*

The ceiling of the Garden Court is a glittering masterpiece of glass.

⑤ ★ Embarcadero Promenade. The 1989 Loma Prieta earthquake encouraged city leaders to decommission the ugly elevated freeway that once obscured this lovely stretch of waterfront that extends from AT&T Park to Fisherman's Wharf. The wide sidewalk and scenic views make this a favored destination for pedestrians, bikers, and joggers. Notice the Embarcadero Ribbon, a 2½-mile (4km) continuous line of glass encased in concrete. The 13-foot-tall (3.9m) metal pylons and bronze plaques embedded in the sidewalk are imprinted with photographs, drawings, poetry, and historical facts. ⏱ *30 min.–1 hr.; a walk in either direction is pleasant at any time of day, but avoid the traffic on weekday afternoons 4–6pm. Return to Market St. to catch the F-Market streetcar to the Montgomery St. station, or walk.*

⑥ Garden Court. The extravagant Palace Hotel astounded San Franciscans and bankrupted its owner, who allegedly committed suicide a day before the 1875 grand opening. Three decades later, the hotel was ravaged by one of the many fires following the 1906 earthquake. The hotel was restored and reopened in 1909, along with the magnificent Garden Court. This impressive atrium's domed ceiling is made from 80,000 glass panes and houses the Garden Court Restaurant (p 180). After absorbing Garden Court's grandeur, step into the Pied Piper Bar to glimpse the $2.5-million Maxfield Parrish painting of the same name. ⏱ *20 min. 2 New Montgomery St. (at Market St.).* ☎ *415/546-5089. Daily 6:30am–2pm; tea Sat 1–3pm. BART/Muni: Powell or Montgomery.*

⑦ ★★ SoMa (South of Market). This former industrial area south of Market Street has become a major center for art and entertainment, museums, galleries, and major-league baseball. ⏱ *2–4 hr. to stroll through the neighborhood; visit during daylight hours. Note: SFMOMA (see bullet ⑨) is closed Wed.*

⑧ ★ kids Yerba Buena Center for the Arts is SoMa's cultural anchor. It serves as a major arts-and-entertainment center, with cultural programs, oasis-like gardens, and recreational facilities. Pay tribute at the **Martin Luther King Jr. Memorial** and its 50-foot (15m) waterfall, or see a movie at the **Sony Metreon Entertainment Center.** *Best time: daylight hours.* ⏲ *1 hr. 101 4th St.* ☎ *415/978-2787. www.ybca.org* ⏲ *1–3 hr. Between 3rd, 4th, Mission & Folsom sts.*

⑨ ★★★ San Francisco Museum of Modern Art (SFMOMA). In 1995, SFMOMA moved into its $62-million home designed by architect Mario Botta. Its permanent collection includes more than 15,000 works by the likes of Henri Matisse, Jackson Pollock, and Georgia O'Keeffe. The first major museum to have recognized photography as an art form, SFMOMA also exhibits the works of Ansel Adams, Man Ray, and others. Not enough of the permanent collection is on display at any one time, but temporary exhibits are usually superb. ⏲ *1½ hr. 151 3rd St. (between Mission & Howard sts.).* ☎ *415/357-4000. www.sfmoma.org. Admission $12.50, $8 seniors 62+, $7 students with ID, free for kids under 13. Half price Thurs 6–9pm. Free to all 1st Tues of the month. Thurs 11am–8:45pm; Fri–Tues 11am–5:45pm. Closed Wed & major holidays. Opens at 10am in summer. Bus: 15, 30, 45. BART/Muni: Montgomery St. Best time: weekdays.*

🔟 Caffe Museo. SFMOMA's on-site cafe has excellent soups, sandwiches, and salads. *151 3rd St.* ☎ *415/357-4500. $.*

SFMOMA's skylight is just one of the museum's architectural highlights.

⑪ ★ kids California Academy of Sciences. The country's fourth-largest natural-history museum will be in SoMa until 2008 while a new facility is built in Golden Gate Park. The temporary location is not as expansive as its old home, but does include terrific exhibits, fascinating animal life in the Steinhart Aquarium, and twice-daily narrated penguin feedings. ⏲ *1–2 hr.; weekday afternoons are best, as mornings are full with school tours. 875 Howard St. (at 5th St.).* ☎ *415/321-8000. www.calacademy.org. Admission $7, $4.50 seniors & kids 12–17 & students, $2 kids 4–11, free for kids under 3, free for all the 1st Wed of the month. Daily 10am–5pm.*

⑫ ★ Civic Center. Less than a decade after the 1906 earthquake destroyed SF's original City Hall, architect Arthur Brown erected a lavish Beaux Arts–style administrative and cultural center to take its place. Buildings here include extravagant City Hall itself, topped with a 308-foot-tall (92m) dome; the 376,000-square-foot (35,000-sq.-m) main public library; the Asian Art Museum, recently transformed by the architect who did France's Musée d'Orsay; and the War Memorial Opera House, where the 1951 U.S.-Japan peace accord was signed. ⏲ *1 hr. Most Civic Center buildings are bordered by Hayes, Franklin & Hyde sts. & Golden Gate Ave. Best time: weekdays during daylight hours.*

⑬ Zuni Café. Splurge on dinner at an SF institution, one of the first purveyors of innovative California cuisine. *1658 Market St.* ☎ *415/552-2522. $$$.* For a delicious (and cheaper) alternative, head to **⑭ Vicolo Pizzeria,** an alley-side gem serving memorable corn-meal-crust pizzas. *150 Ivy Alley.* ☎ *415/863-2382. $.*

San Francisco **Lodging & Dining**

DINING ●

A16 **7**
Aqua **16**
Boogaloos **37**
Boulevard **13**
Chez Papa **36**
Cliff House **43**
Dottie's True Blue Café **30**
Fifth Floor **32**
Fleur de Lys **27**
Foreign Cinema **37**

Garden Court Restaurant **34**
Gary Danko **6**
Ghirardelli Soda Fountain &
  Chocolate Shop **5**
Greens **2**
Hawthorne Lane **35**
Indian Oven **40**
Jardiniere **38**
Kokkari **10**
L'Osteria del Forno **8**
Michael Mina **25**

Millennium **29**
Mitchell's Ice Cream **37**
Moose's **9**
One Market **13**
Postrio **28**
Quince **44**
The Slanted Door **11**
Suppenküche **39**
Tacqueria Pancho Villa **37**
BERKELEY INSET
Chez Panisse **1**

Berkeley

LODGING ■

Adagio **29**

The Archbishop's Mansion **42**

The Argonaut **3**

Campton Place Hotel **22**

Clift Hotel **28**

Fairmont Hotel **17**

Four Seasons **33**

The Huntington Hotel **18**

The Hotel Majestic **44**

Hyatt at Fisherman's Wharf **4**

Hyatt Regency San Francisco **12**

InterContinental
  Mark Hopkins **19**

King George Hotel **26**

Mandarin Oriental **16**

Monticello Inn **31**

The Palace Hotel **24**

Ritz-Carlton **20**

Red Victorian **41**

Sir Francis Drake **23**

Hotel Triton **21**

W San Francisco **35**

Westin St. Francis **24**

Lodging A to Z

★ **Adagio** UNION SQUARE This newish property offers sleek charm for a good price. Double queen rooms are a great deal for families. The in-house Cortez restaurant shines. *550 Geary St. (between Jones & Taylor sts.).* ☎ *800/ 228-8830 or 415/775-5000. www. thehoteladagio.com. 173 units. Doubles from $185. AE, DC, DISC, MC, V. Bus: 2, 3, 4, 38. BART/Muni: Powell St. Map p 174.*

★★ **The Archbishop's Mansion** CIVIC CENTER Built in 1904 for SF's archbishop, this flamboyantly decorated mansion is SF's most romantic B&B. *1000 Fulton St. (at Steiner St.).* ☎ *800/543-5820 or 415/563-7872. www.thearchbishops mansion.com. 15 units. Doubles $145–$355 w/breakfast. AE, DC, DISC, MC, V. Bus: 5, 22. Map p 174.*

★★ **kids The Argonaut** FISHERMAN'S WHARF The beautifully restored 1907 building in the Maritime National Historical Park has vibrant nautical-themed decor, a great location, and some bay views. Best choice at the wharf. *495 Jefferson St. (corner of Jefferson & Hyde sts.).* ☎ *866/415-0704. www. argonauthotel.com. 252 units. Doubles $179–$329. AE, DC, MC, V. Bus: 10, 30. Cable car: Powell-Hyde. Map p 174.*

★★ **Campton Place Hotel** UNION SQUARE The epitome of refined opulence and exclusivity. Bathrooms, with Portuguese limestone and deep soaking tubs, are a dream. *340 Stockton St. (between Post & Sutter sts.).* ☎ *800/234-4300 or 415/781-5555. www.campton place.com. 110 units. Doubles $345–$475. AE, DC, DISC, MC, V. Bus: 2, 3, 4. BART/Muni: Montgomery St. Cable car: Powell lines. Map p 174.*

★ **Clift Hotel** UNION SQUARE Hotelier Ian Schrager and designer Philippe Starck created this überhip hotel with modern furnishings and a cool attitude. Most rooms scream minimalism, and bathrooms are stylish but small. The gorgeous Redwood Room is a hopping lounge (p 190). *495 Geary St. (at Taylor St.).* ☎ *800/652-5438 or 415/775-4700. www.clifthotel.com. 389 units. Doubles $295–$355. AE, DC, DISC, MC, V. Bus: 2, 3, 4, 27, 38. Map p 174.*

★★★ **The Fairmont** NOB HILL This 1907 landmark's exterior makes an immediate impression. A recent $85-million restoration recaptured architect Julia Morgan's (of Hearst Castle fame) original design. The Fairmont is where U.S. presidents stay, and where the UN charter was drafted in 1945. For great views, opt for the Tower Building. *950 Mason St. (at California St.).* ☎ *800/ 441-1414 or 415/772-5000. www. fairmont.com. 591 units. Doubles $229–$499. AE, DC, DISC, MC, V. Bus: 1. Cable car: All. Map p 174.*

Muted, pale colors infuse a tranquil vibe at the ultratrendy Clift hotel.

The ultrahip Triton comes with Friday-night freebies like wine parties and chair massages.

★★★ Four Seasons SOMA

This divinely luxurious hotel has plush furnishings and large marble bathrooms. Impeccable service and access to the massive Sports Club/LA add to the wonders. *757 Market St. (at 3rd St.). ☎ 415/633-3000. www.fourseasons. com. 277 units. Doubles begin at $415. AE, DC, DISC, MC, V. BART/Muni: Montgomery St. Map p 174.*

★★ Hotel Majestic PACIFIC

HEIGHTS Ornately furnished with European antiques, the Majestic is an escape from the rough edges of modern living. *1500 Sutter St. (between Octavia & Gough sts.). ☎ 800/869-8966 or 415/922-3200. www.thehotelmajestic.com. 58 units. Doubles $200 w/breakfast. AE, DC, DISC, MC, V. Bus: 2, 3, 4. Map p 174.*

★ Hotel Triton UNION SQUARE

A rock-themed hotel with Wi-Fi-equipped suites designed by famous musicians, eco-friendly floors, and free Friday-night wine parties with tarot-card readings and chair massages. Rooms are tiny. *342 Grant Ave. (at Bush St.). ☎ 800/433-6611 or 415/394-0500. www.hoteltriton.com. 140 units. Doubles $149–$189. AE, DC, DISC, MC, V. Bus: 2, 3, 4, 15, 30. BART/Muni: Montgomery St. Map p 174.*

★★★ The Huntington Hotel & Nob Hill Spa NOB HILL

A discreet but very upscale Nob Hill choice. Rooms are sizable and seven suites have kitchens. The hotel's spa is magnificent. *1075 California St. (at Powell St.). ☎ 800/227-4683 or 415/474-5400. www.huntingtonhotel.com. 135 units. Doubles $315–$375. AE, DC, DISC, MC, V. Bus: 1. Cable car: All. Map p 174.*

kids Hyatt at Fisherman's Wharf FISHERMAN'S WHARF

Best of the wharf chain hotels. All rooms were recently renovated to create a clean, contemporary look. There's new luxury beds, an outdoor pool, and a sports-bar-like restaurant. *555 N. Point St. (between Jones & Taylor sts.). ☎ 415/563-1234. www.fishermanswharf.hyatt.com. 313 units. Doubles $168–$268. AE, DC, DISC, MC, V. Bus: 10, 30. Streetcar: F. Map p 174.*

★ Hyatt Regency San Francisco FINANCIAL DISTRICT

This corporate hotel has a 17-story atrium, spacious rooms, some fine views, the Embarcadero Center next door, and the Ferry Building across the street. *5 Embarcadero Center (at Market St. by The Embarcadero). ☎ 800/233-1234 or 415/788-1234. www.sanfranciscoregency.hyatt.com. 802 units. Doubles $179–$349. AE, DC, DISC, MC, V. BART/Muni: Embarcadero. Map p 174.*

★★★ InterContinental Mark Hopkins NOB HILL

Plush rooms have stellar views and the Top of Mark sky-lounge is a stunning place to dine. An extra $50 per day grants access to the club lounge and free food. *1 Nob Hill (at Mason & California sts.). ☎ 800/327-0200 or 415/392-3434. www.san-francisco.intercontinental.com. 380 units. Doubles $209–$329. AE, DC, DISC, MC, V. Bus: 1. Cable car: All. Map p 174.*

San Francisco

King George Hotel UNION SQUARE Popular with European tourists, this 1912 hotel offers modern amenities and handsome, albeit petite, rooms. On weekends and holidays, English afternoon tea is served in the hotel's Windsor Tea Room. *334 Mason St. (between Geary & O'Farrell sts.).* ☎ *800/288-6005 or 415/781-5050. www.kinggeorge.com. 152 units. Doubles $109–$179. AE, DC, DISC, MC, V. Bus: 2, 3, 4, 38. Cable car: Powell lines. BART/Muni: Powell St. Map p 174.*

★★★ **Mandarin Oriental** FINANCIAL DISTRICT Atop SF's third-tallest building, the Mandarin affords jaw-dropping views. Every room was just redone to have international flavor and an oversized bed. Regal service impresses. *222 Sansome St. (between Pine & California sts.).* ☎ *800/622-0404. www.mandarinoriental.com. 158 units. Doubles $505–$735. AE, DC, DISC, MC, V. BART/Muni: Montgomery St. Cable car: California. Map p 174.*

The Mark Hopkins Hotel (p 177) sits on the site of the former mansion (destroyed in the 1906 earthquake) of Mark Hopkins, one of the founders of the Southern Pacific Railroad.

★ **Monticello Inn** UNION SQUARE A literary-themed hotel with an inviting lobby, tasteful rooms, central location, and decent (for SF) rates. *127 Ellis St. (between Powell & Mason sts.).* ☎ *800/669-7777 or 415/392-8800. www.monticelloinn.com. 91 units. Doubles $139–$309. AE, DC, DISC, MC, V. BART/Muni: Powell St. Cable car: Powell lines. Map p 174.*

★★ **The Palace Hotel** SOMA Over-the-top decor encompasses the landmark Garden Court Restaurant (p 180). Large rooms have 14-foot (4.2m) ceilings and marble bathrooms. *2 New Montgomery St. (at Market St.).* ☎ *415/512-1111. www.sfpalace.com. 552 units. Doubles $499–$539. AE, DC, DISC, MC, V. BART/Muni: Montgomery St. Map p 174.*

Red Victorian HAIGHT There should be a sign in front of this eccentric Haight-Ashbury B&B that reads, "WELCOME BACK TO 1967." Each guestroom has its own flowery theme. *1665 Haight St. (at Belvedere St.).* ☎ *415/864-1978 or 415/296-7465. www.redvic.com. 19 units (6 w/private bath). Doubles $86–$200. AE, DC, DISC, MC, V. Bus: 6, 7, 43, 66, 71. Muni: Carl & Cole. Map p 174.*

★★★ **The Ritz-Carlton** NOB HILL A recent $12.5-million face-lift upgraded every room. But new features—Wi-Fi, flat LCD TVs, 400-thread-count linens, Bvlgari toiletries—don't detract from classic ones: regal decor, 18th-century antiques, a spa and fitness center, and the exceptional Dining Room. Above all, this 1909 landmark that occupies a full city block maintains impeccable service—with prices to match. *600 Stockton St. (at California St.).* ☎ *800/241-3333 or 415/296-7465. www.ritzcarlton.com. 336 units. Doubles $495 & up. AE, DC, DISC, MC, V. Cable car: All. Map p 174.*

Sir Francis Drake UNION SQUARE Despite the grandiose lobby and beefeater-clad doormen, stay here only if you get a great deal. The tiny rooms aren't as well maintained as the lobby. It's always a party, though, at 21st-floor **Harry Denton's Starlight Lounge** (p 189). *450 Powell St. (at Sutter St.).* ☎ *800/227-5490 or 415/392-7755. www.sirfrancisdrake. com. 417 units. Doubles $239–$259. AE, DC, DISC, MC, V. Bus: 2, 3, 4. BART/Muni: Powell St. Cable car: Powell lines. Map p 174.*

★★ kids Westin St. Francis UNION SQUARE The historic "grand dame" of SF hotels, this Westin couldn't be better located; it's right on Union Square. Word is that whichever foreign flag hangs outside the hotel represents the nationality of a dignitary currently inside on a given day. *335 Powell St. (at Geary St.).* ☎ *415/397-7000. www.westin.com. 1,195 units. Doubles $129–$569. AE, DC, DISC, MC, V. Bus: 2, 3, 4, 30, 45. BART/Muni: Powell St. Cable car: Powell lines. Map p 174.*

★★ W San Francisco SOMA This ultrahip hotel next to SFMOMA has sleek rooms, great views, and 24-hour concierge service. New-agey amenities include the Bliss Spa, free poolside yoga, and XYZ restaurant. *181 3rd St. (at Howard St.).* ☎ *415/777-5300. www.whotels. com. 425 units. Doubles start at $259. AE, DC, DISC, MC, V. Bus: 15, 30, 45. BART/Muni: Montgomery St. Map p 174.*

Dining A to Z

★★ A16 MARINA *ITALIAN* A chic crowd comes for wood-fired pizza and an exciting wine list. *2355 Chestnut St. (between Scott & Divisadero sts.).* ☎ *415/771-2216. Entrees $10–$25. AE, DC, MC, V. Lunch Wed–Fri, dinner daily. Bus: 30. Map p 174.*

★★★ Aqua FINANCIAL DISTRICT *SEAFOOD* Resplendent dishes stunningly presented against an opulent backdrop. *252 California St. (between Battery & Front sts.).* ☎ *415/956-9662. Entrees $19–$25. AE, DC, DISC, MC, V. Lunch Mon–Fri, dinner nightly. BART/Muni: Embarcadero. Map p 174.*

★★ Boogaloos MISSION *LATIN* A well-loved brunch cafe with funky mosaic decor and a long wait. *3296 22nd St. (at Valencia St.).* ☎ *415/824-4088. Entrees $4.50–$9.50. DISC, MC, V. Breakfast & lunch daily. BART: 24th St. Mission Station. Map p 174.*

★★★ Boulevard SOMA *AMERICAN* A seasonal globally influenced menu and industrial Belle Epoque decor. *1 Mission St. (at Steuart St.).* ☎ *415/543-6084. Entrees $14–$38. AE, DC, DISC, MC, V. Lunch Mon–Fri, dinner daily. Bus: 12. BART/Muni: Embarcadero. Map p 174.*

Chez Panisse BERKELEY *CALIFORNIA* The famous Alice Water's restaurant still delivers a changing menu with fresh ingredients—the definition of California cuisine (see box p 182). *1517 Shattuck Ave. (between Cedar & Vine sts.).* ☎ *510/548-5525. Entrees $50–$75 (prix-fixe). AE, DC, DISC, MC, V. Dinner Mon–Sat. BART: Downtown Berkeley. Map p 174.*

★★ Chez Papa POTRERO HILL *FRENCH* At this busy bistro, tasty goodies combine with cramped quarters for a very French dining experience. *1401 18th St. (at Missouri St.).* ☎ *415/824-8210. Entrees $17–$30. AE, DC, DISC, MC, V. Lunch Mon–Sat, dinner nightly. Bus: 22. Map p 174.*

Alice Waters, the queen of California Cuisine, in her kitchen at the famed Chez Panisse (p 179).

★★ **Cliff House** SUNSET *AMERICAN* Truly breathtaking ocean views and charming early-20th-century decor make the whole experience here—food is almost an afterthought. *1090 Point Lobos Ave. (just west of 48th Ave. Geary Blvd. turns into Point Lobos Ave. after 43rd Ave.).* ☎ *415/386-3330. Entrees $10–$38. AE, DC, DISC, MC, V. Breakfast, lunch & dinner daily. Bus: 18, 38. Map p 174.*

★ **kids Dottie's True Blue Café** TENDERLOIN *AMERICAN* Ample portions of cornmeal pancakes and

The Cliff House may be pricey, but it is more than worth it for its view of the Pacific Ocean.

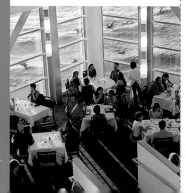

eggs. Lunch features salads and burgers. Kitschy decor. *522 Jones St. (between Geary & O'Farrell sts.).* ☎ *415/885-2767. Entrees $5.75–$11. DISC, MC, V. Breakfast & lunch Wed–Mon. Bus: 2, 3, 4, 27, 38. Map p 174.*

★★ **Fifth Floor** SOMA *FRENCH* An acclaimed restaurant serving well-executed meals in a swank space. *12 4th St. (in the Hotel Palomar, at Market St.).* ☎ *415/348-1555. Entrees $28–$58. AE, DC, DISC, MC, V. Dinner Mon–Sat. Bus: 30, 45. Map p 174.*

★★★ **Fleur de Lys** UNION SQUARE *FRENCH* This epitome of luxury dining is the city's most classic French affair. *777 Sutter St. (between Jones & Taylor sts.).* ☎ *415/673-7779. Prix-fixe from $70. AE, DC, MC, V. Dinner Mon–Sat. Bus: 2, 3, 4, 27. Map p 174.*

★★ **Foreign Cinema** MISSION *CALIFORNIA/MEDITERRANEAN* Eat on this fancy restaurant's patio and watch foreign films while trying interesting dishes. *2534 Mission St. (between 21st & 22nd sts.).* ☎ *415/648-7600. Entrees $16–$30. AE, DISC, MC, V. Dinner daily, brunch Sat–Sun. Bus: 14, 49. BART: 24th St. Map p 174.*

★ Garden Court Restaurant

SOMA *AMERICAN* Elegant service in a lovely historic setting. *Palace Hotel, 2 New Montgomery St. (at Market St.).* ☎ 415/512-1111. Entrees $11–$26.50. AE, DC, DISC, MC, V. Breakfast & lunch daily. BART/Muni: Montgomery St. Map p 174.

★★★ Gary Danko FISHERMAN'S

WHARF *CALIFORNIA* SF's best restaurant boasts flawless service, outstanding wines, and a superlative menu that changes daily. Reserve 4 weeks ahead or try your luck at the bar. *800 N. Point St. (at Hyde St.).* ☎ 415/749-2060. Prix-fixe menu from $61. DC, DISC, MC, V. Dinner daily. Bus: 10, 30. Cable car: Powell-Hyde. Map p 174.

★ kids Ghirardelli Soda Fountain & Chocolate Shop FISHER-

MAN'S WHARF *ICE CREAM* The ever-present line attests to consistently great sundaes—all chocolate-topped, of course. *Ghirardelli Sq., 900 N. Point St. (at Larkin St.).* ☎ 415/771-4903. Desserts $5–$20. AE, DC, DISC, MC, V. Mon–Thurs 10am–11pm; Fri–Sat 10am–midnight. Bus: 10, 30. Cable car: Powell-Hyde. Map p 174.

★★ Greens MARINA *VEGETARIAN*

Fabulous flavors and stunning views impress even dedicated carnivores. *Building A, Fort Mason Center (by Buchanan & Marina sts.).* ☎ 415/

Catch a flick with dinner at Foreign Cinema's alfresco tables.

Gary Danko won the prestigious James Beard Foundation's "Best New Restaurant" award in 2000; today, it still lives up to its acclaim.

771-6222. Entrees $8–$23; Sat prix-fixe $48. AE, DISC, MC, V. Lunch Tues–Sun, dinner Mon–Sat. Bus: 28, 30. Map p 174.

★★★ Hawthorne Lane SOMA

CALIFORNIA This elegant establishment with a quiet, private ambience thrills diners (and often, celebrities) with imaginative dishes and desserts. *22 Hawthorne Lane (off Howard St., between 2nd & 3rd sts.).* ☎ 415/777-9779. Entrees $11–$36. AE, DISC, MC, V. Lunch Mon–Fri, dinner daily. Bus: 10, 15, 30, 45. Map p 174.

★ Indian Oven HAIGHT *INDIAN*

The city's best Indian restaurant. *233 Fillmore St. (between Haight & Waller sts.).* ☎ 415/626-1628. Entrees $8–$19. AE, DC, DISC, MC, V. Dinner daily. Bus: 6, 7, 22, 66, 71. Map p 174.

★ Jardiniere HAYES VALLEY

FRENCH Symphony and opera patrons begin (or complete) a night with dinner at this upscale Civic Center staple. *300 Grove St. (at Franklin St.).* ☎ 415/861-5555. Entrees $29–$41. AE, DC, DISC, MC, V. Dinner daily. Bus: 21. Map p 174.

★★ Kokkari FINANCIAL DISTRICT

GREEK Greek classics in a warm,

California Cuisine

What is California cuisine? The birth of California cuisine can be traced to chef Alice Waters, owner of Berkeley's Chez Panisse (p 179), which has been hailed as the best restaurant in the country. Waters revolutionized American cuisine by championing the use of fresh, seasonal, and local ingredients. Her own culinary revelation came during a year spent in France, where she lived next to a market street that teemed with fresh, high-quality produce.

The fact that Waters's grand vision came while she was overseas highlights California cuisine's multicultural, transnational character. It draws from the entire world, and, as such, it is always evolving. While Waters was inspired by the produce of France, other California chefs have drawn on the cooking of Italy or the Middle East. Today, Asian and South American flavors turn up in many Californian dishes. But the key thread that unites all California cuisine is this: a strong preference for uncomplicated dishes with superior ingredients that change with the seasons.

The Bay Area's location and immigrant history were central to the development of this epicurean style. Today you still find several family farms (many organic) and ranches (specializing in naturally raised meats and poultry) surrounding San Francisco. Add the Pacific's bounty of fresh seafood, and the city's treasure trove of ethnic influences, and you've got what makes San Francisco a perfect city in which to sample California cuisine.

upscale setting. *200 Jackson St. (at Front St.).* ☎ *415/981-0983. Entrees $15–$35. AE, DC, DISC, MC, V. Lunch Mon–Fri, dinner Mon–Sat. Bus: 10. Map p 174.*

★★ **L'Osteria del Forno** NORTH BEACH *ITALIAN* There's always a crowd outside waiting to get into the romantic dining room—this is North Beach's best Italian place, and that's saying a lot. *519 Columbus Ave. (between Union & Green sts.).* ☎ *415/982-1124. Entrees $7–$15. No credit cards. Lunch & dinner Wed–Mon. Bus: 15, 30, 41. Cable car: Powell-Mason. Map p 174.*

★★★ **Michael Mina** UNION SQUARE *CALIFORNIA* A bustling dining room with expert waitstaff, world-class sommeliers, and startlingly vibrant flavors. *335 Powell St.* (in the Westin St. Francis Hotel, at Geary St.). ☎ *415/397-9222. Prix-fixe $88–$120. AE, DC, DISC, MC, V. Dinner daily. Cable car: Powell line. Map p 174.*

★★ **Millennium Restaurant** UNION SQUARE *VEGETARIAN* Nothing at this upscale restaurant is made with animal products, proving that an ethical menu doesn't have to sacrifice taste. *580 Geary St. (at Jones St.).* ☎ *415/345-3900. Entrees $20–$22. AE, DC, DISC, MC, V. Dinner daily. Bus: 2, 3, 4, 27, 38. Map p 174.*

★ **kids** **Mitchell's Ice Cream** MISSION *ICE CREAM* Try the unexpected flavors like avocado, ginger, and sweet corn. *688 San Jose Ave. (at 29th St., just south of where Guerrero St. turns into San Jose Ave.).* ☎ *415/648-2300. $2.10–$5.30.*

No credit cards. Daily 11am–11pm. Bus: 14, 49. Muni: Church & 30th St. Map p 174.

★★ **Moose's** NORTH BEACH *AMERICAN* Local politicos seek out this institution for its innovative take on classic American dishes. *1652 Stockton St. (between Filbert & Union sts.). ☎ 415/989-7800. Entrees $11–$39. AE, DC, DISC, MC, V. Lunch Thurs–Sat, dinner daily, brunch Sun. Bus: 15, 30, 41, 45. Cable car: Powell-Mason. Map p 174.*

★★ **One Market** FINANCIAL DISTRICT *CALIFORNIA* Bradley Ogden's SF outlet, across from the Ferry Building, is larger than life. *1 Market St. (at Steuart St.). ☎ 415/777-5577. Entrees $14.50–$33. AE, DC, DISC, MC, V. Lunch Mon–Fri, dinner Mon–Sat. BART/Muni: Embarcadero. Map p 174.*

★ **Postrio** UNION SQUARE *CALIFORNIA* Wolfgang Puck's creation remains a lovely (and celebrity-studded) place to dine. *545 Post St. (in the Prescott Hotel, between Taylor & Mason sts.). ☎ 415/776-7825. Entrees $16–$39. AE, DC, DISC, MC,*

Open since 1953, Mitchell's Ice Cream's original owner Larry Mitchell imports fresh fruit from the Philippines to make his famous tropical flavors.

The Slanted Door's spring rolls, stuffed with shrimp, pork, and mint, are served with a Vietnamese peanut sauce.

V. Lunch & dinner daily. Bus 2, 3, 4. Map p 174.

★★ **Quince** PACIFIC HEIGHTS *ITALIAN* Seasonal dishes in an elegant, discreet setting. *1701 Octavia St. (at Bush St.). ☎ 415/775-8500. Entrees $16–$30. AE, MC, V. Dinner daily. Bus: 2, 3, 4. Map p 174.*

★★★ **The Slanted Door** FINANCIAL DISTRICT *VIETNAMESE* A perpetual crowd awaits Charles Phan's upscale Vietnamese cooking and his modern restaurant's Embarcadero view. Call ahead. *Ferry Bldg., 1 Ferry Plaza (at The Embarcadero & Market St.). ☎ 415/861-8032. Entrees $10–$27. AE, MC, V. Lunch & dinner daily. BART/Muni: Embarcadero. Map p 174.*

★ **Suppenküche** HAYES VALLEY *GERMAN* An excellent beer selection and well-prepared Bavarian classics. *601 Hayes St. (at Laguna St.). ☎ 415/252-9289. Entrees $10–$19. AE, DISC, MC, V. Dinner daily, brunch Sun 10am–2:30pm. Bus: 21. Map p 174.*

★ **kids Taqueria Pancho Villa** MISSION *MEXICAN* This humble standby is one of SF's best taquerias. *3071 16th St. (between Mission & Valencia sts.). ☎ 415/864-8840. Entrees $1.35–$10. AE, MC, V. Lunch & dinner daily. Bus: 14, 22, 49. BART: 16th St. Map p 174.*

SF **Shopping, Nightlife & Arts**

SHOPPING ●

49 Geary **5**
Ambassador Toys **31**
Amoeba Music **7**
Apple Store San Francisco **4**
Barnes & Noble **21**
Canton Bazaar **33**
Chinatown Kite Shop **15**
City Lights Bookstore **27**
Ferry Building Marketplace **32**

Flight 001 **12**
Ghirardelli Square **18**
Golden Gate Fortune
    Cookies Co. **34**
Good Vibrations **10, 35**
Maiden Lane **3**
Nordstrom **41**
Patagonia **20**
Piedmont **8**

Pumpkin **6**
Rainbow Grocery **10**
Ruby's Artist Coop. **22**
SF Antique & Design Mall **45**
SF Shopping Centre **41**
Shabby Chic **16**
Soko Hardware **15**
Wilkes Bashford **2**
Wine Club San Francisco **44**

SPECTATOR SPORTS ★
Giant's Baseball (AT&T Park) **46**
SF 49ers **45**

NIGHTLIFE & ARTS ■

Beach Blanket Babylon **25**
Boom Boom Room **14**
Buena Vista Café **19**
Curran Theatre **40**
Dalva **10**
Elbo Room **10**
Enrico's Sidewalk Café **26**
Fly Bar **13**
The Fillmore **14**
Gordon Biersch **47**

Greens Sports Bar **24**
Harry Denton's
  Starlight Lounge **1**
Laszlo **10**
La Rondalla **10**
Mad Dog in the Fog **11**
Matrix Fillmore **17**
The Mint **10**
Moby Dick **9**
Redwood Room **38**

Ruby Skye **39**
SF Brewing Co. **28**
SF Opera **42**
SF Symphony **43**
Teatro Zinzanni **23**
The Tonga Room &
  Hurricane Bar **37**
The Top of the Mark **36**
Tosca **30**
Vesuvio **29**

Shopping A to Z

Art
★★ 49 Geary Street UNION SQUARE   You'll find several top galleries here. *49 Geary St. (between Grant Ave. & Kearny St.). Streetcar: F. Most galleries closed Sun–Mon. Bus: 16, 17, 50. BART/Muni: Powell St. Map p 184.*

Books
★ kids Barnes & Noble FISHERMAN'S WHARF   An enormous superstore of this popular chain. *2550 Taylor St. (between Bay & N. Point sts.).* ☎ *415/292-6792. AE, DISC, MC, V. Cable car: Powell/Hyde line. Map p 184.*

★★ City Lights NORTH BEACH Founded by Beat poet Lawrence Ferlinghetti in 1953, this landmark shop still stocks avant-garde and alternative lit. *261 Columbus Ave. (at Broadway St.).* ☎ *415/362-8193. www.citylights.com. AE, DISC, MC, V. Bus: 15, 30, 41. Map p 184.*

Department Store
★ Nordstrom UNION SQUARE Clothes for the whole family and an excellent shoe department. *865 Market St. (at 5th St.).* ☎ *415/243-8500. www.nordstrom.com. AE, DC, DISC, MC, V. Bus: 27, 30, 38, 45. Streetcar: F. Map p 184.*

City Lights contains an impressive selection of art, poetry, and political paperbacks.

Electronics
★★ Apple Store UNION SQUARE This beautiful store houses trendy gear. *1 Stockton St. (at Market St.).* ☎ *415/392-0202. www.apple.com. AE, DC, DISC, MC, V. Bus: 30, 38, 45. Streetcar: F. Map p 184.*

Fashion
★★ Maiden Lane UNION SQUARE Top designers like Marc Jacobs have boutiques on this pedestrian alley. Louis Vuitton, Kate Spade, and others are nearby. *Maiden Lane, off Stockton St. Bus: 30, 38, 45. Map p 184.*

★ Patagonia FISHERMAN'S WHARF An excellent source for high-quality outerwear and a staple in most locals' closets. *770 N. Point St. (between Hyde & Leavenworth sts.).* ☎ *415/ 771-2050. www.patagonia.com. AE, DC, DISC, MC, V. Bus: 10, 30. Cable car: Powell-Hyde. Map p 184.*

★ Piedmont HAIGHT   Absolutely outrageous vintage women's garments—sold mostly to men. The giant fishnet legs over the entrance epitomize The Haight. *1452 Haight St. (at Ashbury).* ☎ *415/864-8075. AE, MC, V. Closed Mon. Bus: 21. Map p 184.*

★★ kids Pumpkin PRESIDIO HEIGHTS   Groovy, well-priced clothes for kids who want to set themselves apart from the Gap-pack. *3366 Sacramento St. (between Walnut St. & Presidio Ave.).* ☎ *415/567-6780. www.pumpkinbabes.com. AE, DISC, MC, V. Bus: 1, 3, 4. Map p 184.*

★★★ Wilkes Bashford UNION SQUARE   SF's best-known men's clothing store with fine European fashions. *375 Sutter St. (at Stockton St.).* ☎ *415/986-4380. www.wilkes bashford.com. AE, DC, DISC, MC, V. Bus: 2, 3, 4, 30, 45. Map p 184.*

The famous red-heeled legs looming over the entrance to Piedmont.

Gifts & Souvenirs

★★ Canton Bazaar CHINATOWN This complex carries Chinese porcelain, jade, antiques, and hand-carved furniture. *616 Grant Ave. (between California & Sacramento sts.).* ☎ *415/362-5750. AE, DISC, MC, V. Bus: 1, 15, 30, 45. Map p 184.*

Good Vibrations MISSION AND NOB HILL The first and probably best pro-woman erotic shop. If you're not shy, the employees give great advice. *603 Valencia St. (at 17th St.).* ☎ *415/522-5460. Bus: 22, 26. Bart to 16th St. 1620 Polk St. (at Sacramento St.).* ☎ *415/345-0400. www.goodvibes.com. Bus: 1, 19. Cable car: California line. AE, DISC, MC, V. Map p 184.*

Housewares & Furnishings

★ Shabby Chic PACIFIC HEIGHTS Rachel Ashwell's airy English designs are now famous because of her TV series and design books. *2185 Fillmore St. (between California & Sacramento sts.).* ☎ *415/771-3881. www.shabbychic.com. AE, DISC, MC, V. Bus: 1, 3, 22. Map p 184.*

★ Soko Hardware JAPANTOWN A great selection of ceramic plates, tea sets, sake cups, and more at bargain prices. *1698 Post St. (at Buchanan St.).* ☎ *415/931-5510. MC, V. Bus: 2, 3, 4, 38. Map p 184.*

Jewelry

★★ Ruby's Artist Cooperative MISSION Local jewelers' one-of-a-kind creations. *3602 20th St. (at Valencia St.).* ☎ *415/550-8052. www.rubygallery.com. MC, V. Bus: 12, 27. Streetcar: J. BART to 16th or 24th St. Map p 184.*

Music

★★ Amoeba HAIGHT The planet's biggest and best independent music store has listening booths and frequent free live performances. Ask staffers for advice, but only about something adequately obscure. *1855 Haight St. (between Shrader & Stanyan sts.).* ☎ *415/831-1200. www.amoebamusic.com. DISC, MC, V. Bus: 6, 7, 66, 71. Map p 184.*

Shopping Centers

★ San Francisco Antique & Design Mall POTRERO HILL More than 200 antiques specialists in a huge warehouse. *701 Bayshore Blvd.* ☎ *415/656-3530. www.sfantique.com. AE, DISC, MC, V. Bus: 9. Map p 184.*

San Francisco Shopping Centre SOMA Anchored by Nordstrom, this attractive mall has some more interesting chains like Kenneth Cole and some less interesting ones. *865 Market St. (at 5th St.).* ☎ *415/495-5656. www.westfield.com/sanfrancisco. Bus: 27, 30, 38, 45. Streetcar: F. Map p 184.*

★★★ Ferry Building Marketplace FINANCIAL DISTRICT All sorts of food-specific shops and mini-restaurants. Don't miss Cowgirl Creamery's Artisan Cheese Shop, Sharffen Berger Chocolates, Recchiuti Confections, or Book Passage.

Amoeba Music carries CDs plus a massive selection of classic LPs (remember those?).

The SF Shopping Center (p 187) downtown is an endlessly entertaining mall to explore on a damp, foggy afternoon.

Go on Saturday or Tuesday, when the humongous farmers' market takes center stage. *The Embarcadero (at Market St.).* ☎ *415/693-0996. www.ferrybuildingmarketplace.com. Streetcar: F. Map p 184.*

★★ kids **Ghirardelli Square** FISHERMAN'S WHARF A former chocolate factory with a priceless view and quaint shops. Ghirardelli's flagship store (p 181) is right here. *900 N. Point St. (at Larkin St.).* ☎ *415/775-5500. www.ghirardellisq.com. Bus: 10, 30. Streetcar: F. Map p 184.*

Specialty Foods & Wines
For Ghirardelli chocolate and the Ferry Building Farmers' Market, see above.

★★ kids **Golden Gate Fortune Cookies Factory** CHINATOWN Buy fortune cookies hot off the press at this tiny Chinatown shop in an alley. Bring your own message and watch it get folded in. *56 Ross Alley (between Washington & Jackson sts.).* ☎ *415/781-3956. No credit cards. Bus: 30, 45. Cable car: Powell-Mason. Map p 184.*

★★ **Rainbow Grocery** MISSION A gargantuan health-food co-op where you can browse through virtually any kind of health food that exists and a mind-boggling selection of bulk spices and teas. *1745 Folsom St. (at 13th St.).* ☎ *415/863-0620. www.rainbowgrocery.org. AE, DISC, MC, V. Bus: 12. Map p 184.*

Wine Club San Francisco
SOMA The West's largest wine merchant; surprisingly affordable. *953 Harrison St. (between 5th & 6th sts.).* ☎ *415/512-9086. www.thewineclub.com. AE, MC, V. Bus: 12, 19, 27. Map p 184.*

Toys
★ kids **Ambassador Toys**
FINANCIAL DISTRICT European dolls, wooden toys, and clever games are among the whimsical playthings. *2 Embarcadero Center (at Sacramento St., between Front & Davis sts.).* ☎ *415/345-8697. AE, DISC, MC, V. Bus: 1. Cable car: California line. Map p 184.*

Travel Goods
Flight 001 HAYES VALLEY Hip travel accessories like sleek luggage, "security-friendly" manicure sets, and other midair must-haves. *525 Hayes St. (between Laguna & Octavia sts.).* ☎ *415/487-1001. www.flight001.com. AE, DISC, MC, V. Bus: 21. Map p 184.*

Your child will be mesmerized by the traditional toys on sale at Ambassador Toys.

Nightlife & Arts A to Z

Bars, Lounges, Pubs & Clubs

★★ The Boom Boom Room
WESTERN ADDITION This dark, steamy joint hosts some of America's best blues bands. *1601 Fillmore St. (at Geary Blvd.).* ☎ *415/673-8000. Cover free–$22. Bus: 22, 38. Map p 184.*

★ The Buena Vista COW HOLLOW It's served more Irish coffees than any other bar in the world. A SF tradition. *2765 Hyde St. (at Beach St.).* ☎ *415/474-5044. Bus: 10, 30. Map p 184.*

★★ Dalva MISSION A dark, intimate cocktail lounge with an eclectic crowd and excellent sangria. *3121 16th St. (between Valencia and Albion sts.).* ☎ *415/252-7740. Bus: 26, 49. BART: 16th St. (before dark). Map p 184.*

★★ Elbo Room MISSION Chill out by the inviting bar or head upstairs for excellent live music (separate cover up to $10). *647 Valencia St. (between Clarion Alley and Sycamore St.).* ☎ *415/552-7788. Bus: 26, 49. BART: 16th St. (before dark). Map p 184.*

★ Enrico's Sidewalk Café
NORTH BEACH Sit on the front patio for people watching and jazz. *504 Broadway (at Kearny St.).* ☎ *415/982-6223. Bus: 12, 15, 41. Map p 184.*

★★ Fly Bar PANHANDLE A neighborhood lounge with interesting soju and sake drinks, great pizzas, and rotating art. *762 Divisadero St. (at Fulton St.).* ☎ *415/931-4359. Bus: 5, 21, 22, 24. Map p 184.*

★ Gordon Biersch SOMA SF's largest brewery restaurant serves tasty German-style beers and garlic fries on the waterfront. *2 Harrison St.* *(at The Embarcadero).* ☎ *415/243-8246. Bus: 12. Map p 184.*

★ Greens Sports Bar RUSSIAN HILL SF's best sports bar boasts 15 TVs and 18 on-tap beers. *2239 Polk St. (at Green St.).* ☎ *415/775-4287. Bus: 19. Cable car: Powell-Hyde. Map p 184.*

★ Harry Denton's Starlight Lounge UNION SQUARE A 1930s-style gathering place with dancing, stellar views, a long appetizer menu, and, on weekends, an orchestra. *Sir Francis Drake Hotel, 450 Powell St. (between Sutter & Post sts.).* ☎ *415/395-8595. Cover varies; call ahead. Bus: 2, 3, 4. Map p 184.*

★ La Rondalla MISSION A seemingly innocuous Mexican diner turns into a chaotic after-hours mariachi fiesta. Open till 3am Tuesday through Sunday. *901 Valencia St. (at 20th St.).* ☎ *415/647-7474. Bus: 12, 27. BART to 16th or 24th St. Map p 184.*

★★ Laszlo MISSION This industrial-chic bar serves funky cocktails. *2534 Mission St. (between 21st & 22nd sts.).* ☎ *415/648-7600. Bus: 14, 49. BART to 24th St. Map p 184.*

Mad Dog in the Fog HAIGHT This quirky British pub is where to watch European soccer. *530 Haight St. (between Steiner & Fillmore sts.).* ☎ *415/626-7279. Bus: 22, 67. Map p 184.*

Boogie down to the blues at the Boom Boom Room.

Matrix Fillmore COW HOLLOW The center of SF's singles' scene. *3138 Fillmore St. (between Greenwich & Filbert sts.).* ☎ *415/563-4180. Bus: 22, 30. Map p 184.*

★ **The Mint Karaoke Lounge** MISSION This once-gay song spot now draws patrons of all orientations, who, after a potent cocktail, take to the stage. *1942 Market St. (between Guerrero & Dolores sts.).* ☎ *415/626-4726. No cover, but a 2-drink minimum. Drinks $4.75–$10. Bus: 22. Streetcar: F, J, N. Map p 184.*

★ **Moby Dick** CASTRO This gay bar is a 25-year-old Castro institution. *4049 18th St. (between Castro & Noe sts.).* ☎ *415/861-1199. Bus: 33. Streetcar: F. Map p 184.*

★ **Redwood Room** UNION SQUARE A historic lounge with famous decor. *Clift Hotel, 495 Geary St. (at Taylor St.).* ☎ *415/775-4700. Bus: 2, 3, 4, 27, 38. Map p 184.*

Ruby Skye UNION SQUARE This former Victorian movie house is SF's biggest dance club. *420 Mason St. (between Post & Geary sts.).* ☎ *415/693-0777. Cover free–$35. Bus: 2, 3, 4, 38. Map p 184.*

★ **San Francisco Brewing Company** NORTH BEACH This old-time saloon with stained-glass windows and a mahogany bar serves homemade brews to a usually packed house. *155 Columbus Ave. (between Jackson St. & Pacific Ave.).* ☎ *415/434-3344. Bus: 12, 14, 15. Map p 184.*

★ **The Tonga Room & Hurricane Bar** NOB HILL Umbrella drinks and faux thunderstorms, plus a $7 all-you-can-eat happy hour. *Fairmont Hotel, 950 Mason St. (at California St.).* ☎ *415/772-5278. Bus: 1. Cable car: All. Map p 184.*

★★★ **The Top of the Mark** NOB HILL A historic venue with the best view in town and a 100-martini menu. Occasional live entertainment. *InterContinental Mark Hopkins, 1 Nob Hill at Mason & California sts.).* ☎ *415/616-6916. Cover $5–$10. Bus: 1. Cable car: All. Map p 184.*

★★ **Tosca** NORTH BEACH This traditional old North Beach institution draws local politicos and celebs. With a dark-wood bar and a jukebox playing only opera, it's a classic. *242 Columbus Ave. (between Broadway St. & Pacific Ave.).* ☎ *415/986-9651. Bus: 12, 15, 41. Map p 184.*

★ **Vesuvio** NORTH BEACH Once the favored beatnik watering hole, famous Vesuvio still draws an artsy crowd. *225 Columbus Ave. (at Pacific Ave.).* ☎ *415/362-3370. Bus: 12, 15, 41. Map p 184.*

The Beautiful People dominate the Redwood Room.

Vesuvio, City Lights Bookstore's neighbor and Jack Kerouac's old haunt, attracts a diverse clientele.

Live Entertainment
★★★ Beach Blanket Babylon
NORTH BEACH   For more than 30 years, BBB's outrageously hatted comedians have spoofed modern pop culture. *Club Fugazi, 678 Green St. (at Columbus Ave.).* ☎ 415/421-4222. *Tickets $25–$72. Bus: 15, 30, 45. Cable car: Powell-Mason. Map p 184.*

★ Curran Theatre UNION SQUARE
Established in 1922 to host European and East Coast productions. Along with the ★ **Orpheum Theater** *(1192 Market St.;* ☎ 415/551-2000 and the **Golden Gate Theater** *(1 Taylor St.;* ☎ 415/551-2000, its "Best of Broadway" series brings NY hits to SF. *445 Geary St. (between Mason & Taylor sts.).* ☎ 415/551-2000. *Tickets $25–$90. Bus: 2, 3, 4, 38. BART/Muni: Powell St. Map p 184.*

★★★ The Fillmore WESTERN
ADDITION   The venue that featured bands like Jefferson Airplane and the Grateful Dead is SF's best rock venue. *1805 Geary Blvd. (at Fillmore St.).* ☎ 415/346-6000. *Tickets $20–$38.50. Bus: 22, 38. Map p 184.*

★★ San Francisco Opera CIVIC
CENTER   North America's second-largest opera company is outstanding. *Tip:* $10 standing-room tickets are sold on the day of the show (cash only; one per person). The season runs from September to December and June to July. Top-notch **San Francisco Ballet** also performs here. *War Memorial Opera House, 301 Van Ness Ave. (at Grove St.).* ☎ 415/864-3330. *Tickets $25–$235. Bus: 5, 21. BART/Muni: Civic Center. Map p 184.*

★★ San Francisco Symphony
CIVIC CENTER   Founded in 1911 and conducted by internationally acclaimed Michael Tilson Thomas. *Davies Symphony Hall, 201 Van Ness Ave. (between Grove & Hayes sts.).* ☎ 415/864-6000. *Tickets $3.50–$107. Bus: 5, 21. BART/Muni: Civic Center. Map p 184.*

★ Teatro Zinzanni EMBARCADERO
Circus artists and a five-course meal come together for a 3-hour dinner extravaganza. *Pier 29, The Embarcadero (at Battery St.).* ☎ 415/438-2668. *Tickets $110–$135. Bus: 10. Streetcar: F. Map p 184.*

Expect the unexpected at Beach Blanket Babylon's comedy show.

Two SF ballet dancers leaping during a performance of Tomasson's Criss-Cross.

Spectator Sports

★★★ kids **Giants Baseball** SOMA AT&T Park is arguably the world's best baseball stadium. Dramatic bay views, lots of kids' amenities, excellent food, and a compellingly entertaining team make a visit here time well spent. *24 Willie Mays Plaza (King & 2nd sts.).* ☎ *415/972-2000. Tickets $6–$85. Bus: 10, 15, 30, 45. Muni: N. Map p 184.*

San Francisco 49ers CANDLE-STICK POINT SF's pro football team. Because there are so many season-ticket holders, single tickets are hard to come by. Check Ticketmaster or Craigslist. *Monster Park, Candlestick Point.* ☎ *415/972-2000. Tickets $59–$94. Map p 184.* ●

A game at AT&T Park comes with an unobstructed view of San Francisco Bay.

The **Savvy Traveler**

Before You Go

Tourist Offices

Napa Valley Conference and Visitors' Bureau (**NVCVB;** 1310 Napa Town Center, Napa, CA 94559; ☎ 707/226-7459; www.napavalley. com). **Yountville Chamber of Commerce** (6484 Washington St.; ☎ 707/944-0904; www.yountville. com). **Santa Rosa Convention & Visitors' Bureau** (9 4th St., Santa Rosa; ☎ 800/404-7673 or 707/577-8674; www.visitsantarosa.com). **Healdsburg Chamber of Commerce and Visitors Bureau** (217 Healdsburg Ave., Healdsburg; ☎ 707/433-6935; www.healdsburg. org). **Russian River Chamber of Commerce & Visitor Center.** More widespread regional information is available at **Sonoma Valley Visitors Bureau,** which offers a free pocket-size visitors guide. 453 1st St. E., Sonoma. ☎ 707/996-1090. www. sonomavalley.com. **Sonoma County Tourism Bureau** (☎ 800/5-SONOMA or 707/576-6662; www.sonoma county.com).

When to Go

Wine country's beauty is striking at any time of year, but it's most memorable during the September and October harvest months, when wineries are in full gear and the landscape is swept with rich autumnal colors. Spring is also a gorgeous time of year; mustard flowers bloom profusely, and since this is when tourist season just begins, there'll be less traffic, thinner crowds, and better deals. Though winter boasts the best rates and fewest people, there's a reason: The days are often chilly and rainy, while miles of bare vines lay dormant. The summer months bring hot weather and lots of traffic.

The Weather

Though the valleys claim a year-round average temperature of 70°F (21°C), if you come with a suitcase packed with T-shirts and shorts during the winter holiday season, you're likely to shiver your way to the nearest department store to stock up on warm clothes and possibly an umbrella. In summer, if you rent a car without air-conditioning, you're liable to want to make a pit stop at every hotel swimming pool you pass. And don't let that morning fog and those early cool temperatures fool you; on most days, come noon, the hot sun sends down plenty of rays. Dress in layers and keep in mind that the temperature can drop dramatically at night.

Festivals & Special Events

SPRING: A favorite Sonoma Valley festival is the **Barrel Tasting Weekend,** held on March's third full weekend. The event, which gives the public a glimpse of Sonoma Valley's finest future releases and raises money for the American Heart Association, is a 2-day celebration that includes demonstrations, pairings, hors d'oeuvres—and all the world-class wine you can drink. Tickets are about $30; buy them well in advance. For details, call the St. Francis Winery. ☎ *800/543-7713. www.heartofsonomavalley.com.* Early April brings the **Sonoma Valley Film Festival,** a 5-day extravaganza featuring more than 75 new independent films, including features, documentaries, and shorts. Day passes are $50 each, and basic passes to the whole festival are $200, but patrons can buy travel packages costing upward of $3,600. *www.cinemaepicuria.org.* ☎ *707/ 933-2600.* In late April, the annual

AVERAGE SEASONAL TEMPERATURES IN WINE COUNTRY

	SPRING	SUMMER	FALL	WINTER
	(MAR–MAY)	(JUNE–AUG)	(SEPT–NOV)	(DEC–FEB)
Average highs (in °F)	78	92	85	72
Average highs (in °C)	26	33	29	22
Average lows (in °F)	64	81	74	61
Average lows (in °C)	18	27	23	16

AVERAGE MONTHLY TEMPERATURES IN SAN FRANCISCO

	JAN	FEB	MAR	APR	MAY	JUNE
High °F/°C	56/13	59/15	60/16	61/16	63/17	64/18
Low °F/°C	46/8	48/19	49/9	49/9	51/11	53/12
	JULY	AUG	SEPT	OCT	NOV	DEC
High °F/°C	64/18	65/18	69/21	68/20	63/17	57/14
Low °F/°C	53/12	54/12	56/13	55/13	52/11	47/8

Vineyard to Vintner (V2V) day includes seminars, blind tastings, and open houses at many wineries. In the evening, Stags' Leap Winery and Manor House hosts barrel tastings, alfresco dining, and live music. It's $175 for the whole day, $100 for the open houses only. *www.stagsleapdistrict.com.* ☎ *707/255-1720.* Calistoga's **Cinco de Mayo Parade & Festival** happens the first weekend of May. It's the valley's largest celebration and features Mexican culture at its best: mariachis in traditional costumes, *charros* performing equestrian feats, elaborate parade floats, and lots of music, dancing, and food. Admission is $5, and proceeds fund scholarships for disadvantaged students. *www.napavalleycincodemayo.com.* ☎ *707/942-8442.*

SUMMER: The **Napa Valley Wine Auction,** held each June, is the area's most renowned—and exclusive—event. The annual charity affair brings about 2,000 deep-pocketed wine aficionados to Napa Valley to schmooze and spend serious cash. Tickets are $2,500 per couple, and they sell out every year. ☎ *707/963-3388.* Another big June attraction is the 10-day **Healdsburg Jazz Festival.** Venues range from

vineyards to restaurants to intimate theaters, and headliners sell out quickly. Admission prices vary, and tickets are available via website or at the venue. *www.healdsburgjazzfestival.com.* ☎ *707/433-4644* Summer is also time for the **Napa Sonoma Wine Country Film Festival,** a monthlong celebration of cinema, cuisine, and wine. Open-air venues screen flicks while film buffs sip, nibble, and socialize. Other activities include symposia, celebrity receptions, and chef demonstrations. Tickets are $10 to $25 per movie. *www.winecountryfilmfest.com.* ☎ *707/935-FILM.*

AUTUMN: The annual **Napa Valley Harvest Festival and Art Exhibition,** takes place in September in a garden setting at Charles Krug Winery. Hundreds of Napa residents and tourists come to check out art, the products of more than 20 wineries, the cuisine of more than 15 restaurants, and constant live music. A large silent auction means you can try to buy any of the art you see. Advance tickets are $50; at the door, they're $60. *www.napakiwanis.com.* ☎ *707/253-2276.* Another major Sonoma event is the **Vintage Festival,** held the last weekend in September at Sonoma's historic plaza.

This is a real party, complete with live music, dancing, parades, art displays, and, of course, copious wine tasting. *www.sonomavinfest.org.* ☎ *707/996-2109.*

WINTER: February's **Napa Valley Mustard Festival** kicks off tourist season with a celebration of the mustard blossoms that speckle the valley. Its 6 weeks' worth of activities range from a formal gourmet gala at the CIA Greystone featuring local restaurants, wineries, and artists to a wine auction, golf benefit, recipe and photography competition, and plenty of food and wine celebrations, including **A Taste of Yountville** in mid-March. ☎ *707/ 259-9020. www.mustardfestival.org.* Right before heavy tourist season kicks off, Healdsburg holds a barrel-tasting weekend at nearly 100 wineries along the **Russian River Wine Road.** If you fall in love with a wine you've sampled, secure your share of bottles—at discounted prices— long before they even hit the stores, never mind buying *futures.*) **Tip:** It's free if you bring your own wine glass, $5 if you need to purchase one to tote from winery to winery. *www.wineroad.com.* ☎ *800/723-6336.*

Useful Websites

www.napachamber.com
www.napadowntown.com
www.napavalleyreservations.com
www.napavintners.com
www.silveradotrail.com
www.sonomavalley.com
www.sonoma.com
www.sonomavalleywine.com
www.staysonoma.com
www.winecountry.com

Cell (Mobile) Phones

One good wireless rental company is **InTouch USA** (☎ 800/872-7626). Though Napa and Sonoma don't have stores that rent cell phones, sometimes hotels' business centers, like the one at **Vintners Inn** (☎ 707/575-7350), will. A store in downtown San Francisco: **Triptel Mobile Rental Phones** (☎ 415/ 474-3330; 1525 Van Ness Ave., between California and Pine sts.) rents cellular phones at $3 per day, or $15 per week. Airtime rates are 95¢ per minute for domestic calls, with an additional $1.25 per minute for international calls. Triptel also sells SIM cards for foreign travelers bringing their own phones. International travelers will be happy to know that cell phones (mobiles) with triband GSM capabilities work in the U.S. Also remember that you will be charged for calls received on a U.K. mobile used abroad. U.K. visitors can rent a U.S. phone before leaving home. Contact **Cellhire.** ☎ 877/ 244-7242 or, from London, 44 20 7490 7799. www.cellhire.co.uk.

Car Rentals

When booking rental cars online, the best deals are usually on rental-car company websites. Major car-rental companies operating in wine country include **Enterprise** (☎ 800/325-8007 or 707/253-8000; www.enterprise.com); **Budget** (☎ 800/527-0700 or 707/224-7846; www.budget.com); and **Hertz** (800/654-3131 or 707/226-2037; www.hertz.com). U.K. visitors should check **HolidayAutos** (online only; www.holidayautos.co.uk). San Francisco International Airport and Oakland International Airport both have car-rental centers at which the above companies are represented. Rates vary depending on season and other factors, but generally, compact cars run about $150 to $300 per week, including taxes and other charges. Most rentals in the U.S. are automatics.

Getting **There**

By Plane

Wine country is easily accessed by the Bay Area's two major airports: San Francisco International (SFO) and Oakland International (OAK), across the Bay Bridge. **San Francisco International Airport** (☎ 650/821-8211. www.flysfo.com) is a 2-hour drive from wine country. **Oakland International Airport** (☎ 510/577-4000. www.oakland airport.com) is less crowded than SFO and more accessible, but offers fewer carriers. It's a bit more than a 1-hour drive from downtown Napa.

Getting to & from the Airport

Rent a car and drive to wine country (see "Car Rentals," above, for companies and "By Car," below, for driving directions). Since there's no useful public transportation in either valley, it's almost impossible to explore the region without wheels, so you might as well rent right at the airport. If you need to, though, for $29, you can ride to Napa Valley from SFO with **Evans Transportation** (☎ 707/255-1559), and the **Sonoma Airporter** (☎ 707/938-4246) offers door-to-door service six times daily from SFO to hotels and inns in most areas of Sonoma ($45 for home pickup, $40 for standard downtown pickup locations).

By Car

All these routes to wine country are well marked.

To Napa Valley

FROM SAN FRANCISCO   Cross the Golden Gate Bridge and go north on U.S. 101; turn east on Highway 37 (toward Vallejo), then north on Highway 29, the main road through Napa Valley. You can also take Highway 121/12 from Highway 37 and follow the signs.

FROM OAKLAND   Head eastbound on I-80 toward Sacramento; a few miles past the Carquinez Bridge ($3 toll) and the city of Vallejo, exit on Highway 12 west, which, after a few miles, intersects with Highway 29 and leads directly into Napa.

To Sonoma Valley

FROM SAN FRANCISCO   Cross the Golden Gate Bridge and stay on U.S. 101 north. Exit at Highway 37; after 10 miles, turn north onto Highway 121. After another 10 miles, turn north onto Highway 12 (Broadway), which will take you directly into the town of Sonoma.

FROM OAKLAND   Head eastbound on I-80 toward Sacramento. A few miles past the city of Vallejo (and after paying a $3 toll to cross the Carquinez Bridge), exit on Highway 12, which, after a few miles, intersects with Highway 29 at the south end of Napa Valley. Just before entering the town of Napa, you'll come to a major intersection, where Highway 29 meets Highway 12/121. Turn left onto Highway 12/121, which will take you directly into Sonoma Valley.

To Northern Sonoma

FROM SAN FRANCISCO   Cross the Golden Gate Bridge and stay on U.S. 101 north. Exit anywhere from Santa Rosa to Healdsburg, depending on your final destination.

FROM OAKLAND   Head eastbound on I-80 toward Sacramento. A few miles past the city of Vallejo (and after paying a $3 toll to cross the Carquinez Bridge), exit on Highway 12, which, after a few miles, intersects with Highway 29 at the south end of Napa Valley. Just before entering the town of Napa, you'll come to a major intersection, where Highway 29 meets Highway 12/121. Turn left onto Highway 12/121, then turn right onto California 116/Arnold Drive. When the road forks, veer right onto Adobe Road. Turn left onto East Washington Street, merge onto U.S. 101 north when you see the on-ramp, and exit at the town of your choice.

By Train & Bus
Amtrak (☎ 800/872-7245 or 800/USA-RAIL. www.amtrak.com.)

doesn't stop in Sonoma, but maintains two stops in Napa. One is at the Napa Wine Train stop (1275 McKinstry St.), but is only for Amtrak Thruway connecting bus service. The other is at 1151 Pearl St. Wine country's only **Greyhound** (☎ 800/231-2222 or 707/545-6495; www.greyhound.com) terminal is located at 435 Santa Rosa Ave. in Santa Rosa and is open daily (except holidays) from 10 to 11:30am and 1:30 to 5pm.

Getting **Around**

With hundreds of wineries scattered amidst Napa and Sonoma's tens of thousands of acres of vineyards, it's understandably difficult to explore wine country without wheels. See "Getting There," above, for details on renting a car.

By Car
Driving in wine country is relatively straightforward and enjoyable. All the streets and highways are well marked and most of them are strikingly beautiful, even when there's traffic. As you drive, keep in mind that one of the preeminent dangers of driving through wine country is that it's an area highly focused on alcohol consumption. The importance of avoiding drinking and driving simply can't be stressed strongly enough. Refrain from driving if you feel even a little tipsy (see "By Cab," below, in case you feel too inebriated). And beware of others on the road who might have consumed too much in the tasting room. The only other bungling factor is that some wine-country highways have many

different names. For example, Highway 12 is also Highway 121 is also Carneros Highway is also Sonoma-Napa Highway. You'll see examples of this kind of multiple street-naming throughout wine country and it may throw you off; if you get confused, pull over and look at a map (or ask your passenger to guide you). A great online resource for getting directions is MapQuest: www.mapquest.com.

By Cab
(No, not cabernet.) You have to call for a taxi in wine country unless you are boarding one from your hotel. Companies: **Napa Valley Cab** (☎ 707/257-6444); **Yellow Cab** (☎ 707/226-3731); **Black Tie Taxi** (☎ 707/-259-1000 or 888/544-8294); and **Wine Valley Taxi** (☎ 707/251-9463). In Sonoma, your best bet is **Vern's Taxi Service** (☎ 707/938-8885) and, in Northern Sonoma, **Healdsburg Taxi Cab** (☎ 707/433-7099). Rates hover at $2.85 for the first mile and $2.50 for each mile thereafter.

On Foot

Many of wine country's treasures within towns can be seen on foot, though you can't easily walk from town to town. See chapter 4 for the area's best walking tours. Though most of these tours traverse flat surfaces, wear comfortable shoes: You'll likely be standing up for a long time, especially if you shop and visit tasting rooms.

Crossing from County to County

The easiest way to get from Napa to Sonoma Valley and vice versa is to head to the Carneros District, which serves as the southern end of both valleys, and cross over along the Sonoma Highway (Calif. 12/121). To get from Napa to Sonoma takes about 20 minutes when there's no traffic. Another option: Take the Oakville Grade (also called Trinity Rd.) over the Mayacamas Range, which links Napa's Oakville to Sonoma's Glen Ellen. It's a steep and windy road, but it can be a real time-saver if you're headed to the northern end of either valley. Getting to northern Sonoma is a snap from Sonoma Valley. Just follow Highway 12 north to get to Santa Rosa. From there, take U.S. 101 north and exit at the town of your choice. From downtown Napa, take California 12/121 (Sonoma Hwy.) to Highway 16 to Adobe Road (veer right) to U.S. 101 North. The trip is about an hour and 15 minutes. From northern Napa towns like Calistoga or St. Helena, it's easier to follow Highway 29 north past downtown Calistoga when it becomes Highway 128. Follow Highway 128 for a few blocks and turn left onto Petrified Forest Road. Turn right onto Porter Creek Road and follow it; it becomes Mark West Springs Road, which leads you to U.S. 101 North.

Getting Around in San Francisco

Driving in San Francisco can be frustrating. Along with aggressive local drivers, one-way streets, no right/left turns when you really need one, and dead ends, there's a lack of parking, period. Fortunately, it isn't necessary to drive to most places. You can call a cab (**Desoto Cab,** ☎ 415/970-1300; **Luxor Cabs,** ☎ 415/282-4141; **Pacific Cab,** ☎ 415/986-7220; **Veteran's Cab,** ☎ 415/552-1300; and **Yellow Cab,** ☎ 415/626-2345; rates are around $2.85 for the first mile and $2.25 for each additional mile) or take **Muni,** a hodgepodge of county-managed transit systems that includes bus, streetcar, cable car, and subway. For detailed route information, call or go online (☎ 415/673-6864; www.sfmuni.com). Most routes run from 6am to midnight and some busy routes have late-night services. Another helpful website is http://transit.511.org, which also lists schedules and route maps for all Bay Area transit systems. Muni Passports can be a bargain for visitors who plan to take buses, streetcars, or cable cars often. **BART,** an acronym for **Bay Area Rapid Transit** (☎ 415/989-2278; www.bart.gov), connects San Francisco with the East Bay (Oakland, Berkeley, Richmond, Concord, and Fremont). Fares range from $1.25 to $7.10, depending on how far you go. Machines in the stations dispense tickets, and computerized exits automatically deduct the correct fare. Children 4 and under ride free. Trains run every 15 to 20 minutes, Monday through Friday from 4am to midnight, Saturday from 6am to midnight, and Sunday from 8am to midnight. Seeing the city on foot, however, is a fantastic way to get around—but remember, the hills can kill you.

Fast **Facts**

APARTMENT & VILLA RENTALS For short-term rentals, your best bet is **www.craigslist.org**. Click on the "apts/housing" link and put "Napa" into the search bar; you'll likely come up with at least 100 very current listings. You'll most likely negotiate a rental directly from the unit's owner (or the person subletting). Also check **www.sublet.com** or **www.californiarental.com**. To research house exchanges, check out **Homelink International** (www.homelink.org), which has more than 14,000 listings in several countries, and **Homebase Holidays** (www.homebase-hols.com).

AREA CODE Both Napa and Sonoma counties use the **707** area code.

ATMS/CASHPOINTS There are ATMs throughout both valleys, although not as many as you'd find in a big city. Unless you go to your bank's ATM, you'll be charged a fee of $1.50 to $3. The **Cirrus** (☎ 800/424-7787; www.mastercard.com) and **PLUS** (☎ 800/843-7587; www.visa.com) networks span the globe; look at the back of your bankcard to see which network you're on, then call or check online for ATM locations in wine country. Find out your daily withdrawal limit before you depart.

BABYSITTING Most hotel concierges will simply provide referrals to a babysitting service, which guests must then call on their own. Local companies supplying short-term sitters are **Nannies of the Valley** (☎ 707/251-8035), **Take A Break** (☎ 707/226-9188), and, a bit farther south, **Bay Area 2nd Mom, Inc.** (☎ 888/926-3666).

BANKS Most banks are open Monday through Friday from 9am to 5pm. Some are also open until midday Saturday. Many banks also have ATMs for 24-hour banking. **Bank of America** has several branches throughout the area, including one at 1001 Adams St. in St. Helena (☎ 707/963-6807). You'll also find **Wells Fargo** throughout the region, including a branch in Napa at 217 Soscol Ave., inside Raley's supermarket (☎ 707/254-8690). The Sonoma Wells Fargo is at 480 W. Napa St. (☎ 707/996-2360). For a complete listing of Wells Fargo branches, call ☎ 800/869-3557.

B&BS Reputable booking services include **Bed & Breakfast Inns Online** (☎ 615/868-1946; www. bbonline.com), **Pamela Lanier's Bed & Breakfasts** (www.lanierbb. com), **BedAndBreakfast.com** (www.bedandbreakfast.com), **Stay Sonoma** (www.staysonoma.com; under "Lodging Type," choose "Bed & Breakfast"), and **NapaValley.com** (www.napavalley.com; click on "Lodging," then "Inns and Bed & Breakfasts"). To read the opinions of those who've already stayed at a place you're considering, enter its name into the search bar at TripAdvisor (www.tripadvisor.com).

BIKE RENTALS One of the best companies is **Napa Valley Bike Tours** (☎ 800/707-BIKE or 707/251.8687; www.napavalleybiketours.com). Daily rentals range from $30 to $50, depending on the type of bike. Kids' bikes are $20 for the day, and tandems (synchronized fun) are $65. Napa Valley Bike Tours also provides excellent guided tours, ranging from $45 to $115, depending on what's included—but if you go this route, choose a package that includes lunch; the company's gourmet picnics are fantastic. Other area companies providing bike rentals include **Getaway Adventures** (Sonoma and Napa; ☎ 800/499-2453; www.getawayadventures.com) and **Wine Country Bike Rentals** (Sonoma; ☎ 866/922-4537 or 707/473-0610; www.winecountrybikes.com). Also remember that sometimes B&Bs and even hotels will lend out bikes for free; ask if that's the case at your accommodations before renting.

CAR RENTALS See "Getting Around," p 198.

CLIMATE See "The Weather," p 194.

CONSULATES & EMBASSIES All embassies are located in the nation's capital, Washington, D.C. For a directory of embassies in Washington, D.C., call ☎ 202/555-1212 or go to www.embassy.org/embassies. Napa's nearest major city is San Francisco; the following are SF consulate addresses for a selection of countries: The **consulate of Australia** is at 625 Market St., Suite 200, San Francisco (☎ 415/536-1970). There is no Canadian consulate in SF. The **embassy of Canada** is at 501 Pennsylvania Ave. NW, Washington, DC 20001 (☎ 202/682-1740; www.canadianembassy.org). The **consulate of Ireland** is at 100 Pine St., San Francisco (☎ 415/392-4214). The **consulate of New Zealand** is at One Maritime Plaza, Ste. 700, San Francisco (☎ 415/399-1255). The **consulate of the U.K.** is at One Sansome St., Ste. 850, San Francisco (☎ 415/617-1300).

CREDIT CARDS Credit cards are a safe way to "carry" money. They provide a convenient record of all your expenses and generally offer good exchange rates. You can also withdraw cash advances from your credit cards at banks or ATMs, provided you know your PIN.

CUSTOMS Visitors arriving by air, no matter what the port of entry, should cultivate patience and resignation before setting foot on U.S. soil. Getting through immigration can sometimes take a very long time, especially on summer weekends. People traveling by air from Canada and certain Caribbean countries can sometimes clear Customs and Immigration at the point of departure, which is much quicker.

DENTISTS If you have dental problems, a nationwide referral service known as **1-800-DENTIST** (☎ 800/336-8478) will provide the name of a nearby dentist or clinic.

DINING Dining in wine country, as in most of California, is generally casual and a jacket is rarely required, except at Napa or Sonoma's most upscale restaurants. **Reservations:** Call the restaurant or try www.opentable.com, a free online reservations site.

DOCTORS See "Emergencies," below.

ELECTRICITY Like Canada, the United States uses 110 to120 volts AC (60 cycles), compared to 220 to 240 volts AC (50 cycles) in most of Europe, Australia, and New Zealand. If your small appliances use 220 to 240 volts, you'll need a 110-volt transformer and a plug adapter with two flat parallel pins to operate them here. Downward converters that change 220 to 240 volts to 110 to 120 volts are difficult to find in the United States, so bring one with you.

EMERGENCIES Dial ☎ **911** for fire, police, and ambulance. No coins are needed from a working public phone. The **Poison Control Center** can be reached at ☎ 800/222-1222 toll-free from any phone. If you encounter serious problems, contact **Traveler's Aid International** (☎ 202/546-1127; www.travelersaid.org).

FAMILY TRAVEL See www.gocitykids.com, www.familyfun.com, or www.sfvisitor.org for good ideas.

GAY & LESBIAN TRAVELERS See www.sfvisitor.org or www.gaywired.com/travel for good ideas.

HOLIDAYS Banks, government offices, post offices, and many stores, restaurants, and museums are closed on the following legal national holidays: January 1 (New Year's Day), the third Monday in January (Martin Luther King Jr. Day), the third Monday in February (Presidents Day), the last Monday in May (Memorial Day), July 4 (Independence Day), the first Monday in September (Labor Day), the second Monday in October (Columbus Day), November 11 (Veterans Day), the fourth Thursday in November (Thanksgiving), and December 25 (Christmas). Also, the Tuesday following the first Monday in November is Election Day and is a federal government holiday in presidential-election years held every 4 years.

INSURANCE   For Domestic Visitors: Trip-cancellation insurance helps you get your money back if you have to back out of a trip or go home early, or if your travel supplier goes bankrupt. Allowed reasons for cancellation can range from sickness to natural disasters to the State Department declaring your destination unsafe for travel. (Insurers usually won't cover vague fears, though, as many travelers discovered when they tried to cancel their Oct. 2001 trips.) Trip-cancellation insurance might be a good buy if you're getting tickets well in advance—who knows what the state of the world, or of your airline, will be in 9 months. Insurance policy details vary, so read the fine print—and make sure that your provider is on the list of carriers covered in case of bankruptcy. For information, contact one of the following insurers: **Access America** (☎ 866/807-3982; www.accessamerica.com), **Travel Guard International** (☎ 800/826-4919; www.travelguard.com), **Travel Insured International** (☎ 800/243-3174; www.travelinsured.com), or **Travelex**

Insurance Services (☎ 888/457-4602; www.travelex-insurance.com). **Medical Insurance:** Insurance policies can cover everything from the loss or theft of your baggage to trip cancellation to the guarantee of bail in case you're arrested. Good policies will also cover the costs of an accident, repatriation, or death. Packages such as Europ Assistance's Worldwide Healthcare Plan are sold by European automobile clubs and travel agencies at attractive rates. **Worldwide Assistance Services, Inc.** (☎ 800/821-2828; www.worldwideassistance.com) is the agent for Europ Assistance in the U.S. Although it's not required of travelers, health insurance is highly recommended. Unlike many European countries, the U.S. does not usually offer free or low-cost medical care to its citizens or visitors. Doctors and hospitals are expensive, and in most cases will require advance payment or proof of coverage before they render their services. Though lack of health insurance may prevent you from being admitted to a hospital in non-emergencies, don't worry about being left injured or ill; the American way is to fix you now and bill you later. **For British Travelers:** Most big travel agents offer their own insurance and will probably try to sell you their package when you book a holiday. Think before you sign. The Consumers' Association recommends that you insist on seeing the policy and reading the fine print before buying travel insurance. **The Association of British Insurers** (☎ 020/7600-3333; www.abi.org.uk) gives advice by phone and publishes *Holiday Insurance,* a free guide to policy provisions and prices. You might also shop around for better deals. **For Canadian Travelers:** Canadians should check with their provincial health plan offices or call Health Canada (☎ 613/957-2991; www.hc-sc.gc. ca) to find out the extent of your coverage and what documentation and receipts you must take home in case you are treated in the U.S. **For Australian Travelers:** Online Travel Insurance (☎ 02/6262-8754; www. travelinsuranceaustralia.com.au) offers a variety of policies for U.S. travel. **Lost-Luggage Insurance:** On domestic flights, checked baggage is covered up to $2,500 per ticketed passenger. On international flights (including U.S. portions of international trips), baggage is limited to approximately $9 per pound, up to approximately $635 per checked bag. If you plan to check items more valuable than the standard liability, see if your valuables are covered by your homeowner's policy, get baggage insurance as part of your comprehensive travel-insurance package, or buy Travel Guard's "BagTrak" product. Don't buy insurance at the airport, as it's usually overpriced. Be sure to take any valuables or irreplaceable items with you in your carry-on luggage, since many valuables (including books, money, and electronics) aren't covered by airline policies. If your luggage is lost, immediately file a lost-luggage claim at the airport, detailing the luggage contents. For most airlines, you must report delayed, damaged, or lost baggage within 4 hours of arrival. The airlines are required to deliver luggage, once found, directly to your house or destination free of charge.

INTERNET ACCESS Internet cafes aren't too prevalent in wine country. In Napa, try Wi-Fi hotspot **Copperfield's Books** (3900A Bel Aire Plaza; ☎ 707/252-8002; www. copperfieldsbooks.com). In Sonoma, wi-fi is available at **Sonoma State Historic Park** (363 3rd St. W.;

☎ 707/938-9560; www.parks. ca.gov); and a coffeehouse called **Barking Dog Roasters** (free; 18133 Sonoma Hwy.; ☎ 707/939-1905). Note that wireless access fees vary; call in advance to verify.

LIMOUSINE SERVICES There are tens of companies chomping at the bit to chauffeur your wine tasting in style. Among the best: **Pure Luxury** (4246 Petaluma Blvd., Petaluma; ☎ 800/ 626-LIMO; www.pureluxury.com), **Beau Wine Tours and Limousine Service** (21707 8th St. E., Sonoma; ☎ 707/938-8001 or 800/387-2328; www.beauwinetours.com), and **Celebrity Limousine** (☎ 707/552-7752 or 800/307-7974; www.celeb limo.com). **Vintage Chrome Tours and Adventures** (☎ 707/225-4943; www.vintagechrometours.com) is unique in that its vehicles are antique Cadillacs and Rolls-Royces. Rates for limos hover around $75 per hour.

LIQUOR LAWS Liquor and grocery stores, as well as some drugstores, are permitted to sell packaged alcoholic beverages between 6am and 2am. Most restaurants, nightclubs, and bars are licensed to serve alcoholic beverages during the same hours. The legal age for purchase and consumption is 21; proof of age is required.

MONEY **Traveler's checks:** You can get traveler's checks at almost any bank. American Express offers denominations of $20, $50, $100, $500, and, for cardholders only, $1,000. You'll pay a service charge ranging from 1% to 4%. You can also get American Express traveler's checks by phone (☎ 800/221-7282; ☎ 0870/600-1060 in the U.K.; Amex gold and platinum cardholders who use this phone number are exempt from the 1% fee). Australians can go to www.americanexpress.com.au. American Automobile Association

(AAA) members can obtain checks without a fee at most AAA branches. In the U.S., Visa (☎ 800/732-1322) offers traveler's checks at Citibank locations nationwide, as well as at several other banks. The service charge ranges between 1.5% and 2%; checks come in denominations of $20, $50, $100, $500, and $1,000. MasterCard also offers traveler's checks (☎ 800/223-9920). Outside the U.S., contact your bank, which will be able to advise you on buying U.S. traveler's checks. If you choose to carry traveler's checks, be sure to keep a record of their serial numbers separate from your checks in the event that the checks are stolen or lost. You'll get a refund faster if you know the numbers.

Credit Cards: See "Credit Cards," p 201.

PASSES **The Wine Country Explorer Pass** (www.explorerpass.com), presented by Smart Destinations (☎ 800/887-9103; www.gocardusa.com), is an excellent deal. For $45, the pass includes 2 days of prepaid admission to Napa and Sonoma wineries and cultural attractions (which would cost $118 if each was purchased separately), plus some shopping savings.

PHARMACIES **Rite Aid,** a drugstore and convenience chain, has stores just about everywhere. Phone ☎ 800/748-3243 for the address and phone number of the nearest store.

SAFETY Don't walk alone at night, stay in well-lighted areas, and carry a minimum of cash and jewels. Though wine country isn't crime-ridden by any means (Napa County had a single homicide from 2005–2006), it's not a 24-hour region. One of the dangers here is drunk driving; avoid it at all costs and keep watch for other motorists who may have consumed too much wine.

SENIOR TRAVELERS Many wine-country attractions offer admission discounts for those over 50; ask if you're not sure. **The Council on Aging Services for Sonoma County Seniors** (730 Bennett Valley Rd., Santa Rosa; ☎ 707/525-0143; www.councilonaging.com) offers day services such as entertainment, gentle exercise, arts and crafts, guest speakers, and current event discussions. The council's special events for active seniors include nature walks, enrichment workshops, and an annual art show (usually in May). Members of **AARP** (601 E St. NW, Washington, DC 20049; ☎ 800/424-3410 or 202/434-2277; www.aarp.org) get discounts on hotels, airfares, and car rentals. Seniors looking to travel with a similarly aged group should visit **Elderhostel's** website, www.elderhostel.com (enter "Napa" or "Sonoma" into the search bar). U.K. seniors can contact **Saga** (☎ 0800/414-525; www.saga.co.uk) for a range of products and services, including holidays and insurance. Australians over 50 should contact the **National Seniors Association** (☎ 1300/76-5050; www.nationalseniors.com.au).

SMOKING California law prohibits smoking in public buildings, restaurants, and bars.

TAXES California sales tax (8.5%) is added to all purchases except snack foods. The hotel tax, known as the transient occupancy tax, is generally 10.5% in Sonoma County and 12% in Napa County (at press time). You won't have to pay sales tax if you have your purchases shipped directly out of state.

TAXIS See "Getting Around," earlier in this chapter.

TELEPHONES For directory assistance, dial ☎ **411.** Pay phones (which are becoming difficult to find) cost 35¢ to 50¢ for local calls, more for long-distance. See "Cell (Mobile) Phones" earlier in this chapter.

TIME California is in the Pacific standard time zone: 8 hours behind Greenwich Mean Time (GMT); 3 hours behind Eastern Standard Time (EST).

TIPPING In hotels, tip bellhops at least $1 per bag and the housekeeping staff $2 to $3 per day (more if you've left a mess); the doorman or concierge $1 to $5 only if he or she has provided you with some specific service (for example, calling a cab or obtaining hard-to-get tickets). Tip the valet-parking attendant $1 each time your car is retrieved. In restaurants, bars, and nightclubs, waitstaff expect 15% to 20% of the check, bartenders 10% to 15%, checkroom attendants $1 per garment, and valet-parking attendants $1 per vehicle. Tip cab drivers 15%, skycaps at airports at least $1 per bag, and hairdressers and barbers 15% to 20%.

TOILETS Public toilets can be hard to find in wine country. Hotels and restaurants are probably the best bet for clean facilities and they're usually friendly about letting stoppers-by use them.

TOURIST INFORMATION See "Tourist Offices," p 194.

TRAVELERS WITH DISABILITIES Many travel agencies offer customized tours and itineraries for travelers with disabilities. Two of them are **Flying Wheels Travel** (☎ 507/451-5005; www.flyingwheelstravel.com) and **Accessible Journeys** (☎ 800/846-4537 or 610/521-0339; www.disabilitytravel.com). From the U.K., **Access Travel** (☎ 01942/888844; www.access-travel.co.uk) offers a variety of holidays for persons with disabilities.

Wine Country: **A Brief History**

1542 Wappo Indians inhabit Napa Valley; **Portuguese explorer** Juan Rodriguez Cabrillo sails up the California coast, the first **European** to investigate the region.

1780 Franciscan missionaries, establishing the first of what would become the state's 21 missions, plant California's first vineyard near San Diego.

1821 Mexico wins independence from Spain and annexes California.

1824 The *padres* of the 21st mission, San Francisco Solano, plant vines near present-day Sonoma.

1825 California's first commercial vineyards are established in Los Angeles.

1825 George Calvert Yount establishes Napa's first homestead (now Yountville) and is the first to plant vineyards in Napa.

1840 California missions become secular and Mission San Francisco Solano's vines become the region's first commercial vineyard.

1846 The Bear Flag Revolt: Americans capture **Sonoma,** arresting and imprisoning resident Mexican governor Mariano Guadalupe Vallejo. The Americans then declare an independent **California Republic.**

1846–48 The Mexican-American War rages between the U.S. and Mexico; Mexico loses about half its territory.

1850 Mariano Guadalupe Vallejo is elected to California's first **State Senate.**

1857 "Count" Agoston Haraszthy plants the first major vineyard of European varieties in Sonoma Valley.

1858 Sonoma's first commercial wines are produced when Charles Krug makes a few gallons for Napa pioneer John Patchett.

1861 Charles Krug goes on to establish Napa's first commercial winery.

1861 Schramsberg is founded.

1875 Sonoma supplants Los Angeles as the state's leading wine region (as measured by acreage).

1875 Beringer is founded.

1885 Napa ousts Sonoma as the state's leading wine region (as measured by acreage). Both valleys' wine industries continue to grow and prosper.

1889 Sonoma has 100 wineries; Napa has more than 140.

1890S Napa loses roughly 75% of its acreage to a plant louse *(phylloxera vastatrix)* epidemic that attacks vineyards.

1919 The 18th Amendment is enacted: "the manufacture, sale, or transportation of **intoxicating liquors...** is hereby prohibited." President Woodrow Wilson vetoes the accompanying Volstead Act but the amendment is made anyway.

1920 Prohibition begins and is enforced. Most of California's wineries shut down, though a few keep operating to produce sacramental and medicinal wine.

1933 The 18th Amendment is repealed by the 21st Amendment, making it the Constitution's only provision to be explicitly modified.

1934 Americans pay almost no attention to dry European-style table wines; the bulk of domestically consumed wines are ports and sherries. This lack of interest persists for 35 years.

1937 Napa has only 37 wineries; Sonoma has 91.

1944 Napa Valley Vintners Association is founded with the mission of promoting local wine worldwide.

1960 Napa dwindles to 25 wineries; Sonoma has even fewer (just 9, by one account).

1960 Robert Mondavi leaves Charles Krug winery to found his own. He develops new winemaking techniques and aggressive marketing strategies.

1972 Wineries start burgeoning again in Napa: This year and next, big players appear on the scene, including Chateau Montelena, Stag's Leap Wine Cellars, Clos du Val, Franciscan, Trefethen, Joseph Phelps, and Domaine Chandon. In Sonoma, Kenwood, Chateau St. Jean, and St. Francis arise.

1976 At a blind tasting in Paris, French wine experts unwittingly award top honors to Chateau Montelena's chardonnay and Stag's Leap Wine Cellars' cabernet, shocking France and waking the world up to California wines.

EARLY 1980S Vintners in both valleys discover *phylloxera vastatrix* again, requiring replanting of most of their acreage. Wine sales level off.

1981 The first annual Auction Napa Valley takes place, starting a tradition that has raised more than $60 million for charity and helped establish Napa as a prestigious region capable of drawing considerable wealth.

1981 Sonoma Valley is designated an American Viticulture Area (AVA).

1982 Napa Valley is designated an AVA. Since then, more than a dozen other AVAs have been defined.

1990 Replanting continues and new labels steadily emerge; restyled red wines become particularly popular.

1992 Sonoma Valley Vintners & Growers Alliance is formed to promote Sonoma wines and grapes.

2006 Napa Valley boasts more than 300 wineries; Sonoma has about 45.

A Quick Guide to **Wine Varietals**

Major Grape Varietals

Below is a list of some of California wine country's most prevalent grape varietals.

Cabernet sauvignon This transplant from Bordeaux has become California's best-known varietal. The small, deep-colored, thick-skinned berry is a complex grape, yielding medium- to full-bodied red wines that are highly tannic when young and usually require a long aging period to achieve their greatest potential. Cabernet is often blended with other related red varietals, such as merlot and cabernet franc (see below), into full-flavored red table wines. These blends, if sanctioned by The Meritage Association, are often called Meritage wines. Cabernet is often matched with red-meat dishes and strong cheeses. If you're looking to invest in several cases of wine, cabernet sauvignon is always a good long-term bet.

Chardonnay The most widely planted grape variety in wine country produces exceptional medium- to full-bodied dry white wines. In fact, it was a California chardonnay that revolutionized the world of wine when it won the legendary 1976 Paris tasting test. You'll find a range of chardonnays in wine country, from delicate, crisp wines that are clear and light in color to buttery, fruity, and oaky (no other wine benefits more from the oak aging process) wines that tend to have deeper golden hues as they increase in richness. This highly complex and aromatic grape is one of the few grapes that doesn't require blending; it's also the principal grape for making sparkling wine. Chardonnay goes well with a variety of dishes, including seafood, poultry, pork, veal, and pastas made with cream or butter.

Merlot Traditionally used as a blending wine to smooth out other grapes' rough edges, merlot has gained popularity in California since the early 1970s—enough so that wineries such as Sonoma's St. Francis are best known for producing masterful merlots. Though it got a bad rap in the 2004 film "Sideways," it's still America's most popular red (at least by sales figures, if not by chicness). The merlot grape is a relative of cabernet sauvignon, but it's fruitier and softer, with a pleasant black-cherry bouquet. Merlots tend to be simpler and less tannic than most cabernets, and they are drinkable at an earlier age, though these wines, too, gain complexity with age. Serve this medium- to full-bodied red with any dish you'd normally pair with a cabernet—it's great with pizza.

Pinot noir   It's taken California vintners decades to make relatively few great wines from pinot noir grapes, which are difficult to grow and vinify. Even in their native Burgundy, the wines are excellent only a few years out of every decade, and they are a challenge for winemakers to master. Recent attempts to grow the finicky grape in the Carneros District's cooler climes have had promising results. During banner harvest years, California's pinot grapes produce complex, light- to medium-bodied red wines with such low tannins and silky textures that they're comparable to the world's finest reds. Pinots are fuller and softer than cabernets and can be drinkable at 2 to 5 years of age, though the best improve with additional aging. Pinot noir is versatile at the dinner table, but goes best with lamb, duck, turkey, game birds, semisoft cheeses, even fish.

Riesling   Also called Johannisberg Riesling or white Riesling, this is the grape from which most of Germany's great wines are made. It was introduced to California in the mid–19th century by immigrant vintners and is now used mainly to produce floral and fruity white wines of light to medium body, ranging from dry to very sweet. It's also often used to make late-harvest dessert wine. Well-made Rieslings, of which California has produced few, have a vivid fruitiness and lively balancing acidity, as well as a potential to age for many years. Suggested food pairings include crab, pork, sweet-and-sour foods, Asian cuisine, and anything with a strong citrus flavor.

Sauvignon blanc   Also labeled as fumé blanc, sauvignon blanc grapes are used to make crisp, dry whites of medium to light body that vary in flavor from slightly grassy to tart or fruity. The grape grows well in Napa and Sonoma and has become increasingly popular due to its distinctive character and pleasant acidity; indeed, it's recently become a contender to the almighty chardonnay. Because of their acidity, sauvignon blancs pair well with shellfish, seafood, and salads.

Zinfandel   Often called the "mystery" grape because its origins are uncertain, "Zinfandel" first appeared on California labels in the late 1800s. Hence, it's come to be known as California's grape. In fact, most of the world's zinfandel acreage is in northern California, and some of the best zinfandel grapes grow in cool coastal locations and on century-old vines in California's more eastern Gold Country. Zinfandel is by far wine country's most versatile grape, popular as blush wine (the ever-quaffable white zinfandel: a light, fruity wine, usually served chilled); as dark, spicy, and fruity red wines; even as a port. Premium zins, like those crafted by Sonoma's Ravenswood winery, are rich and peppery, with a lush texture and nuances of raspberries, licorice, and spice. Food-wise, it's a free-for-all, though premium zins go well with beef, lamb, hearty pastas, pizza, and stews.

Lesser-Known Grape Varietals

Cabernet franc   A French black grape that's often blended with and overshadowed by the more widely planted cabernet sauvignon, cabernet franc was recently discovered to be one of the grape species that gave rise to cabernet sauvignon. The grape grows best in cool, damp conditions and tends to be lighter in color and tannins than cabernet sauvignon; therefore, it matures earlier in the bottle. These wines have a deep purple color with an herbaceous aroma.

Chenin blanc Planted mainly in France, chenin blanc runs the gamut from cheap, dry whites with little discernible character to some of the world's most subtle, fragrant, and complex wines. In wine country, the grape is mostly used to create fruity, light- to medium-bodied and slightly sweet wines. Chenin blanc lags far behind chardonnay and sauvignon blanc in popularity, though in good years it's known for developing a lovely and complex bouquet, particularly when aged in oak. It's often served with pork and poultry, Asian dishes with soy-based sauces, mild cheeses, and vegetable and fruit salads.

Gewürztraminer The gewürztraminer grape produces whites with strong floral aroma and litchinut-like flavor. Slightly sweet yet spicy, it's somewhat similar in style to Johannisberg Riesling and is occasionally used to make late-harvest, dessert-style wine. The grape grows well in California's cooler coastal regions, particularly Mendocino County. The varietal is particularly appreciated for its ability to complement Asian foods; its sweet character stands up to flavors that would diminish a drier wine's flavors and make it seem more tart.

Petite sirah Widely grown throughout warmer regions of California, petite sirah's origins are a mystery. The grape, which produces rich, high-tannin reds, serves mainly as the backbone for Central Valley "jug" wines. Very old vines still exist in cooler northern regions, where grapes are often made into robust and well-balanced reds of considerable popularity.

Pinot blanc A mutation of pinot gris, the pinot blanc grape is prevalent in France's Alsace region, where it's used to make dry, crisp white wines. In California, pinot blanc produces a fruity wine similar to chardonnay's simpler versions. It's also blended with champagne-style sparkling wines, thanks to its acid content and clean flavor.

Sangiovese This is Italy's favorite grape; it makes everything from chianti and Brunello di Montalcino to "Super Tuscan" blends. Now it's also making a name for itself in California. Its style varies depending on where it's grown, but it's commonly described as anything from "fruity," "smooth," "spicy," "good acidity," and "medium-bodied" to "structured" and "full-bodied."

Syrah This red varietal is best known for producing France's noble and age-worthy Rhône Valley reds such as côte-rôtie and hermitage. Syrah vines produce dark, blackish berries with thick skins, resulting in typically dark, rich, dense, medium- to full-bodied wines with distinctive pepper, spice, and fruit flavors (particularly cherry, blackcurrant, and blackberry).

Index

See also Accommodations, Restaurant, and Wineries indexes, below.

A

AARP, 204
Access America, 202
Accessible Journeys, 205
Access Travel, 205
Accommodations, 115–128.
   See also Accommodations
   Index
      Napa Valley, 118–124
      San Francisco, 176–179
      Sonoma Valley,
         124–128
Adventures Aloft, 19, 64
Airlines, 197
Airports, 197
Alcatraz Island, 167–168
Ambassador Toys (San
   Francisco), 188
American Indian Trading Co.
   (Calistoga), 103–104
Amoeba (San Francisco), 187
Antique Fair (Yountville), 95
Apartment and villa rentals,
   200
Apples, 47
Apple Store (San Francisco),
   186
Armstrong Redwoods State
   Reserve, 110
Artefact Design & Salvage
   (Sonoma), 48
Art galleries, 48, 59
      Calistoga, 104, 105
      Napa, 74
      St. Helena, 83
      San Francisco, 186
      Sonoma, 79
Art on Main (St. Helena), 83
Arts and entertainment, San
   Francisco, 189–192
Arts Guild of Sonoma, 59
ATMs (automated teller
   machines), 200
Austin Creek State Recre-
   ation Area, 110

B

Babysitting, 200
Baksheesh (Healdsburg), 89
Bale Grist Mill State Historic
   Park, 54–55
Ballooning, 4, 18–19, 64–65
Bank of America, 200
Banks, 200
Barking Dog Roasters
   (Sonoma), 203
Barnes & Noble (San Fran-
   cisco), 186
Barn Gallery (Sonoma), 48
Barrel Tasting Weekend, 194
BART (Bay Area Rapid Tran-
   sit; San Francisco), 199
Basque Boulangerie
   (Sonoma), 79
Bay Area 2nd Mom, Inc., 200
Beach Blanket Babylon (San
   Francisco), 191
Beard Plaza (Yountville), 95
Bear Flag Monument
   (Sonoma), 51
Bear Flag Revolt (1846), 3, 17
Beau Wine Tours and Limou-
   sine Service, 65, 203
BedAndBreakfast.com, 200
Bed & Breakfast Inns Online,
   200
Bed & breakfasts (B&Bs), 200
Bell Wine Cellars (Yountville),
   95
Ben & Jerry's (Napa), 39
Benziger Family Winery, 3
Bicycling, 61
Biking, 3, 108–109
      rentals, 200–201
Blue Wing Inn (Sonoma),
   51, 80
Boat tours and cruises, San
   Francisco, 168
Bodega Bay, 112–113
Bonaventura Balloon Co.,
   18–19, 65
The Boom Boom Room (San
   Francisco), 189
Bothe-Napa Valley State
   Park, 55
Bouchon Bakery (Yountville),
   95
Bounty Hunter Rare Wine &
   Provisions (Napa), 74
Budget car rentals, 196
Budget tour, 68–70
The Buena Vista (San Fran-
   cisco), 189
Bullfrog Pond, 111
Burbank Circle, 111
Bus travel, 198
Buying wines, 7. See also
   Wineries Index; Wine tast-
   ing and tasting rooms

C

Cabernet franc, 208–209
Cabernet sauvignon, 207
Cable Car Museum and Pow-
   erhouse (San Francisco),
   168–169
Cable cars, San Francisco,
   163, 168–169
California Academy of Sci-
   ences (San Francisco), 173
California Palace of the
   Legion of Honor (San Fran-
   cisco), 168
California Wine Tours, 65
Calistoga, 102–106
      lodging, 118–121, 123
Calistoga Creamery & Bak-
   ery, 105
Calistoga Roastery, 105
The Cannery (San Francisco),
   164
Canoeing, 29, 114
Canton Bazaar (San Fran-
   cisco), 187
Carneros District, 199
Car rentals, 62–63, 196, 201
Carriage House (Oakville), 66
Car travel, 197–198
Castle Vineyards & Winery
   Tasting Room (Sonoma),
   80
Ca'toga Galleria d'Arte (Calis-
   toga), 105
Celebrity Limousine, 203
Cellar 360 World Wine
   Estates (Healdsburg), 88
Cellhire, 196
Cell (mobile) phones, 196
Chardonnay, 207
Charles Creek Vineyard Tast-
   ing Room & Gallery
   (Sonoma), 80–81
Charles M. Schulz Museum
   (Santa Rosa), 4, 37
Chateau Felice (Healdsburg),
   89
Chauffeured cars, 65
The Cheesemaker's Daugh-
   ter (Sonoma), 49, 79
Chenin blanc, 209
Chinatown (San Francisco),
   165
Cinco de Mayo Parade & Fes-
   tival (Calistoga), 194
City Lights Booksellers &
   Publishers (San Francisco),
   165, 186

Civic Center (San Francisco), 173

Coit Tower (San Francisco), 165

Colonel Armstrong Tree, 111

Community Presbyterian Church (Calistoga), 104

Consulates, 201

Coolers, 7–8

COPIA: The American Center for Wine, Food & the Arts (Napa), 22–23, 34–35, 69

Copperfield's Books (Napa), 203

Cornerstone Festival of Gardens (Sonoma), 48

Costeaux French Bakery (Healdsburg), 88

The Council on Aging Services for Sonoma County Seniors, 204

Courthouse (Napa), 75

Cravings (Yountville), 95

Credit cards, 201

Cuisine, California, 182

The Culinary Institute of America (St. Helena), 33

Curran Theatre (San Francisco), 191

Customs regulations, 201

D

Dalva (San Francisco), 189

Dean & Deluca (St. Helena), 33

Dentists, 201

Depot Park (Sonoma), 52

Desoto Cab (San Francisco), 199

Dining. *See also* Restaurant Index
  Calistoga, 105–106
  Glen Ellen, 100–101
  Guerneville, 93
  Healdsburg, 89–91
  Napa, 76–77
  St. Helena, 84–85
  San Francisco, 179–183
  Sonoma, 81
  Yountville, 96–97

Di Rosa Preserve (Napa), 3, 57–58

Disabilities, travelers with, 205

Discovery Trail, 111

Division Street (Napa), 75

Downtown
  Glen Ellen, 99
  Napa, 11–12

Downtown Bakery & Creamery (Healdsburg), 88

Dr. Wilkinson's Hot Springs Resort (Calistoga), 103

Dry Creek Band of Pomo Indians, 21

Dwight Murray Plaza (Napa), 11, 73

E

East Ridge Trail., 111

Elbo Room (San Francisco), 189

Elderhostel, 204

Electricity, 201

Embarcadero Promenade (San Francisco), 172

Embassies and consulates, 201

Emergencies, 201

Enrico's Sidewalk Café (San Francisco), 189

Enterprise car rentals, 196

Enterprise Rent-A-Car (Sonoma), 62–63

Eric Ross Winery tasting room (Glen Ellen), 100

Et Cetera (Guerneville), 93

Etre (Sonoma), 79

Evans Designs (Calistoga), 103

Evans Designs Gallery (Healdsburg), 89

Evans Transportation, 197

F

Families with children, 36–39

Family travel, 201

Farmers' markets, 3, 21
  San Francisco, 171

Ferry Building Marketplace (San Francisco), 187

Ferry Building (San Francisco), 171

Ferry Plaza Farmers Market (San Francisco), 171

Festivals and special events, 194–195

Film festivals, 194, 195

The Fillmore (San Francisco), 191

Findings (St. Helena), 84

First Presbyterian Church (Napa), 75

First United Methodist Church (Napa), 75

Fisherman's Wharf (San Francisco), 164

Fly Bar (San Francisco), 189

Flying Goat Coffee (Healdsburg), 88

Flying Wheels Travel, 205

F-Market streetcar (San Francisco), 171

Food For Humans (Guerneville), 93

Foodies, tours for, 32–35

Fort Ross State Historic Park, 28, 113

49 Geary Street (San Francisco), 186

Fuller Park (Napa), 76

G

Galleries, 48, 59
  Calistoga, 104, 105
  Napa, 74
  St. Helena, 83
  San Francisco, 186
  Sonoma, 79

Gallo Family Vineyards (Healdsburg), 89

Garden Court (San Francisco), 172

Garden Valley Ranch (Petaluma), 47–48

Gay and lesbian travelers, 28, 201

George C. Yount Pioneer Cemetery (Napa), 55

Getaway Adventures, 200–201

Gewürztraminer, 209

Ghirardelli Square (San Francisco), 164, 188

Giants Baseball (San Francisco), 192

Glen Ellen, 98–101
  lodging, 124–126

Glen Ellen Village Market, 99

Goat Rock Beach, 113

Golden Gate Fortune Cookie Factory (San Francisco), 165, 188

Golden Gate Theater (San Francisco), 191

Good Vibrations (San Francisco), 187

Gordon Biersch (San Francisco), 189

Grace Cathedral (San Francisco), 169

Grape varietals, 207–209

Greens Sports Bar (San Francisco), 189

Guerneville, 28, 92–93

H

Hand Fan Museum (Healdsburg), 87
Haraszthy, Agoston, 52
Harry Denton's Starlight Lounge (San Francisco), 189
Hayman House (Napa), 75
Healdsburg, 27, 86–91
  lodging, 126–128
  restaurants, 89–91
  visitor information, 194
Healdsburg Jazz Festival, 195
Healdsburg Museum, 27, 88
Health insurance, 202–203
Helicopter tours, 41
Hertz car rentals, 196
High season, 7
Hwy. 1, 28
  along Sonoma Coast State Beach, 113–114
Historic Napa Mill (Napa), 75–76
HolidayAutos, 196
Holidays, 201–202
Holy Assumption Monastery & Orthodox Religious Center (Calistoga), 104
Hot-air ballooning, 4, 18–19, 64–65
Hotel St. Helena, wine bar at, 83
Huntington Park (San Francisco), 169
Hurd Beeswax Candles (Calistoga), 104–105
Hyde Street Pier (San Francisco), 164

I

Icicle Tree, 111
Insurance, 202–203
Internet access, 203
InTouch USA, 196
I. wolk gallery (St. Helena), 84

J

Jack London State Historic Park, 53
Jack London Village (Glen Ellen), 100
Jan de Luz (St. Helena), 84
Jeanine's Coffee & Tea Co. (Sonoma), 79
Jelly Belly store (Petaluma), 35
Johnson's Beach (Guerneville), 93

K

Kayaking, 4, 29, 114
Kendall-Jackson (Healdsburg), 87

L

Lachryma Montis (Sonoma), 51–52
La Crema (Healdsburg), 87
La Haye Art Center (Sonoma), 59
Lamdin Cottage (Napa), 75
La Rondalla (San Francisco), 189
Laszlo (San Francisco), 189
Lime Stone (Healdsburg), 89
Limousine services, 65, 203
Lincoln Park (San Francisco), 168
Lincoln Theater (Yountville), 54
Liquor laws, 203
Locals (Geyserville), 29
Lodging, 115–128. See also Accommodations Index
  Napa Valley, 118–124
  San Francisco, 176–179
  Sonoma Valley, 124–128
Lombard Street (San Francisco), 163
London, Jack, 53
Long Meadow Ranch (St. Helena), 33–34
Lost-luggage insurance, 203
Luxor Cabs (San Francisco), 199

M

Mad Dog in the Fog (San Francisco), 189
Maiden Lane (San Francisco), 186
Main Element Gallery (Calistoga), 104
The Maritime Museum (San Francisco), 164
Market (St. Helena), 83
Martin Luther King Jr. Memorial (San Francisco), 172
Martin (St. Helena), 84
Matrix Fillmore (San Francisco), 190
Mayo on the Plaza (Sonoma), 79
Medical insurance, 202–203
Merlot, 207–208

The Mint Karaoke Lounge (San Francisco), 190
Mission San Francisco Solano (Sonoma), 51, 80
Moby Dick (San Francisco), 190
Mondavi, Robert, 57
Money matters, 203–204
Mudd Henns (Calistoga), 105
Municipal Pier (San Francisco), 164
Muni (San Francisco), 199
Murray n' Gibbs (St. Helena), 82

N

Nannies of the Valley, 200
Napa, 72–77
  downtown, 11–12
  lodging, 118–123
Napa Downtown Farmers' Market, 21
Napa Downtown Trolley, 72–73
Napa Firefighters Museum, 39, 74
Napa General Store, 11–12, 76
Napa River, 104
Napa Sonoma Wine Country Film Festival, 195
Napa Town Center, 11, 73
Napa Valley, 6–7
  best full-day tours of, 11–13
  crossing to or from Sonoma Valley, 199
  foodie tour of, 32–35
  lodging, 118–124
  traveling to, 197
  visitor information, 194
Napa Valley Bike Tours, 109, 200
Napa Valley Cab, 67
Napa Valley Coffee Roasting Co. (Napa), 74
Napa Valley Coffee Roasting Co. (St. Helena), 82
NapaValley.com, 200
Napa Valley Conference and Visitors Bureau, 73
Napa Valley Harvest Festival and Art Exhibition (St. Helena), 195
Napa Valley Lavender Co. (Napa), 76
Napa Valley Museum (Yountville), 3, 53–54

Napa Valley Mustard Festival, 195
Napa Valley Opera House (Napa), 73
Napa Valley Railroad Depot (Calistoga), 103
Napa Valley Wine & Cigar (Napa), 42
Napa Valley Wine Auction, 195
Napa Valley Wine Train (Napa), 67
National Seniors Association, 204
Navillus Birney Tasting Room (Glen Ellen), 99
A New Leaf Gallery (Sonoma), 48
Nob Hill (San Francisco), 169
Nordstrom (San Francisco), 186
North Beach (San Francisco), 165

O

Oak Hill Farm (Glen Ellen), 49
Oakville Grocery, 110
   Healdsburg, 91
   Oakville, 34
Off-season, 7
Off the Preserve! (Napa), 74
Old Faithful Geyser of California (Calistoga), 3, 19, 38
Olive oils, 32–34, 49, 137
The Olive Press (Glen Ellen), 35, 100
Olivier (St. Helena), 33, 83
OnThEdge Winery (Calistoga), 105
Opera House (Napa), 11
Orpheum Theater (San Francisco), 191
Outdoor activities, 107–114
Out of the Past (Guerneville), 92

P

Pacific Cab (San Francisco), 199
Pamela Lanier's Bed & Breakfasts, 200
Parson Jones Tree, 111
Passes, 204
Patagonia (San Francisco), 186
Petaluma Adobe State Historic Park, 50–51
Petite sirah, 209

Petrified Forest, 20, 37–38
Pharmacies, 204
Picnic, 3
Picnic fare, 61
Piedmont (San Francisco), 186
Pier 39 (San Francisco), 164
Pinot blanc, 209
Pinot noir, 208
Pioneer Cemetery (Napa), 55
Pioneer Trail, 110–111
Plaza Farms (Healdsburg), 87
Plaza Park (Healdsburg), 27, 87
Poison Control Center, 201
Pool Ridge Trail, 111
Potter Schoolhouse (Bodega Bay), 112
Powell-Hyde Cable Car (San Francisco), 163
Powell's Sweet Shoppe (Healdsburg), 27, 89
Pumpkin (San Francisco), 186
Pure Luxury, 203

R

Rainbow Grocery (San Francisco), 188
Ranch Market Too (Yountville's), 109
Ravenswood (Sonoma), 61
Raven Theater (Healdsburg), 91
Red & White Fleet Bay Cruise (San Francisco), 168
Red Barn Store (Glen Ellen), 49
Redwood Empire Ice Arena (Santa Rosa), 37
Redwood Forest Theater, 111
Redwood Room (San Francisco), 190
Restaurants. See also Restaurant Index
   Calistoga, 105–106
   Glen Ellen, 100–101
   Guerneville, 93
   Healdsburg, 89–91
   Napa, 76–77
   St. Helena, 84–85
   San Francisco, 179–183
   Sonoma, 81
   Yountville, 96–97
Riesling, 208
River House Books (St. Helena), 82
River Mist (Guerneville), 93

River Reader (Guerneville), 93
River Rock Casino (Geyserville), 21
River's Edge (Healdsburg), 29, 114
Roses, 47–48
Round Pond Estate (Rutherford), 34
Ruby's Artist Cooperative (San Francisco), 187
Ruby Skye (San Francisco), 190
Russian River, 4, 29, 114
Russian River Wine Road, 196

S

Safari West Wildlife Preserve (Santa Rosa), 24–25
Safety, 204
Saga, 204
St. Helena, 82–85
   lodging, 118, 121, 122, 124
   restaurants, 84–85
St. Helena Olive Oil Co., 33, 83
St. Helena's Farmers' Market, 21
St. Helena Wine Center, 42, 83
San Francisco, 161–192
   average temperatures, 195
   lodging, 176–179
   restaurants, 179–183
   shopping, 184–188
   transportation, 199
San Francisco Antique & Design Mall, 187
San Francisco Ballet, 191
San Francisco Brewing Company, 190
San Francisco 49ers (San Francisco), 192
San Francisco Museum of Modern Art (SFMOMA), 173
San Francisco Opera, 191
San Francisco Shopping Centre SOMA, 187
San Francisco Symphony, 191
Sangiovese, 209
Santa Rosa
   farmers' markets, 21
   visitor information, 194
Sauvignon blanc, 208

Scenic drives, 4
 Hwy. 1, 28
Seasons, 7, 194
Seconds First (Guerneville), 92
Seguin Moreau Napa Cooperage (Napa), 39
Senior travelers, 204
SFMOMA (San Francisco Museum of Modern Art), 173
Shabby Chic (San Francisco), 187
Sharpsteen Museum (Calistoga), 104
The Silverado Museum (St. Helena), 69
Smoking, 204
Soko Hardware (San Francisco), 187
SoMa (South of Market; San Francisco), 172
Sonoma, 78–81
 lodging, 125, 127, 128
 restaurants, 81
 shopping, 79–80
Sonoma Airporter, 197
Sonoma Barracks, 48–49, 80
Sonoma Cheese Factory, 49, 80
Sonoma Coast State Beach, 113–114
Sonoma County Farm Trails, 35
Sonoma-Enoteca, 79
Sonoma Market, 61
Sonoma Mission, 80
Sonoma Overlook Trail, 23
Sonoma Plaza, 17
Sonoma State Historic Park, 51, 203
Sonoma Valley, 6–7
 best full-day tours of, 14–17
 crossing to or from Napa Valley, 199
 foodie tour of, 35
 lodging, 124–128
 special events, 194
 traveling to, 197–198
 visitor information, 194
Sonoma Valley Cyclery, 61
Sonoma Valley Farmers' Market (Sonoma), 21
Sonoma Valley Film Festival, 194
Sonoma Valley Friday Farmers' Market (Sonoma), 21
Sonoma Valley Museum of Art (Sonoma), 59

Sonoma Valley Regional Park (Glen Ellen), 99, 100
Sony Metreon Entertainment Center (San Francisco), 173
Spectator sports, San Francisco, 192
Spice Islands Marketplace, 3
Spirits in Stone
 Healdsburg, 89
 Sonoma, 79
Stay Sonoma, 200
Swiss Hotel (Sonoma), 52, 80
Syrah, 209

T

Take A Break, 200
A Taste of Yountville, 196
Tasting on Main (St. Helena), 84
Taxes, 204
Taxis, 67, 198
Teatro Zinzanni (San Francisco), 191
Telephones, 204–205
Temperatures, average seasonal, 195
Thirty-Four North (Healdsburg), 89
Tiddle E. Winks Vintage 5 & Dime (Sonoma), 79
Time zone, 205
Tipping, 205
Toad Hollow Vineyards (Healdsburg), 88
Toilets, 205
The Tonga Room & Hurricane Bar (San Francisco), 190
The Top of the Mark (San Francisco), 190
Tosca (San Francisco), 190
Tourist offices, 194
Toyon Books (Healdsburg), 89
Train Town (Sonoma), 38
Train travel, 198
Translations (Sonoma), 48
Transportation, 198–199
Traveler's Aid International, 201
Traveler's checks, 203–204
Travelex Insurance Services, 202
Travel Goods Flight 001 (San Francisco), 188
Travel Guard International, 202

Travel Insured International, 202
Triptel Mobile Rental Phones, 196
Twin Hill Ranch (Sebastopol), 47

U

Union Square (San Francisco), 163

V

Vesuvio (San Francisco), 190
Veteran's Cab (San Francisco), 199
Veterans Home of California (Yountville), 54
Veterans Memorial Park (Napa), 75
Victorian Park (San Francisco), 164
Villa rentals, 200
Vine Life (Guerneville), 93
Vineyard to Vintner (V2V) day, 194
Vintage Chrome Tours and Adventures, 203
Vintage 1870 (Yountville), 95
Vintage Festival (Sonoma), 195
Vintage Home (St. Helena), 84
Vintage Sweet Shoppe (Napa), 76
Vintner's Collective (Napa), 11, 74
Vintners Inn, 196
Visitor information, 194

W

Washington Square Park (San Francisco), 165
Weather, 196
Wells Fargo, 200
West Coach Limousine, 65
Whale Point, 113
Wildflowers, 3, 111, 113
Wilkes Bashford (San Francisco), 186
Wine Club San Francisco, 188
Wine Country Bike Rentals, 201
The Wine Country Explorer Pass, 204
Wine Country Helicopters (Napa), 41

Wineries, 8. *See also* Wineries Index
buying wines at, 7
The Wine Shop (Healdsburg), 89
Wine tasting and tasting rooms. *See also* Wineries Index
fees, 7
Glen Ellen, 99
Healdsburg, 87–89
like a pro, 30
Napa, 74
St. Helena, 84
Sonoma, 79
Yountville, 95
Wine varietals, 207–209
Winship Building (Napa), 74
Woodhouse Chocolate (St. Helena), 33, 83
Worldwide Assistance Services, 202

Y
Yellow Cab (San Francisco), 199
Yerba Buena Center for the Arts (San Francisco), 172
Yount, George C., 55
Yountville, 94–97
lodging, 120, 122–124
visitor information, 194
Yountville's Farmers' Market, 21

Z
Zinfandel, 208

Accommodations
Adagio (San Francisco), 176
Adagio Inn (St. Helena), 118
Ambrose Bierce House (St. Helena), 118
Applewood Inn (Guerneville), 124
The Archbishop's Mansion (San Francisco), 176
The Argonaut (San Francisco), 176
Auberge du Soleil (Rutherford), 118
Aurora Park Cottages (Calistoga), 118
Beazley House (Napa), 118
Beltane Ranch (Glen Ellen), 124
Best Western Stevenson Manor Inn (Calistoga), 118

Blackbird Inn (Napa), 118–119
Bungalows 313 (Sonoma), 125
Calistoga Ranch (Calistoga), 119
Campton Place Hotel (San Francisco), 176
Candlelight Inn (Napa), 119
The Carneros Inn (Napa), 119
CasaLana (Calistoga), 119
Castle in the Clouds (Yountville), 120
Cedar Gables Inn (Napa), 120
Chateau de Vie (Calistoga), 120
Churchill Manor (Napa), 120
Clift Hotel (San Francisco), 176
Cottage Grove Inn (Calistoga), 120
The Cottage Inn & Spa Mission B&B (Sonoma), 125
The Cottages of Napa Valley (Napa), 121
Dr. Wilkinson's Hot Springs Resort (Calistoga), 121
1801 First Inn (Napa), 121
El Dorado Hotel (Sonoma), 125
Embassy Suites (Napa), 121
The Fairmont (San Francisco), 176
Fairmont Sonoma Mission Inn & Spa (Boyes Hot Springs), 125
Four Seasons (San Francisco), 177
The Gables Wine Country Inn (Santa Rosa), 125
Gaige House Inn (Glen Ellen), 125
Glenelly Inn & Cottages (Glen Ellen), 126
Grape Leaf Inn (Healdsburg), 126
Harvest Inn (St. Helena), 121
Healdsburg Inn on the Plaza, 126
Hennessey House (Napa), 121
Honor Mansion (Healdsburg), 126
Hotel Healdsburg, 127
Hotel Majestic (San Francisco), 177
Hotel Triton (San Francisco), 177

The Huntington Hotel & Nob Hill Spa (San Francisco), 177
Hyatt at Fisherman's Wharf (San Francisco), 177
Hyatt Regency San Francisco, 177
Indian Springs (Calistoga), 121–122
InterContinental Mark Hopkins, 177
The Kenwood Inn & Spa, 127
King George Hotel (San Francisco), 180
La Belle Epoque (Napa), 122
Lavender (Yountville), 122
Ledson Hotel (Sonoma), 127
Les Mars Hotel (Healdsburg), 127
The Lodge at Sonoma, 127–128
MacArthur Place (Healdsburg), 128
Maison Fleurie (Yountville), 122
Mandarin Oriental (San Francisco), 178
Meadowood Napa Valley (St. Helena), 122
The Meritage Resort (Napa), 122–123
Milliken Creek Inn & Spa (Napa), 123
Monticello Inn (San Francisco), 178
Mount View Hotel (Calistoga), 123
Napa River Inn (Napa), 123
The Palace Hotel (San Francisco), 178
Poetry Inn (Yountville), 123
Ramekins (Healdsburg), 128
Rancho Caymus Inn (Rutherford), 123
Red Victorian (San Francisco), 178
The Ritz-Carlton (San Francisco), 178
Roman Spa Hot Springs Resort (Calistoga), 123
Safari West Tent Camp (Santa Rosa), 123
Silverado Resort (Napa), 123
Sir Francis Drake (San Francisco), 179
Toscano Hotel (Sonoma), 51, 80
Trojan Horse Inn (Sonoma), 128

Villagio Inn & Spa (Yountville), 124
Villa Verotto (Carneros), 128
Vine Hill Inn (Sebastopol), 128
Vintage Inn & Spa (Yountville), 124
Westin St. Francis (San Francisco), 179
White Sulphur Springs Inn & Spa (St. Helena), 124
W San Francisco (San Francisco), 179

Restaurants

All Seasons Bistro (Calistoga), 45, 105
American Market Café (Napa), 23
Ana's Cantina (St. Helena), 84
Angèle (Napa), 53, 76
Aqua (San Francisco), 179
A16 (San Francisco), 179
Barndiva (Healdsburg), 89
Bear Republic Brewing Co. (Healdsburg), 30, 89–90
Bistro Don Giovanni (Napa), 76
Bistro Jeanty (Yountville), 42, 96
Bistro Ralph (Healdsburg), 90
Boogaloos (San Francisco), 179
Boon Fly Café (Napa), 69, 76
Bosko's (Calistoga), 105
Bouchon (Yountville), 13, 96
Boudin Sourdough Bakery & Café (San Francisco), 168
Boulevard (San Francisco), 179
Bovolo (Healdsburg), 90
Brannan's (Calistoga), 105
Brix (Yountville), 42
Café Citti (Kenwood), 70
Café La Haye (Sonoma), 24, 59, 81
Caffe Museo (San Francisco), 173
The Cantina (Santa Rosa), 37
Cantinetta (St. Helena), 85
Cena Luna (Healdsburg), 90
Center Street Café & Deli (Healdsburg), 90
Checkers (Calistoga), 38, 105–106
Chez Panisse (Berkeley), 179
Chez Papa (San Francisco), 179–180
Cindy's Backstreet Kitchen (St. Helena), 84

Cliff House (San Francisco), 180
Compadres Bar & Grill (Yountville), 96
Cornerstone Market Café (Sonoma), 48
The Culinary Institute of America (St. Helena), 33
Cyrus (Healdsburg), 30, 90
Della Santina's (Sonoma), 35, 62
Depot Hotel-Cucina Rustica (Sonoma), 52
Deuce (Sonoma), 58
Dottie's True Blue Café (San Francisco), 180
Downtown Joe's (Napa), 39, 76–77
Dry Creek Kitchen (Healdsburg), 90
El Dorado Kitchen (Sonoma), 24, 35, 81
Fifth Floor (San Francisco), 180
the fig café & winebar (Glen Ellen), 100
Fleur de Lys (San Francisco), 180
Foreign Cinema (San Francisco), 180
Franciscan Pier (San Francisco), 168
French Laundry (Yountville), 3
The French Laundry (Yountville), 13, 34, 43, 94, 96
Fresh Choice (Santa Rosa), 37, 70
Frog Hollow Farm (San Francisco), 171
Garden Court Café (Glen Ellen), 100
Garden Court Restaurant (San Francisco), 180
Gary Danko (San Francisco), 180–181
The General's Daughter (Sonoma), 55, 63, 81
Ghirardelli Soda Fountain & Chocolate Shop (San Francisco), 181
the girl and the fig (Sonoma), 17, 48, 81
Giugni's (St. Helena), 84
Glen Ellen Inn Restaurant, 49, 100–101
Gordon's (Yountville), 97
Greens (San Francisco), 181
Harmony (Sonoma), 62, 81
Hawthorne Lane (San Francisco), 181

Healdsburg Bar & Grill, 91
High Tech Burrito (Napa), 66
Hoffman House Café (Geyserville), 29
Hurley's Restaurant and Bar (Yountville), 97
Hydro Grill (Calistoga), 106
Indian Oven (San Francisco), 181
Jack's Bistro & Wine Bar (Glen Ellen), 16, 101
Jardiniere (San Francisco), 181
Julia's Kitchen (Napa), 23, 77
Kitani Sushi (Calistoga), 106
Kokkari (San Francisco), 181
La Estancia Argentine Grill (Glen Ellen), 101
LaSalette (Sonoma), 81
La Toque (Rutherford), 63
L'Osteria del Forno (San Francisco), 181
Main Street Station (Guerneville), 93
Manzanita (Healdsburg), 91
Mario's Bohemian Cigar Store Café (San Francisco), 165
Martini House (St. Helena), 85
Mary's Pizza Shack (Sonoma), 81
Michael Mina (San Francisco), 182
Millennium Restaurant (San Francisco), 182
Mitchell's Ice Cream (San Francisco), 182
Moose's (San Francisco), 182–183
Moving On Cafe (Geyserville), 20
Napa Valley Grille (Yountville), 97
Olive and Vine Culinary Adventures (Glen Ellen), 16
Olive & Vine Culinary Adventures (Glen Ellen), 101
One Market (San Francisco), 183
Pacifico (Calistoga), 38, 106
Pat's Restaurant & Bar (Guerneville), 93
Pearl (Napa), 25, 77
Postrio (San Francisco), 183
Quail Run Restaurant (Geyserville), 20
Quince (San Francisco), 183
Redd (Yountville), 25, 97
The Red Grape (Sonoma), 17

Restaurant at Domaine Chandon (Yountville), 97

Restaurant Charcuterie (Healdsburg), 91

Saffron (Glen Ellen), 101

Savannah Café (Santa Rosa), 25

Seaweed Café (Bodega Bay), 113

The Slanted Door (San Francisco), 183

Soo Yuan (Calistoga), 106

Stomp (Calistoga), 106

Sunflower Caffe (Sonoma), 52

Suppenküche, 183

Taqueria El Sombrero (Healdsburg), 91

Taqueria Pancho Villa (San Francisco), 183

Taqueria Rosita (Napa), 39

Taste of the Himalayas (Sonoma), 81

Taylor's Automatic Refresher (St. Helena), 45, 85

Terra (St. Helena), 85

The Tides Wharf & Restaurant (Bodega Bay), 28

Tra Vigne (St. Helena), 85

Uva Trattoria (Napa), 59, 77

Vicolo Pizzeria (San Francisco), 173

Villa Corona (Napa), 77

Wappo Bar & Bistro (Calistoga), 106

Willi's Seafood & Raw Bar (Healdsburg), 91

Wine Spectator Greystone Restaurant (St. Helena), 84

Wolf House (Glen Ellen), 49, 101

Zin (Healdsburg), 91

Zuni Café (San Francisco), 173

ZuZu (Napa), 66, 77

Wineries

Acacia Vineyard (Napa), 132

Alderbrook (Healdsburg), 132–133

Alexander Valley Vineyards (Healdsburg), 133

Andretti Winery (Napa), 133

Arista Winery (Healdsburg), 133

Arrowood Vineyards & Winery (Glen Ellen), 63, 133

Artesa Vineyards & Winery (Napa), 65–66, 134

Baldacci Family Vineyards (Napa), 134

Bartholomew Park Winery (Sonoma), 62, 134

Beaulieu Vineyard (Healdsburg), 134–135

Bella Vineyards (Glen Ellen), 135–136

Benessere Vineyards (St. Helena), 135

Benziger Family Winery (Glen Ellen), 15, 39, 99, 135–136

Beringer Vineyards (St. Helena), 45, 54, 136

Blackstone Winery (Kenwood), 136

Bouchaine Vineyards (Napa), 137

B.R. Cohn Winery (Glen Ellen), 49, 137

Buena Vista Carneros (Sonoma), 23, 52, 62, 137

Cakebread Cellars (Rutherford), 137–138

Chalk Hill Estate Vineyards and Winery (Healdsburg), 138

Chappellet Vineyard & Winery (St. Helena), 138–139

Charles Creek (Sonoma), 139

Charles Krug Winery-Peter Mondavi Family (St. Helena), 54, 139

Chateau Montelena (Calistoga), 139

Chateau St. Jean (Kenwood), 15, 63, 139

Cliff Lede Vineyards (Yountville), 57, 108, 140

Cline Cellars (Sonoma), 16, 69–70, 140

Clos du Bois (Geyserville), 140

Clos du Val (Napa), 12, 109, 141

Clos Pegase (Calistoga), 57, 141

Conn Creek Napa Valley (St. Helena), 141–142

Corison Winery (St. Helena), 142

Cosentino Winery (Yountville), 142

Cuvaison Winery (Calistoga), 142

Darioush (Napa), 25, 41, 142

De La Montanya Winery and Vineyards (Healdsburg), 143

DeLoach Vineyards (Santa Rosa), 143

Domaine Carneros (Napa), 66, 143

Domaine Chandon (Yountville), 12, 44, 109, 143–144

Duckhorn Vineyards (St. Helena), 144

Dutch Henry (Calistoga), 32

Far Niente Winery (Oakville), 66

Ferrari-Carano Vineyards and Winery (Healdsburg), 30, 144

Flora Springs Winery (St. Helena), 144

Foppiano Vineyards (Healdsburg), 144–145

Franciscan Oakville Estate (Rutherford), 145

Frank Family Vineyards (Calistoga), 45, 145

Freemark Abbey Winery (Napa), 145–146

Gallo of Sonoma (Healdsburg), 146

Gary Farrell Vineyards & Winery (Healdsburg), 146

Geyser Peak Winery (Geyserville), 146

Gloria Ferrer Champagne Caves (Sonoma), 16–17, 146

Grgich Hills Cellar (Rutherford), 147

Gundlach Bundschu (Sonoma), 16, 62, 147

Hagafen Cellars (Napa), 147

Hall Winery (St. Helena), 147–148

Harvest Moon Estate & Winery (Santa Rosa), 148

The Hess Collection Winery (Napa), 11, 58, 148

Honig Vineyard & Winery (Rutherford), 148

Hop Kiln Winery (Healdsburg), 27, 149

Huntington (Healdsburg), 149

Imagery Estate Winery & Art Gallery (Glen Ellen), 58–59, 149

Jordan Vineyard & Winery (Healdsburg), 20, 149

Joseph Phelps Vineyards (St. Helena), 150

Kaz Vineyard & Winery (Kenwood), 150

Kendall-Jackson Wine Center (Santa Rosa), 150

Kenwood Vineyards, 70, 150

Korbel Champagne Cellars (Guerneville), 27–28, 151

Kuleto Estate Family Vineyards (St. Helena), 66–67
Kunde Estate Winery & Vineyards (Kenwood), 151
La Crema (Healdsburg), 87
Ladera Vineyards (Angwin), 151
Ledson Winery & Vineyards (Kenwood), 63, 151
Louis M. Martini Winery (St. Helena), 152
Mahoney Vineyards (Napa), 152
Monticello Vineyards/Corley Family Napa Valley (Napa), 152
Mumm Napa (Rutherford), 25, 57, 152
Navillus Birney Winery & Vineyards (Glen Ellen), 70, 153
Opus One (Oakville), 153
Paradise Ridge Winery (Santa Rosa), 153
Paraduxx Winery (Yountville), 25, 42, 153–154
Peju Province Winery (Rutherford), 154

PlumpJack Winery (Oakville), 154
Provenance Vineyards (Rutherford), 154
Ravenswood Winery (Sonoma), 155
Raymond Vineyards (St. Helena), 155
Robert Craig Wine Cellars (Napa), 155
Robert Mondavi Winery (Oakville), 12, 44, 155
Roshambo Winery + Gallery (Healdsburg), 155
Roshambo Winery (Healdsburg), 114
Rubicon Estate (Rutherford), 12–13, 156
St. Clement Vineyards (St. Helena), 156
St. Francis Winery & Vineyards (Santa Rosa), 156
St. Supéry Winery (Rutherford), 39, 45, 156
Schramsberg Vineyards (Calistoga), 19, 55, 157
Schug Carneros Estate Winery (Kenwood), 63, 157

Sebastiani Vineyards & Winery (Sonoma), 62, 157
Sebastopol Vineyards/Dutton Estates, 157
Shafer Vineyards, 42, 157
Simi Winery (Healdsburg), 158
Sterling Vineyards (Calistoga), 20, 38, 43, 158
Stryker Sonoma (Geyserville), 159
Sutter Home Winery (St. Helena), 68, 159
Thumbprint Cellars (Healdsburg), 87
Tin Barn Vineyards (Sonoma), 159
Trefethen Vineyards (Napa), 159
Viader Vineyards (St. Helena), 42, 160
Viansa Winery (Sonoma), 160
V. Sattui Winery (St. Helena), 68, 159–160
ZD Wines (Rutherford), 160

Photo **Credits**

p viii: © Jerry Alexander/Lonely Planet Images; p 3, top: © Garry Gay/Alamy; p 3, bottom: © Jerry Alexander/Lonely Planet Images; p 4, top: © Judy Bellah/ Lonely Planet Images; p 4, bottom: © Rick Samuels/Charles M. Schulz Museum and Research Center; p 5: © Mike Dobel/Alamy; p 7, bottom: © MedioImages/Getty Images; p 8, top: © Roger Ressmeyer/Corbis; p 8, bottom: © MedioImages/Alamy; p 9: © Michael Orton/Getty Images; p 11, bottom: © Richard Gross/Corbis; p 12, top: © Tim Andrews; p 13, top: © Pierre Vauthey/Corbis Sygma; p 13, bottom: © Ed Kashi/Corbis; p 15, bottom: © Roland & Karen Muschenetz/Cephas Picture Library/Alamy; p 16, bottom: © Courtesy Gloria Ferrer Champagne Caves/Freixenet USA; p 17, top: © Phil Schermeister/Corbis; p 19, top: © Mick Rock/Cephas Picture Library/Alamy; p 20, bottom: © Morton Beebe/Corbis; p 23, bottom: © Kim Kulish/Corbis; p 24, top: © Paul A. Souders/Corbis; p 24, bottom: © Robert Holmes/Alamy; p 25, top: © Laura Norcia Vitale; p 27, top: © Robert Holmes/ AGStockUSA, Inc./Alamy; p 27, bottom: © Dave G. Houser/Post-Houserstock/ Corbis; p 28, top: © Stephen Saks Photorgaphy/Alamy; p 29, bottom: © Gary Crabbe/Alamy; p 30, bottom: © Courtesy Ferrari-Carano Vineyards & Winery; p 31: © Lisa Romerein/Jupiterimages; p 33, top: © C/B Productions/Corbis; p 33, bottom: © Malcolm Sewell/Alamy; p 34, bottom: © Courtesy Round Pond; p 35, top: © foodfolio/Alamy; p 37, bottom: © Rick Samuels/Charles M. Schulz Museum and Research Center; p 38, bottom: © Morton Beebe/Corbis; p 39, top: © Courtesy Benziger Family Winery; p 41, middle: © Aerial Archives/ Alamy; p 42, top: © Apply Pictures/Alamy; p 42, bottom: © Courtesy The French Laundry; p 43, bottom: © Uripos/eStock Photo; p 45, top: © Tim Andrews; p 45, bottom: © Jerry Alexander/Lonely Planet Images; p 47, bottom: © Elmtree Images/Alamy; p 48, bottom: © Courtesy The Girl & the Fig; p 51, bottom: © Robert Holmes/Corbis; p 52, top: © Dave G. Houser/Post-Houserstock/Corbis; p 52, bottom: © Stephen Saks Photography/Alamy; p 53, bottom: © Thomas Hallstein/Alamy; p 54, top: © Courtesy Napa Valley Museum; p 55, top: © Cephas Picture Library/Alamy; p 55, bottom: © John Elk III/Alamy; p 57, top: © Tim Andrews; p 57, bottom: © Courtesy Mumm Napa; p 58, bottom: © Courtesy The Hess Collection; p 59, top: © Courtesy Imagery Estate Winery; p 61, bottom: © Kim Karpeles/Alamy; p 62, top: © Matthew X. Kiernan/Strata Art; p 63, bottom: © Robert Holmes/Alamy; p 65, top: © John Elk III/Lonely Planet Images; p 65, bottom: © Lee Foster/Lonely Planet Images; p 66, bottom: © Courtesy Far Niente; p 67, top: © Courtesy Napa Valley Wine Train; p 67, bottom: © Nik Wheeler/Corbis; p 69, bottom: © Loren Irving/AGE Fotostock; p 70, top: © Courtesy Cline Cellars; p 71: © Brent Miller/WineCountry.com; p 73, top: © Bill Bachmann/Alamy; p 74, top: © Courtesy Napa Valley Opera House; p 74, bottom: © Danita Delimont/Alamy; p 75, top: © Stephen Saks Photography/Alamy; p 77, bottom: © Faith Echtermeyer/COPIA: © The American Center for Wine, Food & the Arts; p 79, bottom: © Courtesy Cheesemaker's Daughter; p 80, top: © Robert Holmes/Alamy; p 80, bottom: © Stephen Saks Photography/Alamy; p 83, top: © Brent Miller/WineCountry.com; p 83, bottom: © Chuck Place/Alamy; p 85, top: © Chuck Place/Alamy; p 85, bottom: © Chuck Place/Alamy; p 87, bottom: © Robert Holmes/Corbis; p 88. Bottom: © Clay McLachlan/Cephas Picture Library/Alamy; p 90, top: © Courtesy Cyrus Restaurant; p 93, top: © Bob Croxford/Atmosphere Picture Library/Alamy; p 95, top: © Robert Holmes/Corbis; p 96, bottom: © Danita Delimont/Alamy; p 97, top: © Danita Delimont/Alamy; p 99, middle: © Peter Horree/Alamy; p 99, bottom: © Roland & Karen Muschenetz/Cephas Picture Library/Alamy; p 101, top: © Courtesy the girl & the fig; p 103, top: © Catherine Karnow/Corbis; p 103, bottom: © Danita Delimont/Alamy; p 104, top: © Stephen Saks Photography/Alamy; p 106, top: © Blinkstock/Alamy; p 106, bottom: © Stephen Saks Photography/Alamy; p 107: © Morton Beebe/Corbis; p 109, top: © Jerry Alexander/Cephas Picture Library/Alamy; p 111, bottom: © Bob Croxford/Atmosphere Picture Library/Alamy; p 113, top: © Gary Crabbe/Alamy; p 113, bottom: © David Sanger Photorgaphy/Alamy; p 114, top: © image100/Alamy; p 115: © Courtesy Gaige House Inn; p 118, bottom: © Courtesy Auberge du Soleil; p 119, top: © Courtesy Calistoga Ranch; p 119, bottom: © Courtesy Napa River Inn; p 121, bottom: © Catherine Karnow/Corbis; p 122, bottom: © Courtesy Meadowood Napa Valley; p 124, top: © Courtesy Villagio Inn & Spa; p 125, bottom: © Courtesy The Fairmont Sonoma Mission Inn & Resort; p 126, top: © Courtesy Honor Mansion; p 126, bottom: © Courtesy Gaige House Inn; p 127, top: © Courtesy Les Mars Hotel; p 127, bottom: © Courtesy The Lodge at Sonomoa; p 128, bottom: © Courtesy MacArthur Place; p 129: © Cephas Picture Library/Alamy; p 133, top: © Courtesy Alexander Vallery Vineyards; p 134, bottom: © Courtesy Artesa Winery; p 135, top: © Danita Delimont/Alamy; p 135, bottom: © Cephas Picture Library/Alamy; p 136, top: © Bruce Fleming/Cephas Picture Library/Alamy; p 136, bottom: © Danita Delimont/Alamy; p 137, top: © Vladpans/eStock Photo; p 138, top: © Nathan Benn/Corbis; p 138, bottom: © Courtesy Chateau Montelena Winery; p 139, bottom: © Cephas Picture Library/Alamy; p 140, bottom: © Ted Stefanski/Cephas Picture Library/Alamy; p 141, top: © Cephas Picture Library/Alamy; p 141, bottom: © Vladpans/eStock Photo; p 142, bottom: © Jerry Alexander/Getty Images; p 143, top: © Cephas Picture Library/Alamy; p 144, bottom: © Ben Mangor/SuperStock; p 145, top:

© Swerve/Alamy; p 146, top: © Courtesy Gloria Ferrer Champagne Caves/ Freixenet USA; p 147, bottom: © Courtesy Gundlach Bundschu; p 148, bottom: © Phil Schermeister/Corbis; p 150, top: © Clay McLachlan/Cephas Picture Library/Alamy; p 150, bottom: © Courtesy Kendall-Jackson Wines; p 151, bottom: © Danita Delimont/Alamy; p 152, top: © Courtesy Ledson Winery & Vineyard; p 152, bottom: © Robert Holmes/Alamy; p 153, top: © Vladpans/ eStock Photo; p 154, top: © Courtesy Provenance Vineyards; p 154, bottom: © Courtesy Provenance Vineyards; p 155, bottom: © Courtesy Robert Mondavi Winery; p 156, top: © Roland & Karen Muschenetz/Cephas Picture Library/Alamy; p 157, bottom: © Robert Holmes/Corbis; p 158, top: © Charles O'Rear/Corbis; p 158, bottom: © Cephas Picture Library/Alamy; p 159, top: © Brad Perks Lightscapes/Alamy; p 160, top: © Courtesy Viansa Winery; p 161: © Mitchell Funk/Getty Images; p 163, bottom: © Phil Schermeister/ Corbis; p 165, top: © Mark Newman/Index Stock; p 165, bottom: © Allenn Russell/Index Stock Imagery; p 167, bottom: © Courtesy San Francisco CVB; p 168, top: © Ed Young/AGStockUSA, Inc./Alamy; p 169, top: © Thomas Winz/ Index Stock Imagery; p 171, bottom: © David Wasserman/Index Stock Imagery; p 172, top: © Courtesy The Palace Hotel; p 173, bottom: © Walter Bibikow/Index Stock Imagery; p 176, bottom: © Courtesy Clift Hotel; p 177, top: © Courtesy Hotel Triton; p 178, bottom: © Mark Gibson/Index Stock Imagery; p 180, top: © Roger Ressmeyer/Corbis; p 180, bottom: © Courtesy Cliff House; p 181, top: © Courtesy Gary Danko; p 181, bottom: © Courtesy Foreign Cinema; p 183, top: © Courtesy The Slanted Door; p 183, bottom: © Courtesy Mitchell's Ice Cream; p 186, bottom: © Thomas Winz/Index Stock Imagery; p 187, top: © Garry Gay/Alamy; p 187, bottom: © Reid Neubert/ Index Stock Imagery; p 188, top: © E. Smith/Alamy; p 188, bottom: © S.T. Yiap/Alamy; p 189, bottom: © Courtesy The Boom Boom Room; p 190, bottom: © Courtesy Clift Hotel; p 191, top: © Anthony Pidgeon/Lonely Planet Images; p 191, bottom: © Morton Beebe/Corbis; p 192, top: © Julie Lenberger/ Corbis; p 192, middle: © Lee Foster/Lonely Planet Images; p 193: © Judy Bellah/ Lonely Planet Images